Beginning Android Games Development

From Beginner to Pro

Fourth Edition

Ted Hagos
Mario Zechner
J.F. DiMarzio
Robert Green

Apress®

Beginning Android Games Development: From Beginner to Pro

Ted Hagos
Makati, Philippines

Mario Zechner
Graz, Steiermark, Austria

J.F. DiMarzio
Kissimmee, FL, USA

Robert Green
Portland, OR, USA

ISBN-13 (pbk): 978-1-4842-6120-0
https://doi.org/10.1007/978-1-4842-6121-7

ISBN-13 (electronic): 978-1-4842-6121-7

Managing Director, Apress Media LLC: Welmoed Spahr
Acquisitions Editor: Spandana Chatterjee
Development Editor: Laura Berendson
Coordinating Editor: Divya Modi

Cover designed by eStudi Pixabay

Distributed to the book trade worldwide by Springer Science+Business Media New York, 233 Spring Street, 6th Floor, New York, NY 10013. Phone 1-800-SPRINGER, fax (201) 348-4505, e-mail orders-ny@springer-sbm.com, or visit www.springeronline.com. Apress Media, LLC is a California LLC and the sole member (owner) is Springer Science + Business Media Finance Inc (SSBM Finance Inc). SSBM Finance Inc is a **Delaware** corporation.

For information on translations, please e-mail booktranslations@springernature.com; for reprint, paperback, or audio rights, please e-mail bookpermissions@springernature.com.

Apress titles may be purchased in bulk for academic, corporate, or promotional use. eBook versions and licenses are also available for most titles. For more information, reference our Print and eBook Bulk Sales web page at http://www.apress.com/bulk-sales.

Any source code or other supplementary material referenced by the author in this book is available to readers on GitHub via the book's product page, located at www.apress.com/978-1-4842-6120-0. For more detailed information, please visit http://www.apress.com/source-code.

Printed on acid-free paper

For Adrianne and Stephanie.

Table of Contents

About the Authors

Ted Hagos is a software developer by trade. At the moment, he's Chief Technology Officer and Data Protection Officer of RenditionDigital International, a software development company based out of Dublin. He wore many hats in his 20+ years in software development, for example, team lead, project manager, architect, and director for development. He also spent time as a trainer for IBM Advanced Career Education, Ateneo ITI, and Asia Pacific College.

Mario Zechner runs Badlogic Games, a game development shop focused on Android.

J.F. DiMarzio is a seasoned Android developer and author. He began developing games in Basic on the TRS-80 Color Computer II in 1984. Since then, he has worked in the technology departments of companies such as the US Department of Defense and The Walt Disney Company. He has been developing on the Android platform since the beta release of version .03, and he has published two professional applications and one game on the Android marketplace. He is also an accomplished author. Over the last 10 years, he has released eight books, including *Android: A Programmer's Guide*. His books have been translated into four languages and published worldwide. His writing style is very easy to read and understand, which makes the information on the topics that he presents more retainable.

Robert Green is a mobile video game developer from Portland, Oregon, who develops and publishes mobile games under the brand Battery Powered Games. He has developed over a dozen mobile games and graphically interactive apps for himself and clients in the last two years, which include 2D and 3D action, puzzle, racing, and casual games. Before diving full time into video game development, he worked for software companies in Minneapolis, Minnesota, and Chicago, Illinois, including IBM Interactive. His current focus is on cross-platform game development and high-performance mobile gaming.

About the Technical Reviewer

 **Nishant Srivastava** is primarily an Android Engineer, but also has experience writing firmware code for custom wearable hardware, building mobile SDKs for enabling DSP on Android, and constantly contributing to the community by giving talks, writing blog posts, coauthoring books, and so on. He is a listed inventor on two patents for using mobile tech in the cross-device mobile ad retargeting domain.

You can find more about him at www.nisrulz.com.

Introduction

Welcome to *Beginning Android Games Development*. This book will help you get started in your game programming journey with the little green robot.

Who This Book is For

The book is aimed at beginner game programmers, but not quite that new to Android (nor Java). If you're an applications programmer who has some experience with Java and wants to get into Android game programming, this book is perfect for you. While we assumed you have some experience with Android programming, we've devoted some chapters for those who are completely new to Android.

If you have a passing knowledge of Java and a bit of Android programming, you should be fine. If you're new to both, there are plenty of Apress books on Java and Android introduction.

Chapter Overview

Chapter 1—This chapter is about the setup and configuration of Android Studio, the tool we'll be using throughout the book for game development. If you're already using this and are quite familiar with the tool, you can safely skip this chapter.

Chapter 2—This chapter walks through how a basic project is created, set up, and compiled in Android Studio. It also discusses how to set up an emulator, which you will need when you test your app.

Chapter 3—This chapter is about the IDE. Android Studio is a full-featured IDE; it's got a lot of parts. This is a good chapter to read if you need to familiarize yourself with Android Studio. In the chapters where we actually build the game, I'll be making some references to various parts of the IDE, for example, the Project tool window, Attributes window, Logcat, and so on.

Chapter 4—Programming for the Android platform is not the same as programming for the desktop or the Web; in fact, even if you come from an iOS background, the Android platform may still feel foreign to you. This chapter gives an overview of the platform and how it is structured architecturally. It's not an extensive introduction to Android components, but it talks about the components that we will need for our games.

Chapter 5—It's a quick tour on game genres and a short overview on how most games are structured logically. If you're new to game programming, I suggest don't skip this chapter. It might give you ideas for your next game.

Chapter 6—This is the chapter where we build the first game. It's a card game called Crazy Eights; you might have played it in the past. This is a long chapter. It's best to download the source code for the game, then keep it open in Android Studio while you're reading through the chapter. That, I think, is the best way to get the most out of it. We will build a turn-based card game, and we're to handle most of the graphics ourselves; we won't use built-in Android View objects, so it's quite a chore—but it's a good learning experience on how to move around in Android graphics.

Chapter 7—In this chapter, we build another game called Pop Balloons. The game has simpler mechanics than Crazy Eights. The player basically just pops balloons as they float to the top of the screen. You'll be introduced to built-in Animator objects in the Android SDK, for example, ValueAnimator, and how to use it as a timing engine. We'll also use audio and sound effects in this chapter.

Chapter 8—This chapter introduces some techniques on how to do testing in Android Studio and what kind of testing you can apply for game apps.

Chapter 9—This chapter provides an easy-to-understand introduction to OpenGL ES. It includes a small exercise on how to draw something in 3D space.

Chapter 10—This chapter talks about options on how to monetize your game app. It's not a how-to chapter, but it provides a high-level discussion on the possible routes on how to get paid if you're a game programmer.

Chapter 11—When you're ready to distribute your app, you'll need to sign it and list it in a marketplace like Google Play. This chapter walks you through the steps on how to do it.

Chapter 12—This chapter talks about some areas of interest that you can add to your game programming arsenal.

CHAPTER 1

Setup

Welcome. Let's start our journey at the beginning—setup. In this chapter, we will cover

- Getting Android Studio
- Setting up the IDE
- Basic configuration

Building Android apps wasn't always as convenient as today. Back in 2008, when Android was first released, what we got by way of a development kit was no more than a bunch of command-line tools and Ant build scripts. Building apps with a plain editor, Android CLI tools, and Ant wasn't so bad if you're used to that kind of thing, but many developers were not. The lack of capabilities of a modern IDE like code hinting, completion, project setup/scaffolding, and integrated debugging was somewhat of a barrier to entry.

Thankfully, the Android Development Tools (ADT) for the Eclipse IDE was released, also in 2008. Eclipse was (and still is) a favorite and dominant choice of IDE for many Java developers. It felt very natural that it would also be the go-to IDE for Android developers.

From 2009 up until 2012, Eclipse remained to be the choice IDE for development. The Android SDK has undergone both major and incremental changes in structure and in scope. In 2009, the SDK manager

© Ted Hagos, Mario Zechner, J.F. DiMarzio and Robert Green 2020
T. Hagos et al., *Beginning Android Games Development*,
https://doi.org/10.1007/978-1-4842-6121-7_1

was released; we use this to download tools, individual SDK versions, and Android images that we can use for the emulator. In 2010, additional images were released for the ARM processor and x86 CPUs.

2012 was a big year because Eclipse and ADT were finally bundled. This was a big deal because until that time, developers had to install Eclipse and the ADT separately; the installation process wasn't always smooth. So, the bundling of the two together made it a whole lot easier to get started with Android development. 2012 is also memorable because it marked the last year of Eclipse being the dominant IDE for Android.

In 2013 Android Studio was released. To be sure, it was still on beta, but the writing on the wall was clear. It will be the official IDE for Android development. Android Studio is based on JetBrains's IntelliJ. IntelliJ is a commercial Java IDE that also has a community (nonpaid) version. It would be the community version that will serve as the base for Android Studio.

Installing Android Studio

At the time of writing, Android Studio is on version 3.5; hopefully, by the time you read this book, the version won't be too far away. You can download it from https://developer.android.com/studio. It's available for Windows (both 32- and 64-bit), macOS, and Linux. I ran the installation instructions on macOS (Catalina), Windows 10 64-bit, and Ubuntu 18. I work primarily in a macOS environment, which explains why most of the screenshots for this book looks like macOS. Android Studio looks, runs, and feels (mostly) the same in all three platforms, with very minor differences like key bindings and the main menu bar in macOS.

Before we go further, let's look at the system requirements for Android Studio. At a minimum, you'll need either of the following:

- Microsoft Windows 7/8/10 (32- or 64-bit)

- macOS 10.10 (Yosemite or higher)

- Linux (Gnome or KDE Desktop), Ubuntu 14.04 or higher; 64-bit capable of running 32-bit applications

- GNU C Library (glibc 2.19 or later) if you're on Linux

For the hardware, your workstation needs to be at least

- 3GB RAM (8GB or more recommended)

- 2GB of available HDD space

- 1280 x 800 minimum screen resolution

These requirements came from the official Android website; of course more is better. If you can snag a 32GB RAM, 1TB SSD, and a Full HD (or UHD) monitor, that wouldn't be bad; not at all.

And now we come about the Java Development Kit (JDK) requirement. Starting with Android Studio 2.2, the installer comes with OpenJDK embedded. This way, a beginner programmer won't have to bother with the installation of a separate JDK; but you can still install a separate JDK if that's your preference. In this book, I'll assume that you will use the embedded OpenJDK which comes with Android Studio.

Download the installer from https://developer.android.com/studio/; get the proper binary file for your platform.

If you have a Mac, do the following:

1. Unpack the installer zipped file.

2. Drag the application file into the Applications folder.

3. Launch Android Studio.

4. Android Studio will prompt you to import some settings if you have a previous installation. You can import that—it's the default option.

If you're using Windows, do the following:

1. Unzip the installer file.

2. Move the unzipped directory to a location of your choice, for example: `C:\Users\myname\AndroidStudio`.

3. Drill down to the "AndroidStudio" folder; inside it, you'll find "studio64.exe". This is the file you need to launch. It's a good idea to create a shortcut for this file—if you right-click *studio64. exe* and choose "Pin to Start Menu," you can make Android Studio available from the Windows Start menu; alternatively, you can also pin it to the Taskbar.

The Linux installation requires a bit more work than simply double-clicking and following the installer prompts. In future releases of Ubuntu (and its derivatives), this might change and become as simple and frictionless as its Windows and macOS counterparts, but for now, we need to do some tweaking. The extra activities on Linux are mostly because Android Studio needs some 32-bit libraries and hardware acceleration.

Note The installation instructions in this section are meant for Ubuntu 64-bit and other Ubuntu derivatives, for example, Linux Mint, Lubuntu, Xubuntu, and Ubuntu MATE. I chose this distribution because I assumed that it is a very common Linux flavor for the readers of this book. If you are running a 64-bit version of Ubuntu, you will need to pull some 32-bit libraries for Android Studio to function well.

To start pulling the 32-bit libraries for Linux, run the following commands on a terminal window:

```
sudo apt-get update && sudo apt-get upgrade -y
sudo dpkg --add-architecture i386
sudo apt-get install libncurses5:i386 libstdc++6:i386
zlib1g:i386
```

When all the prep work is done, you need to do the following:

- Unpack the downloaded installer file. You can unpack the file using command-line tools or using the GUI tools—you can, for example, right-click the file and select the "Unpack here" option, if your file manager has that.

- After unzipping the file, rename the folder to "AndroidStudio".

- Move the folder to a location where you have read, write, and execute privileges. Alternatively, you can also move it to /usr/local/AndroidStudio.

- Open a terminal window and go to the AndroidStudio/ bin folder, then run ./studio.sh.

- At first launch, Android Studio will ask you if you want to import some settings; if you have installed a previous version of Android Studio, you may want to import those settings.

Configure Android Studio

If this is the first time you've installed Android Studio, you might want to configure a couple of things first before diving into coding work. In this section, I'll walk you through the following:

- Get some more software that we'll need so we can create programs that target specific versions of Android.

- Make sure we have all the SDK tools we need.

Launch the IDE if you haven't done so yet, then click "Configure," as shown in Figure 1-1. Choose "Preferences" from the drop-down list.

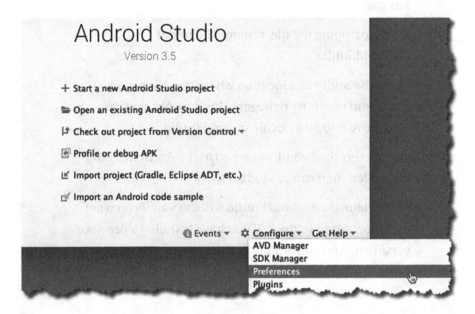

Figure 1-1. *Go to "Preferences" from the Android Studio's opening dialog*

When you click the "Preferences" option, it will open the Preferences dialog, as shown in Figure 1-2. On the left-hand side of the dialog, select the "Android SDK" section.

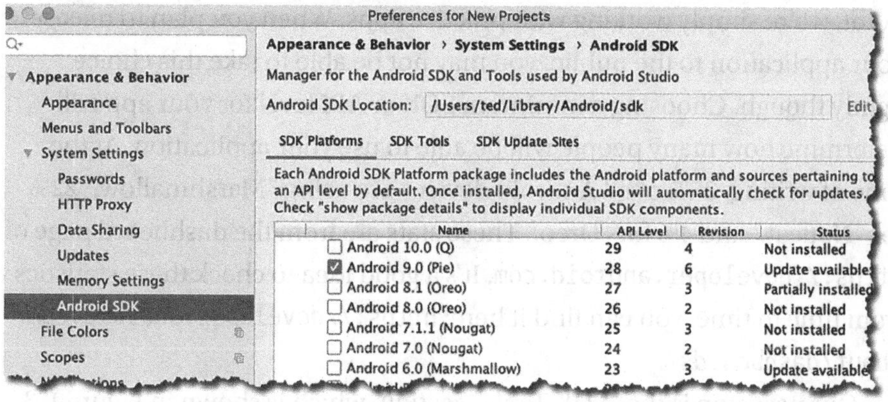

Figure 1-2. *SDK Platforms*

The "Android SDK" section has three tabs: the "SDK Platforms," "SDK Tools," and "SDK Update Sites"; their headings are self-explanatory.

When you get to the "SDK Platforms" section, enable the "Show Package Details" option so you can see a more detailed view of each API level. We don't need to download everything in the SDK window. We will get only the items we need.

SDK levels or platform numbers are specific versions of Android. Android 9 or "Pie" is API level 28, Android 8 or "Oreo" is API levels 26 and 27, and Nougat is API levels 24 and 25. You don't need to memorize the platform numbers, at least not anymore because the IDE shows the platform number with the corresponding Android nickname.

You will notice that only Android 9 (Pie) is selected in my setup. You may choose to install as many SDK platforms as you like, but for the purposes of this book, I will use either Android 9 or 10, as these versions are the latest at the time of writing. That's what we will use for the sample projects. Make sure that together with the platforms, you will also download "Google APIs Intel x86 Atom_64 System Image." We will need those when we get to the part where we test run our applications.

Choosing an API level may not be a big deal right now because at this point, we're simply working with practice apps. When you plan to release your application to the public, you may not be able to take this choice lightly though. Choosing a minimum SDK or API level for your app will determine how many people will be able to use your application. At the time of writing, 25% of all Android devices are using "Marshmallow," 22% for "Nougat," and 4% for "Oreo." These stats are from the dashboard page of https://developer.android.com. It's a good idea to check these statistics from time to time, you can find it here: https://developer.android.com/about/dashboards/.

Our next stop is the "SDK Tools" section, which is shown in Figure 1-3.

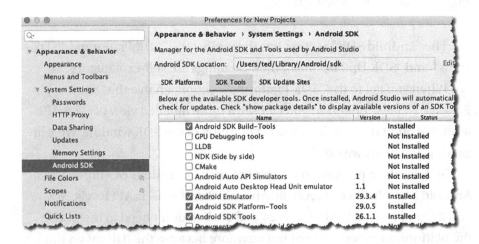

Figure 1-3. *SDK Tools*

You don't need to change anything on this window, but it wouldn't hurt to check if you have the tools, as shown in the following list, marked as "Installed."

- Android SDK Build Tools

- Android SDK Platform Tools

- Android SDK Tools

- Android Emulator

- Support Repository

- HAXM Installer

Checking these tools ensures that we get tools like *adb*, *sqlite*, *aapt*, *zipalign*, and so on. These tools help us in debugging, creating builds, working with databases, running emulations, and so on.

Note   If you are on the Linux platform, you cannot use HAXM even if you have an Intel processor. KVM will be used in Linux instead of HAXM.

Once you're happy with your selection, click the "OK" button to start downloading the packages.

Hardware Acceleration

As you write your apps, it will be useful to test and run it from time to time in order to get immediate feedback and find out if it is running as expected, or if it is running at all. To do this, you will use either a physical or a virtual device. Each option has its pros and cons, and you don't have to choose one over the other; in fact, you will have to use both options eventually.

An Android Virtual Device, or AVD, is an emulator where you can run your apps. Running on an emulator can sometimes be slow; this is the reason why Google and Intel came up with HAXM. It is an emulator acceleration tool that makes testing your app a bit more bearable. This is a boon to developers. That is if you are using a machine that has an Intel processor which supports virtualization and that you are not on Linux. But don't worry if you're not lucky enough to fall on that part of the pie, there are ways to achieve emulator acceleration in Linux, as we'll see later.

macOS users probably have it the easiest because HAXM is automatically installed with Android Studio. They don't have to do anything to get it, the installer took care of that for them.

Windows users can get HAXM either by

- Downloading it from `https://software.intel.com/en-us/android`. Install it like you would any other Windows software, double-click, and follow the prompts.

- Alternatively, you can get HAXM via the SDK manager; this is the recommended method.

For Linux users, the recommended software is KVM (Kernel-based Virtual Machine); it's a virtualization solution for Linux. It contains virtualization extensions (Intel VT or AMD-V).

To get KVM, we need to pull some software from the repos; but even before you can do that, you need to do the following first:

- Make sure that virtualization is enabled on your BIOS or UEFI settings. Consult your hardware manual on how to get to these settings. It usually involves shutting down the PC, restarting it, and pressing an interrupt key like F2 or DEL as soon as you hear the chime of your system speaker, but like I said, consult your hardware manual.

- Once you made your changes, and rebooted to Linux, find out if your system can run virtualization. This can be accomplished by running the following command from a terminal: egrep -c '(vmx|svm)' /proc/cpuinfo. If the result is a number higher than zero, that means you can go ahead with the installation.

To install KVM, type the commands, as shown in Listing 1-1, in a terminal window.

Listing 1-1. Commands to install KVM

```
sudo apt-get install qemu-kvm libvirt-bin ubuntu-vm-builder
bridge-utils
sudo adduser your_user_name kvm
sudo adduser your_user_name libvirtd
```

You may have to reboot the system to complete the installation.

Hopefully, everything went well, and you now have a proper development environment.

Key Takeaways

- You can get Android and Android Studio for macOS, Windows, and Linux. Each platform has an available precompiled binary available on the Android website.

- HAXM gives us a way to accelerate emulation on Android Virtual Devices. You will automatically get HAXM when you're on macOS or Windows (with an Intel processor). If you're on Linux, you can use KVM instead of HAXM.

CHAPTER 2

Project Basics

You will build many interesting apps, to be sure. Whether it be a gaming app, line of business app, or some other kind, we need to learn the basics of creating, building, and testing an app in Android Studio first; this chapter is all about that. In here, we'll cover the following:

- Create a simple project.

- Create an Android Virtual Device (emulator), so we can run and test projects.

Create a Project

Launch Android Studio, if you haven't done so yet. Click "Start a new Android Studio project," as shown in Figure 2-1. You need to be online when you do this because Android Studio's Gradle (a project build tool) pulls quite a few files from online repositories when starting a new project.

© Ted Hagos, Mario Zechner, J.F. DiMarzio and Robert Green 2020
T. Hagos et al., *Beginning Android Games Development*,
https://doi.org/10.1007/978-1-4842-6121-7_2

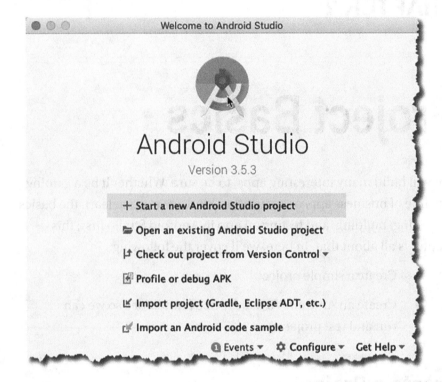

Figure 2-1. *Welcome to Android Studio*

During the creation process, Android prompts for what kind of project we want to build; choose "Phone and Tablet" ➤ "Empty Activity," as shown in Figure 2-2—we'll discuss Activities in the coming chapters, but for now, think of an Activity as a screen or form; it's something that the user sees and interacts with.

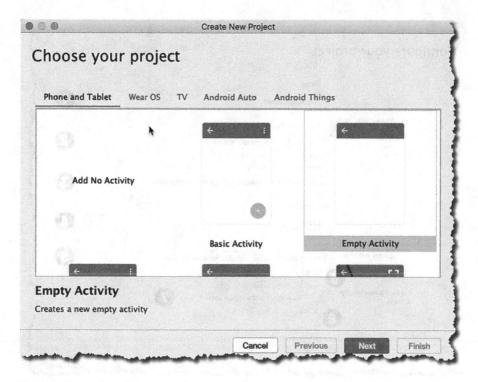

Figure 2-2. *Create a new project, choose an Activity type*

In the next screen, we get to configure the project. We set the app's name, package name (domain), and the target Android version. Figure 2-3 shows the annotated picture of the "Create New Project" screen.

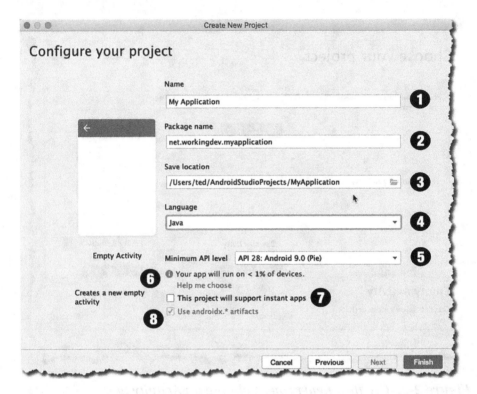

Figure 2-3. *Create New Project*

❶ **NAME**—This is what you want to call the application; this is also known as the project name. This name becomes the name of the top-level folder which contains all of the project's files. This name also becomes part of your application's identity, should you release it in the Play Store.

❷ **PACKAGE NAME**—This is your organization or company's domain name in reverse DNS notation. If you don't have a company name, you can use anything that resembles a web domain. At the moment, it won't matter if we use a real company name or not, since we won't release this to the Play Store.

❸   **SAVE LOCATION**—This is a location in your local directory where the project files will be kept.

❹   **LANGUAGE**—You can use either Kotlin or Java; for this project, we will use Java.

❺   **MINIMUM API LEVEL**—The min API level will determine the lowest version of Android which your application can run on. You need to choose wisely and prudently because it can severely limit the potential audience for your app.

❻   **HELP ME CHOOSE**—This shows the percentage of Android devices that your app can run on. If you click the "Help me choose" link, it will open a window that shows the distribution of Android devices, per Android version.

❼   **INSTANT APPS**—If you want your app to be playable, without the user installing your app, enable this check box. Instant apps allow a user to browse and "try out" your app in Google Play without downloading and installing the app.

❽   **ANDROID.X**—These are support libraries. They're included so that you can use modern Android libraries (like the ones included in Android 9) but still allow your app to be run on devices with lower Android versions.

When you're all done, click "Finish" to begin the project creation. Android Studio scaffolds the project and creates startup files like the main Activity file, Android Manifest, and other files to get the project propped up. The build tool (Gradle) will pull quite a few files from online repos—it can take some time.

After all that, hopefully the project is created, and you get to see Android Studio's main editor window, as shown in Figure 2-4.

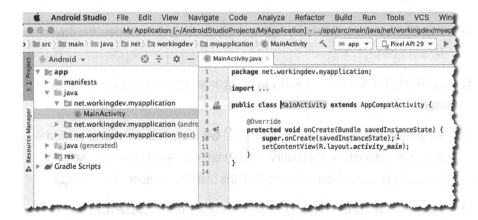

Figure 2-4. *Main editor window*

Android Studio's screen is composed of several sections which can collapse and expand, depending on your needs. The section on the left (Figure 2-4) is the Project Panel; it's a tree-like structure that shows all the (relevant) files in the project. If you want to edit a particular file, simply select it in the Project Panel and double-click; at that point, it will be opened for editing in the main editor window. In Figure 2-4, you can see the *MainActivity.java* file available for editing. In the course of time, we will spend a lot of hours doodling in the main editor window, but for now, we simply want to go through the basic process of application development. We won't add or modify anything in this Java file nor any other in the project. We'll leave it as is.

Create an AVD

We can test the application either by running it in an emulator or plugging a physical Android device into the workstation. This section covers setting up an emulator.

From Android Studio's main menu bar, go to **Tools ➤ AVD Manager**, as shown in Figure 2-5.

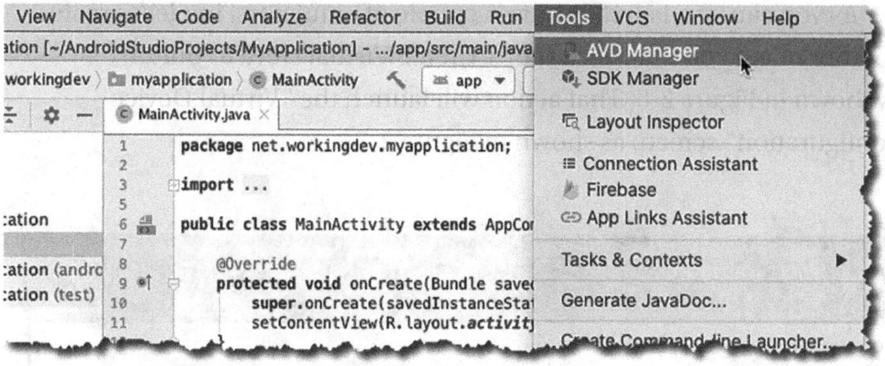

Figure 2-5. *Menu bar, Tools, AVD Manager*

The AVD manager window will launch. AVD stands for Android Virtual Device; it's an emulator that runs a specific version of the Android OS which we can use to run the apps on. The AVD manager (shown in Figure 2-6) shows all the defined emulators in our local development environment.

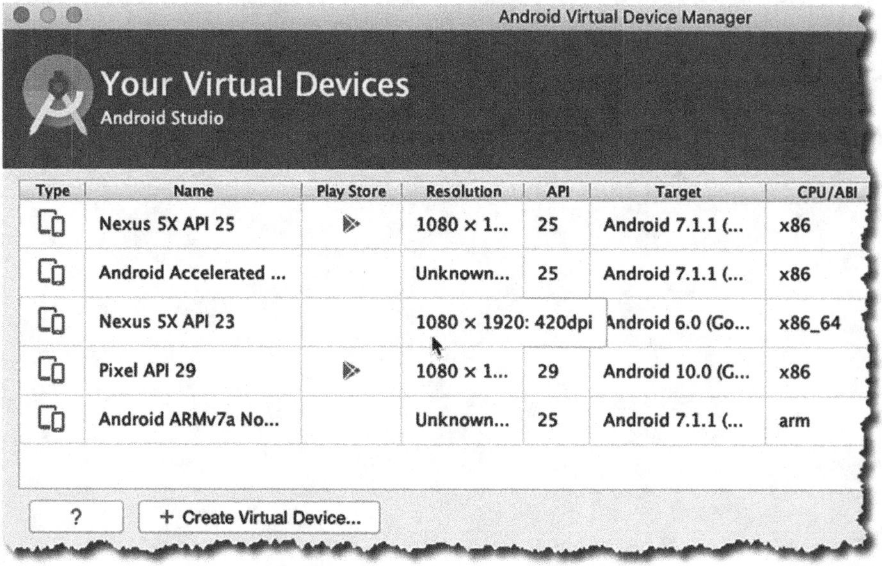

Type	Name	Play Store	Resolution	API	Target	CPU/ABI
	Nexus 5X API 25	▶	1080 × 1...	25	Android 7.1.1 (...	x86
	Android Accelerated ...		Unknown...	25	Android 7.1.1 (...	x86
	Nexus 5X API 23		1080 × 1920: 420dpi		Android 6.0 (Go...	x86_64
	Pixel API 29	▶	1080 × 1...	29	Android 10.0 (G...	x86
	Android ARMv7a No...		Unknown...	25	Android 7.1.1 (...	arm

Figure 2-6. *AVD manager*

As you can see, I already have a couple of emulators; but let's create another one; to do that, click the "+ Create Virtual Device" button, as shown in Figure 2-6. That action will launch the "Virtual Device Configuration" screen, as shown in Figure 2-7.

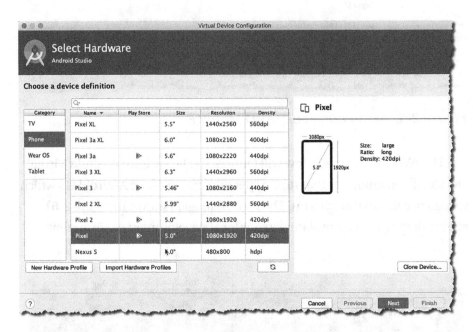

Figure 2-7. *Virtual Device Configuration*

Choose the "Phone" category, then choose the device resolution. I chose the Pixel 5.0" 420dpi screen. Click the "Next" button, and we get to choose the Android version we want to run on the emulator; we can do this on the "System Image" screen, shown in Figure 2-8.

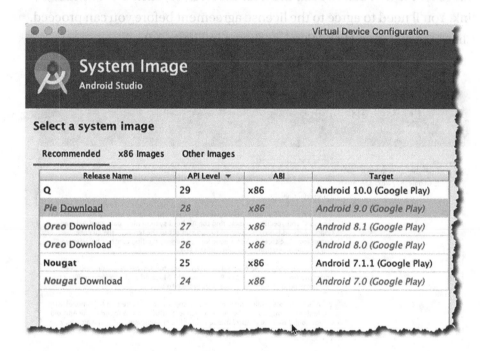

Figure 2-8. *Virtual Device Configuration*

21

I want to use Android 9 (API level 28) or Pie, as some may call it; but as you can see, I don't have the Pie system image in my machine just yet—when you can see the "download" link next to the Android version, that means you don't have that system image yet. I need to get the system image for Pie first before I can use it for the AVD; so, click the "download" link. You'll need to agree to the license agreement before you can proceed. Click "Accept," then click "Next," as shown in Figure 2-9.

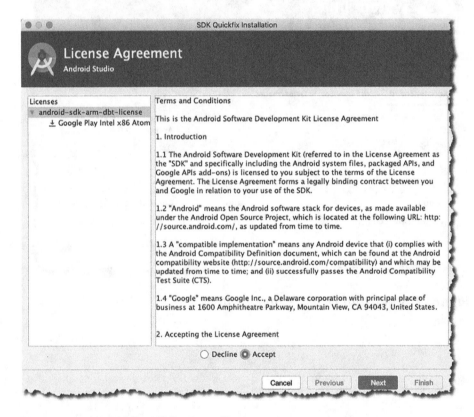

Figure 2-9. SDK Quickfix Installation

The download process can take some time, depending on your Internet speed; when it's done, you'll get back to the "System Image" selection screen, as shown in Figure 2-10.

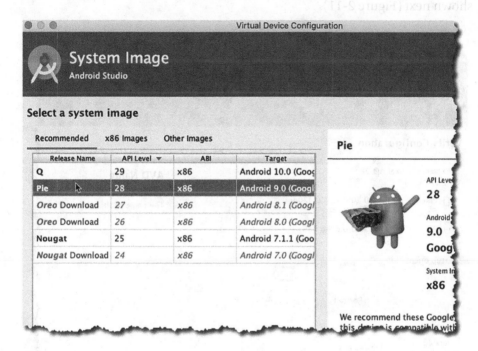

Figure 2-10. *Virtual Device Configuration*

As you can see, we can now use Pie as a system image for our emulator. Select Pie, then click "Next." The next screen shows a summary of our past choices for creating the emulator; the "Verify Configuration" screen is shown next (Figure 2-11).

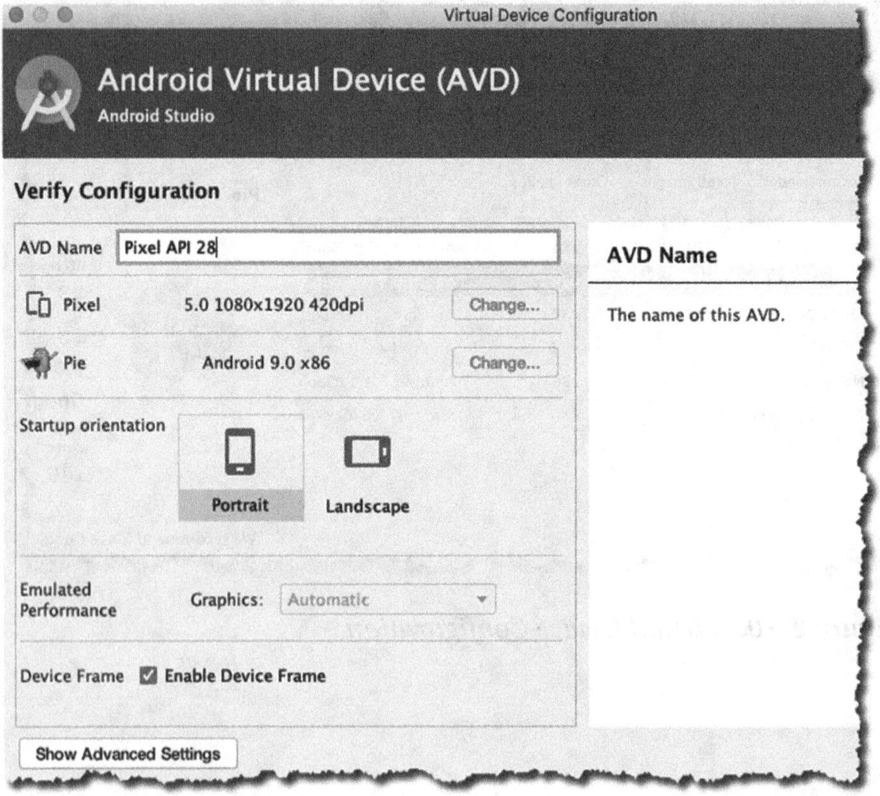

Figure 2-11. *Verify Configuration*

The "Verify Configuration" screen not only shows the summary of our past choices, you can configure some additional functionalities here. If you click the "Show Advanced Settings" button, you can also configure the following:

- Front and back camera

- Emulated network speed

- Emulated performance

- Size of internal storage

- Keyboard input (whether enabled or disabled)

When you're done, click the "Finish" button. When Android Studio finishes provisioning the newly created AVD, we'll be back in the "Android Virtual Device Manager" screen, as shown in Figure 2-12.

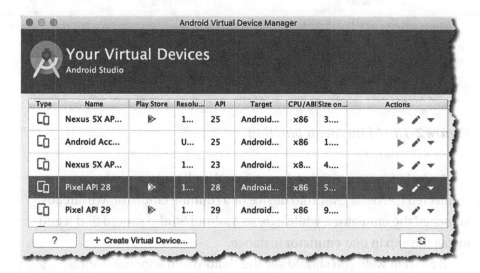

Figure 2-12. *Android Virtual Device Manager*

Now we can see the newly created emulator (Pixel API 28). You can launch it by clicking the little green arrow on the "Actions" column—the pencil icon edits the configuration of the emulator, the green arrow launches it.

When the emulator launches, you'll see an image of the Pixel phone pop up on the desktop; it needs time to boot up completely. Go back to the main editor window of Android Studio to run the app.

From the main menu bar, go to **Run ➤ Run 'app'**, as shown in Figure 2-13.

Figure 2-13. *Main menu bar, Run*

Android Studio compiles the project; then it looks for either a connected (physical) Android device or a running emulator. We already launched the emulator a while ago, so Android Studio should find it and install the app in that emulator instance.

If all went well, you should see the Hello World app that Android Studio scaffolded for us, as shown in Figure 2-14.

Figure 2-14. *Hello World*

Key Takeaways

- Android projects almost always have an Activity. If you want to start with a basic project, choose one with an "Empty Activity" and build from there.

- Pay some attention to what you put in the project details during creation; if you do release the project to Google Play, those project information will be part of your application, and many people will see it.

27

- Choose the minimum SDK carefully; it will limit the number of potential users of your app.

- You can use an emulator to run your app and see how it's shaping up. Testing using an emulator is much better if you have HAXM (emulator accelerator) enabled on your system; if you're on Linux, acceleration can be achieved using KVM.

CHAPTER 3

Android Studio

In the previous chapter, we built a simple app by creating a project, opened it in the main editor window, and ran it in an emulator. In this chapter, we'll take a closer look at the parts of Android Studio where we'll spend most of our time. We'll look at the following:

- Working with files in Android Studio

- Parts of the main editor

- Editing layout files

- The Project tool window

The IDE

From the opening dialog of Android Studio, you can launch the previous project we created. Links to existing projects appear on the left panel of the opening dialog, as shown in Figure 3-1.

© Ted Hagos, Mario Zechner, J.F. DiMarzio and Robert Green 2020
T. Hagos et al., *Beginning Android Games Development*,
https://doi.org/10.1007/978-1-4842-6121-7_3

Figure 3-1. *Welcome to Android Studio*

When you open a project, you'll see the main editor window, the project panel, and other panels that Android Studio opens by default. An annotated picture of an opened project is shown in Figure 3-2.

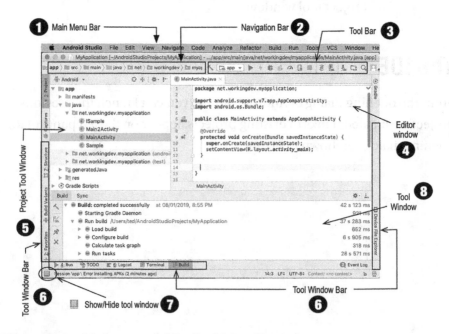

Figure 3-2. *Main parts of Android Studio*

❶   **Main menu bar**—You can navigate Android Studio in various ways. Often, there's more than one way to do a task, but the primary navigation is done in the main menu bar. If you're on Linux or Windows, the main menu bar sits directly at the top of the IDE; if you're on macOS, the main menu bar is disconnected from the IDE (which is how all macOS software works).

❷   **Navigation bar**—This bar lets you navigate the project files. It's a horizontally arranged collection of chevrons that resembles some sort of breadcrumb navigation that you can find on some websites. You can open your project files either through the navigation bar or the Project tool window.

❸   **Toolbar**—This lets you do a wide range of actions (e.g., save files, run the app, open the AVD manager, open the SDK manager, undo, redo actions, etc.).

❹   **Main editor window**—This is the most prominent window and has the most screen real estate. The editor window is where you can create and modify project files. It changes its appearance depending on what you are editing. If you're working on a program source file, this window will show just the source files. When you are editing layout files, you may see either the raw XML file or a visual rendering of the layout.

❺   **Project tool window**—This window shows the contents of the project folders; you'll be able to see and launch all your project assets (source code, XML files, graphics, etc.) from here.

❻   **Tool window bar**—The tool window bar runs along the perimeter of the IDE window. It contains the individual buttons you need to activate specific tool windows, for example, TODO, Logcat, Project window, Connected Devices, and so on.

❼   **Show/hide tool window**—It shows (or hides) the **tool window bar**. It's a toggle.

❽   **Tool Window**—You will find tool windows on the sides and bottom of the
Android Studio workspace. They're secondary windows that let you look at the
project from different perspectives. They also let you access the typical tools you
need for development tasks, for example, debugging, integration with version
control, looking at the build logs, inspecting Logcat dumps, looking at TODO
items, and so on. Here are a couple of things you can do with the Tool Windows:

- You can expand or collapse them by clicking the tool's name in the tool
  window bar. You can also drag, pin, unpin, attach, and detach the tool
  windows.
- You can rearrange the tool windows, but if you feel you need to restore the
  tool window to the default layout, you can do so from the main menu bar;
  click **Window ➤ Restore Default Layout**. Also, if you want to customize
  the "Default Layout," you rearrange the windows to your liking, and then
  from the main menu bar, click **Window ➤ Store Current Layout as
  Default**.

Main Editor

Like in most IDEs, the main editor window lets you modify and work with
source files. What makes it stand out is how well it understands Android
development assets. Android Studio lets you work with a variety of file types,
but you'll probably spend most of your time editing these types of files:

- Java source files
- XML files
- UI layout files

When you're working with Java source files, you get all the code hinting
and completions that you've come to expect from a modern editor. What's
more, it gives you plenty of early warnings when something is wrong with

your code. Figure 3-3 shows a Java class file opened in the main editor. The class file is an Activity, and it's missing a semicolon on one of its statements. You could see Android Studio peppering the IDE with (red) squiggly lines which indicates that the class won't compile.

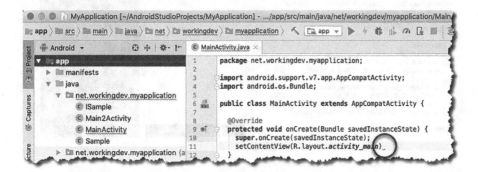

Figure 3-3. *Main editor showing error indicators*

Android Studio places the squiggly lines very near the offending code. As you can see in Figure 3-3, the squiggly lines are placed right at the point where the semicolon is expected.

Editing Layout Files

The screens that the user sees are made up of Activity source files and layout files. The layout files are written in XML. Android Studio, undoubtedly, can edit XML files, but what sets it apart is how intuitively it can render the XML files in a WYSIWYG mode (what you see is what you get). Figure 3-4 shows the two ways you can work with layout files.

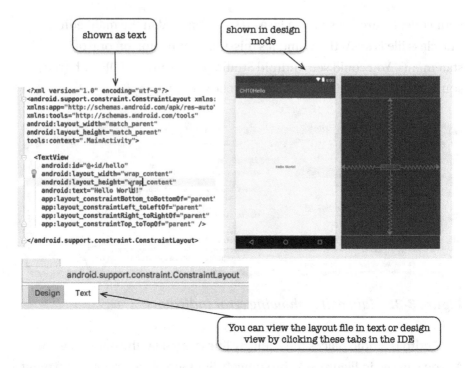

Figure 3-4. *Design mode and text mode editing of layout files*

Figure 3-5 shows the various parts of Android Studio that are relevant when working on a layout file during design mode.

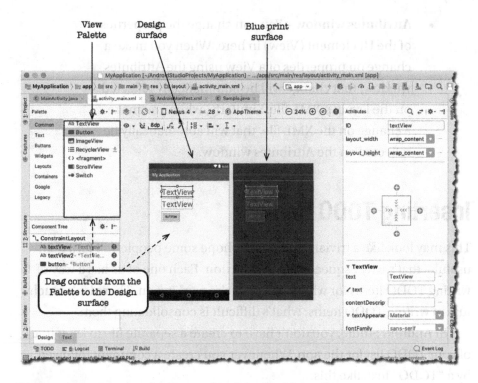

Figure 3-5. *Layout design tools of Android Studio*

- **View palette**—The View palette contains the Views (widgets) that you can drag and drop on either the Design surface or Blueprint surface.

- **Design surface**—It acts like a real-world preview of your screen.

- **Blueprint surface**—Similar to the Design surface, but it only contains the outlines of the UI elements.

- **Attributes window**—You can change the properties of the UI element (View) in here. When you make a change on properties of a View using the Attributes window, that change will be automatically reflected on the layout's XML file. Similarly, when you make a change on the XML file, that will automatically be reflected on the Attributes window.

Inserting TODO Items

This may look like a trivial feature, but I hope some people will find this useful—that's why I squeezed in this section. Each one of us has a way of writing TODO items for whatever app we're working on. There isn't much fuss in writing TODO items; what's difficult is consolidating them.

In Android Studio, you don't have to create a separate file to keep track of your TODO list for the app. Whenever you create a comment followed by a "TODO" text, like this:

```
// TODO This is a sample todo
```

Android Studio will keep track of all the TODO comments in all of your source files. See Figure 3-6.

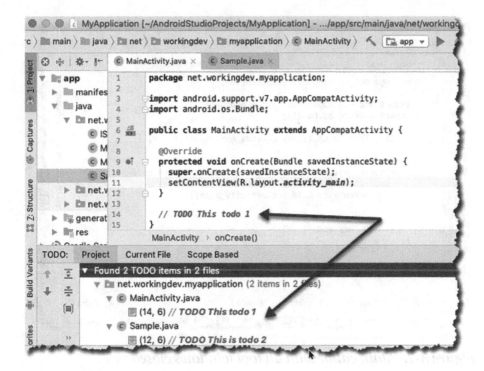

Figure 3-6. *TODO items*

To view all your TODO items, click the "TODO" tab in the tool window bar.

How to get more Screen Space for Code

You can have more screen real estate by closing all Tool Windows. Figure 3-7 shows a Java source file opened in the main editor window while all the Tool Windows are closed. You can collapse any tool window by simply clicking its name, for example, to collapse the Project tool window, click "Project."

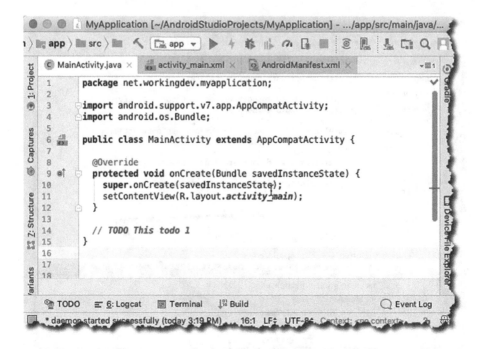

Figure 3-7. *Main editor with all tool windows closed*

You can even get more screen real estate by hiding all the tool window bars, as shown in Figure 3-8.

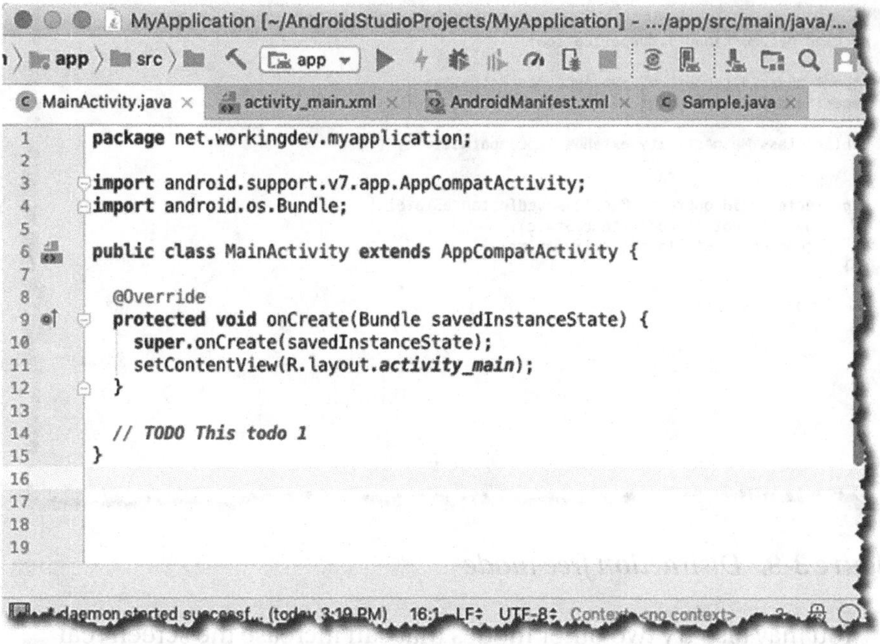

```
● ● ●  ⚙ MyApplication [~/AndroidStudioProjects/MyApplication] - .../app/src/main/java/...

⟩ ⬛ app ⟩ ⬛ src ⟩ ⬛  ⟨  ⟨⬛ app ▾⟩  ▶  ⚡ ⅋  ⬛ ⬛ ⬛ ⬛ ⬛ ⬛ ⬛ ⬛ ⬛ Q ⬛

ⓒ MainActivity.java ×   🔲 activity_main.xml ×   🔲 AndroidManifest.xml ×   ⓒ Sample.java ×

  1        package net.workingdev.myapplication;
  2
  3        import android.support.v7.app.AppCompatActivity;
  4        import android.os.Bundle;
  5
  6        public class MainActivity extends AppCompatActivity {
  7
  8            @Override
  9            protected void onCreate(Bundle savedInstanceState) {
 10                super.onCreate(savedInstanceState);
 11                setContentView(R.layout.activity_main);
 12            }
 13
 14            // TODO This todo 1
 15        }
 16
 17
 18
 19

⬛...daemon started successf... (today 3:19 PM)   16:1  LF⧉  UTF-8⧉  Context <no context>   ⬛ ◯
```

Figure 3-8. *Main editor with all tool windows closed and toolbars hidden*

You can get even more screen space by entering "Distraction Free Mode," as shown in Figure 3-9. You can enter distraction free mode from the main menu bar; click **View ➤ Enter Distraction Free Mode**. To exit the mode, click **View** from the main menu bar, then **Exit Distraction Free Mode**.

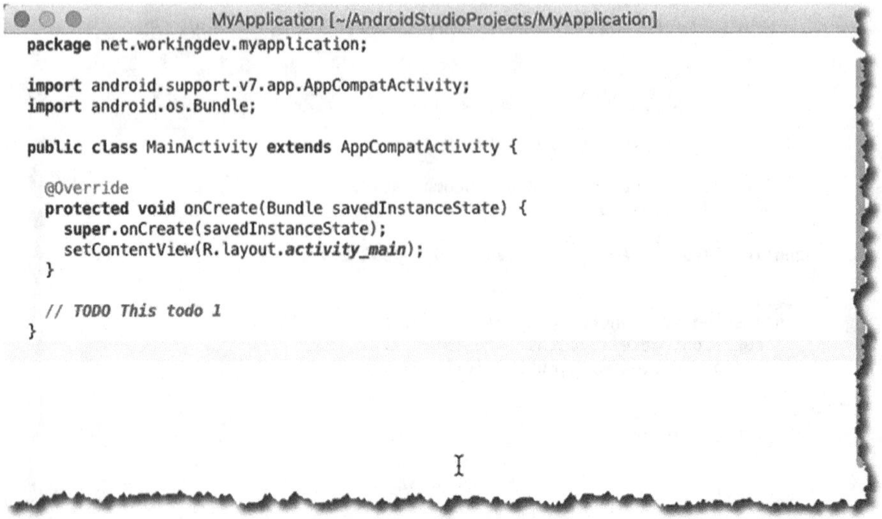

```
• ○ ○                MyApplication [~/AndroidStudioProjects/MyApplication]
package net.workingdev.myapplication;

import android.support.v7.app.AppCompatActivity;
import android.os.Bundle;

public class MainActivity extends AppCompatActivity {

  @Override
  protected void onCreate(Bundle savedInstanceState) {
    super.onCreate(savedInstanceState);
    setContentView(R.layout.activity_main);
  }

  // TODO This todo 1
}
```

Figure 3-9. *Distraction free mode*

You may also try two other modes that can increase the screen real estate. They're also found on the View menu from the main menu bar.

- Presentation mode

- Full screen

Project Tool Window

You can get to your project's files and assets via the **Project tool** window, shown in Figure 3-10. It has a tree-like structure, and the sections are collapsible. You can launch any file from this window. If you want to open a file, you simply need to double-click that file from this window.

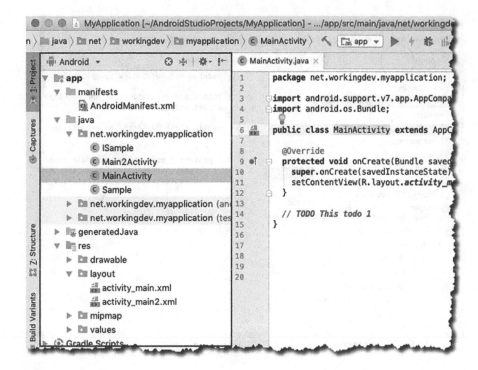

Figure 3-10. *Project tool window*

By default, Android Studio displays the **Project Files** in *Android View*, as shown in Figure 3-10. The "Android View" is organized by modules to provide quick access to the project's most relevant files. You change how you view the project files by clicking the down arrow on top of the Project window, as shown in Figure 3-11.

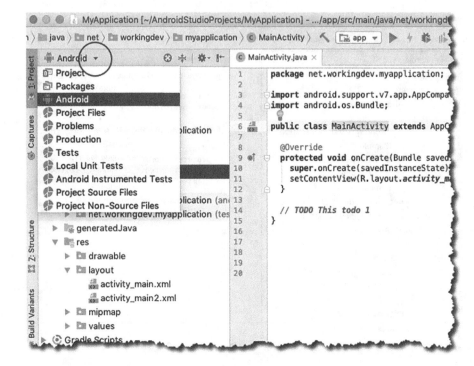

Figure 3-11. *How to change Views in the Project tool window*

Preferences/Settings

If you want to customize the behavior or look of Android Studio, you can do so in its Settings or Preferences window; it's called **Settings** if you're on Windows or Linux, and it's called **Preferences** if you're on macOS.

For Windows and Linux users, you can get to the Settings window in one of two ways:

- From the main menu bar, click **File ➤ Settings**.

- Use the keyboard shortcut **Ctrl+Alt+S**.

For macOS users, you can do it this way:

- From the main menu bar, click **Android Studio ➤ Preferences**.

- Use the keyboard shortcut **Command+,**.

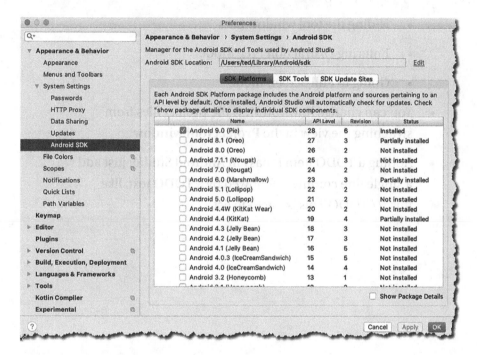

Figure 3-12. *Settings/Preferences window*

You can access a variety of Settings in this window, ranging from how Android Studio looks, whether to use spaces or tabs on the editor, how many spaces to use for tabs, which version control to use, what API to download, what system images to use for AVD, and so on.

Key Takeaways

- You can see more of your code by increasing the screen real estate for the main editor. You can do this by

  - Collapsing all the Tool Windows

  - Hiding the tool window bars

  - Entering Distraction Free Mode

  - Going to Full Screen mode

- You can change how you view the project files from switching the view in the **Project tool window**.

- Adding a TODO item is easy in Android Studio; just add a single line comment followed by a TODO text, like this: // TODO This is my todo list

CHAPTER 4

What's in an Android Application

We already know how to create a basic project, and we took a tour of Android Studio. In this chapter, we'll look at what makes up an Android application.

The Android application framework is vast and can be confusing to navigate. Its architecture is different than a desktop or web app, if you're coming from that background. Learning the Android framework can take a long time; fortunately, we don't have to learn all of it. We only need a few, and that's what this chapter is about, those few knowledge areas that we need to absorb so we can build an Android game:

- What makes up an Android project

- Overview of Android components

- Android Manifest file

- Intents

© Ted Hagos, Mario Zechner, J.F. DiMarzio and Robert Green 2020
T. Hagos et al., *Beginning Android Games Development*,
https://doi.org/10.1007/978-1-4842-6121-7_4

What makes up an Android Project

An Android app may look a lot like a desktop app; some may even think of them as miniature desktop apps, but that wouldn't be correct. Android apps are structurally different from their desktop or web counterparts. A desktop app generally contains all the routines and subroutines it needs in order to function; occasionally, it may rely on dynamically loaded libraries, but the executable file is self-contained. An Android app, on the other hand, is made up of loosely coupled components that communicate to each other using a message-passing mechanism. Figure 4-1 shows the logical structure of an Android app.

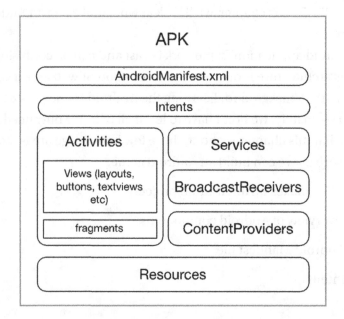

Figure 4-1. Logical representation of an Android app

The app shown in Figure 4-1 is a big one—it's got everything in it. Our app won't be as big; we don't have to use all the kinds of components in Android, but we need to learn how to use some of them, like Activities and Intents.

Activities, Services, BroadcastReceivers, and ContentProviders are called *Android components.* They are the key building blocks of an application. They are high-level abstractions of useful things like showing a screen to a user, running a task in the background, broadcasting an event so that interested applications may respond to them, and so on. Components are precoded or prebuilt classes with very specific behavior, and we use them in our application by extending them so that we can add the behavior that will be unique to our application.

Building an Android app is a lot like building a house. Some people build houses the traditional way; they assemble beams, struts, floor panels, and so on. They build the doors and other fittings from raw materials by hand, like an artisan. If we built android applications this way, it could take us a long time, and it might be quite difficult. The skill necessary to build applications from the scratch could be out of reach for some programmers. In Android, applications are built using components. Think of it as prefabricated pieces of a house. The parts are manufactured in advance, and all it requires is assembly.

An **Activity** is where we put together things that the user can see. It's a focused thing that a user can do. For example, an Activity may be purposely made to enable a user to view a single email or fill up a form. It's where the user interface elements are glued together. As you can see in Figure 4-1, inside the Activity, there are *Views* and *Fragments.* Views are classes that are used to draw content into the screen; some examples of View objects are *Buttons* and *TextViews.* A Fragment is similar to an Activity in that it's also a composition unit but a smaller one. Like Activities, they can also hold View objects. Most modern apps use Fragments in order to address the problem of deploying their app on multiple form factors. Fragments can be turned on or off depending on the available screen real estate and/or orientation.

Services are classes that allow us to run a program logic without freezing up the user interface. Services are code that run in the background; they can be very useful when your app is supposed to download a file from the Web or maybe play music.

BroadcastReceivers allow our application to listen for specific messages from either the Android system or from other applications—yes, our apps can send messages and broadcast it systemwide. You might want to use BroadcastReceivers if you want to display a warning message when the battery dips to below 10%, for example.

ContentProviders allow us to create applications that may be able to share data to other applications. It manages access to some sort of central data repository. Some ContentProviders have their own UI but some don't. The main idea why you would use this component is to allow other applications access to your app's data without them going through some SQL acrobatics. The details of the database access are completely hidden from them (client apps). An example of a prebuilt application that is a ContentProvider is the "Contacts" app in Android.

Your application may need some visual or audio assets; these are the kinds of things we mean by "Resources" in Figure 4-1.

The AndroidManifest is exactly what its name implies; it's a manifest and it's in XML format. It declares quite a few things about the application, like

- The name of the app.

- Which Activity will show up first when the user launches the app.

- What kind of components are in the app. If it has activities, the manifest declares them—names of classes and all. If the app has services, their class names will also be declared in manifest.

- What kinds of things can the app do? What are its permissions? Is it allowed to access the Internet or the camera? Can it record GPS locations and so on?

- Does it use external libraries?

- Does it support a specific type of input device?

- Are there specific screen densities that this application requires?

As you can see, the manifest is a busy place; there's a lot of things to keep an eye on. But don't worry too much about this file. Most of the entries here are automatically taken care of by the creation wizards of Android Studio. One of the few occasions you will interact with it is probably when you need to add permissions to your app.

Note   Google Play filters out incompatible applications from the list of available applications for a specific device. It uses the project's manifest file to do this filtering. Your app won't be seen by devices that cannot meet the requirements stipulated in the manifest file.

Application Entry Point

An app typically interacts with a user, and it does so using Activity components. These apps usually have at least these three things:

1. An Activity class that serves as the first screen that the user will see

2. A layout file for the Activity class which contains all the UI definitions like text views, buttons, and so on

3. The AndroidManifest file, which ties all the project resources and components together

When an application is launched, the Android runtime creates an Intent object and inspects the manifest file. It's looking for a specific value of the intent-filter node (in the xml file). The runtime is trying to see if the application has a defined entry point, something like a *main function*. Listing 4-1 shows an excerpt from the Android manifest file.

Listing 4-1. Excerpt from AndroidManifest.xml

```
<activity android:name=".MainActivity">
  <intent-filter>
    <action android:name="android.intent.action.MAIN" />
    <category android:name="android.intent.category.LAUNCHER" />
  </intent-filter>
</activity>
```

If the application has more than one Activity, you will see several activity nodes in the manifest file, one node for each Activity. The first line of the definition has an attribute called android:name. This attribute points to the class name of an Activity. In this example, the name of the class is "MainActivity".

The second line declares the *intent-filter*; when you see something like android.intent.action.MAIN, on the intent-filter node, it means the Activity is the entry point for the application. When the app is launched, this is the Activity that will interact with the user.

Activities

You can think of an Activity as a screen or a window. It's something that a user can interact with. This is the UI of the app. An Activity is a class that inherits from the *android.app.Activity* (one way or another), but we usually extend the *AppCompatActivity* class (instead of the Activity) so we can use modern UI elements but still make the app run on older Android versions; hence, the "Compat" in the name AppCompatActivity, it stands for "compatibility."

An Activity component has two parts, a Java class (or Kotlin if that's your language of choice) and a layout file in XML format. The layout file is where you put all the definitions of the UI, for example, the text box, button, labels, and so on. The Java class is where you code all the behavior parts of the UI, for example, what happens when the button is clicked, when text is entered into the field, when the user changes the orientation of the device, when another component sends a message to the Activity, and so on.

An Activity, like any other component in Android, has a life cycle. Each lifecycle event has an associated method in the Activity's Java class; we can use these methods to customize the behavior of the application. Figure 4-2 shows the Activity life cycle.

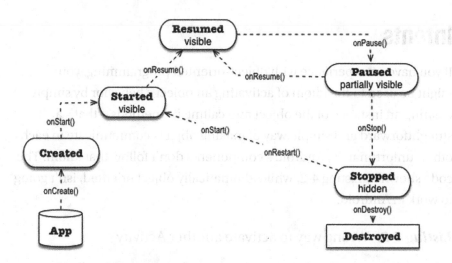

Figure 4-2. *Activity life cycle*

In Figure 4-2, the boxes show the state of an Activity on a particular stage of existence. The name of the method calls is embedded in the directional arrows which connect the stages.

When the runtime launches the app, it calls the onCreate() method of the main Activity which brings the state of the Activity to "created." You can use this method to perform initialization routines like preparing event handling code and so on.

The Activity proceeds to the next state which is "started"; the Activity is visible to the user at this point, but it's not yet ready for interaction. The next state is "resumed"; this is the state where the app is interacting with the user.

If the user clicks anything that may launch another Activity, the runtime pauses the current Activity, and it enters the "paused" state. From there, if the user goes back to the Activity, the onResume() function is called and the Activity *runs* again. On the other hand, if the user decides to open a different application, the Android runtime may "stop" and eventually "destroy" the application.

Intents

If you have an experience with object-oriented programming, you might be used to the idiom of activating an object's behavior by simply creating an instance of the object and calling its methods—that's a straightforward and simple way of making objects communicate to each other; unfortunately, Android's components don't follow that idiom. The code shown in Listing 4-2, while idiomatically object oriented, isn't going to work in Android.

Listing 4-2. Wrong way to activate another Activity

```
public class MainActivity extends AppCompatActivity {

  @Override
  protected void onCreate(Bundle savedInstanceState) {
    super.onCreate(savedInstanceState);
    setContentView(R.layout.activity_main);
```

```
  Button b = (Button) findViewById(R.id.button);
  b.setOnClickListener(new View.OnClickListener() {
    @Override
    public void onClick(View v) {
      new SecondActivity(); // WON'T WORK
    }
  });
 }
}
```

Android's architecture is quite unique in the way it builds application. It has this notion of components instead of just plain objects. Android uses *Intents* as a way for its components to communicate; it also uses Intents to pass messages across components.

The reason Listing 4-2 won't work is because an Android Activity isn't a simple object; it's a component. You cannot simply instantiate a component in order to activate it. Component activation in Android is done by creating an Intent object and then passing it to the component you want to activate, which, in our case now, is an Activity.

There are two kinds of Intents, an explicit Intent and an implicit Intent. For our purposes, we will only need the explicit Intent. Listing 4-3 shows a sample code on how to create an explicit Intent and how to use it to activate another Activity.

Listing 4-3. How to activate another Activity

```
public class MainActivity extends AppCompatActivity {

  @Override
  protected void onCreate(Bundle savedInstanceState) {
    super.onCreate(savedInstanceState);
    setContentView(R.layout.activity_main);
```

```
Button b = findViewById(R.id.button);
b.setOnClickListener(new View.OnClickListener() {
  @Override
  public void onClick(View v) {
    Intent i = new Intent(v.getContext(), SecondActivity.
    class);
    v.getContext().startActivity(i);
  }
});
}
}
```

It may look like there's a lot of things to unpack on our sample code, but don't worry, I'll explain the code with more context as we move further along in the coming chapters.

Key Takeaways

- Android applications are made up of loosely coupled components. These components communicate via Intent objects.

- An app's entry point is usually a launcher Activity. This launcher Activity is designated in the app's AndroidManifest file.

- The manifest file is like a glue that holds together the components of the application; everything the application has, can do, or cannot do is reflected in the manifest.

CHAPTER 5

Introduction to Game Development

There are an estimated 2.8 million apps on Google Play (at the time of writing), and 300,000 of them are games. That's a lot of games; and it will still grow. Anyone thinking of writing a novel game will be hard-pressed, considering that programmers have been writing games for a long time now. If you're hunting for ideas for a new game, it might be best to survey the existing games; see what kinds of ideas you can pick and combine.

In this chapter, we'll look at some of the popular games in Google Play. We'll also discuss a high-level overview of what kind of functionalities we'll need to bake into our game code. We'll cover the following areas:

- Game genres

- Game engine

- Game loop

© Ted Hagos, Mario Zechner, J.F. DiMarzio and Robert Green 2020
T. Hagos et al., *Beginning Android Games Development*,
https://doi.org/10.1007/978-1-4842-6121-7_5

A Quick Tour of Game Genres

If you looked at the Wikipedia page for game genres, you'll see the many (and still growing) categories of games. A game genre is a specific category of games related by their gameplay characteristics. We won't describe all the games here, but let's look at some of the popular ones.

Casual Games

Casual games are fast becoming a favorite for both experienced and non-experienced gamers. These games usually have very simple rules, play techniques, and degree of strategy. You don't need to commit extra-long hours for these games, nor do you need special skills to enjoy them; that's probably the reason why these games are very popular, because they're easy to learn and play as a pastime.

I'm sure you've seen some of these games already; you might have played a couple of them. *Minion Rush* (Figure 5-1) is a runner game, based loosely on the very popular *Temple Run*, where you guide a figure—in this case, a minion—through hoops and obstacles. Swipe left and the minion goes left, swipe right and it goes right, swipe down to slide, and swipe up to jump; it really is simple. There are many derivatives of this game, but the mechanics rarely changes. Usually, the objective is to run for as long as possible and collect some tokens along the way.

Figure 5-1. *Minion Rush*

Another example of a casual game is *Candy Crush Saga* (Figure 5-2). It's a "match three" game. The gameplay revolves around swapping two adjacent candies among several on the game board so that you can make a row or column of three matching colored candies. By the way, while *Candy Crush Saga* is considered a casual game, it also belongs to another category called puzzle games; sometimes, a game may belong to more than one category.

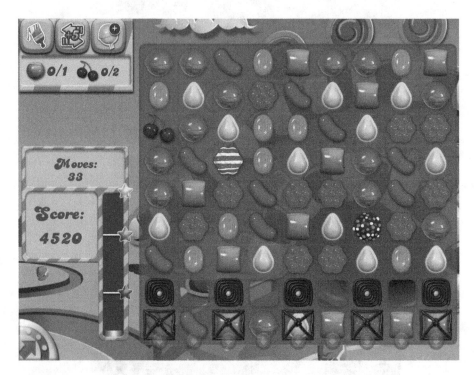

Figure 5-2. *Candy Crush Saga*

Puzzle Games

Puzzle or logic games require the player to solve logic puzzles or navigate challenging locations such as mazes. This genre frequently crosses over with adventure, educational, or even casual games. I'm sure you've heard of *Tetris* (Figure 5-3) or *Bejeweled;* these two are the best examples I can think of for puzzle games.

Tetris is largely credited for popularizing the puzzler genre. *Tetris*, originally, came from the Soviet Union and came to life sometime in 1984. The goal in this game is simple; the player must destroy lines of block before the blocks pile up and reaches the top. A tetromino is the shape of the four connected blocks that falls from the top of the screen and settles at the bottom. There are generally seven kinds of tetrominoes (Figure 5-4). You can guide the tetrominoes as they fall; swiping left or right guides the blocks to the desired location, and (usually) double tapping rotates the tetrominoes.

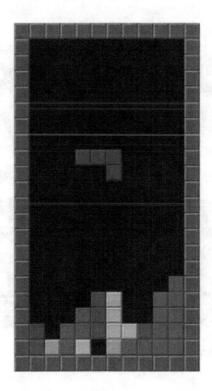

Figure 5-3. *Tetris*

Figure 5-4. *Tetrominoes*

Bejeweled (Figure 5-5) is another popular puzzler. The goal is to clear gems of the same color, potentially causing a chain reaction; this is done by swapping one gem with an adjacent gem to form a horizontal or vertical chain of three or more gems of the same color. When chains are formed, the gems disappear and some other gems fall from the top to fill in the gaps—sometimes, "cascades" are triggered when chains are formed by the falling gems.

Figure 5-5. *Bejeweled*

As you can see from the *Tetris* and *Bejeweled* examples, matchers make for good puzzle gameplay; but there are other kinds of puzzlers. Take "*Cut the Rope*" (Figure 5-6) by ZeptoLab as an example; it's a physics puzzler. The goal of the game is to feed the candy to "Om Nom" (the little green creature). The candy must be guided toward Om Nom by cutting ropes the candy is attached to; the candy may be blown or put inside bubbles, so it avoids obstacles. Every game object is physically simulated to some degree. The game is powered by Box2D, a 2D physics engine.

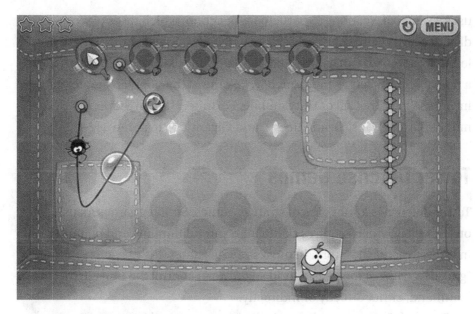

Figure 5-6. Cut the Rope

Action Games

Action games usually require hand-eye coordination and motor skills. These games center around a player who is in control of most of the action. This genre has many subgenres such as platformers, shooting games, fighting games, stealth, survival games, battle royale, and rhythm games.

Platformers usually involve a character that jumps and climbs to navigate the environment. There are usually enemies and obstacles that the character must avoid. The most popular platform games are usually released either in consoles or PCs (Mario Bros., Donkey Kong, Crash Bandicoot, Sonic Mania, Limbo, etc.), but some platformers are making their way into Google Play (Adventure Island, Blackmoor 2, Dandara, etc.).

Shooter games (or simply, shooters) are another popular subgenre of action games. The genre is very descriptive, you can guess what these games are all about just from their genre, and you would be right; you shoot things, people, aliens, monsters, zombies, and so on. The player uses a range of weapons to participate in action, which takes place at a distance. This genre is usually characterized by violent gameplay and lethal weaponry (with some notable exceptions like Splatoon, which have a nonviolent objective and gameplay). Some of the popular shooter games in Google Play are Call of Duty mobile, Fortnite, Hitman Sniper, PUBG mobile, Critical Ops, Dead Effect 2, and Gigantic X, to name a few.

Tower Defense Games

Tower defense is a subgenre of strategy games. Strategy games focus on gameplay which requires skillful and careful thinking and planning in order to achieve victory. In most strategy games, the player is given "god-like" view of the game world so they can control the units in their command, either directly or indirectly.

Tower defense gameplay typically features an evil force that sends out waves of critters, zombies, balloons, or what have you. Your task is to defend some strategic area in the game world (your tower) by mounting defenses, whether that be turrets, monkeys, guns, and so on. These defenses will shoot the incoming waves of the enemy, and you get points for each kill. The points are converted into game currency that you can use either to upgrade your weapons or buy new weapons.

At the time of writing, the popular tower defense games in Google Play are Bloons TD 6, Defenders 2, Defense Zone 3, Digfender, Element TD, Kingdom Rush, and Grow Castle, to name a few.

This is in no way a compendium of the game genres; it's a small list of what kinds of games you can find in Google Play. If you're looking for an inspiration for your next game (or first game), try to play the games analytically, and set aside the entertainment part. Do it clinically. Try to get a feel of how the game flows and try to deconstruct it in your mind. That may give you some ideas for your game.

Game Engine

Once you have an idea what game you want to build, and presumably, you've gone through the exercise of designing your game through storyboarding, mocking the graphics, and drawing some screen wireframes—you know, the planning stage—you probably want to spend some time on how to organize the code. The organization of the code is what makes up the game engine and the game loop.

At the core of every game is the game engine. This is the code that powers the game; this is the one that handles all the grunt work. A typical game engine will handle the following tasks:

- Window management

- Graphics rendering

- Animation

- Audio

- Collision detection

- Physics

- Threading and memory

- Networking

- Input/output

- Storage

The game loop is a block of code within the game engine. As its name suggests, it loops. It runs repeatedly and perpetually; it doesn't stop until the player quits. You may have heard gamers talked about frame rates before; the speed at which your game loop can run affects the frame rate of the game. The faster your code executes within the loop, the more responsive it will be and the smoother the game will be.

A typical game loop does the following:

- **Get inputs from the user**—This is the command interpreter; you need to set up your code to listen to user inputs, whether they be double taps, long clicks, button clicks, swipes, gestures, keyboard inputs, or others. These inputs affect the characters and the overall game, for example, if the game was *Minion Rush* or *Temple Run*, swiping left, right, up, or down moves the runner.

- **Collision detection**—This is where you track the characters as they move through the game world. When they reach the edges of the game world, you decide what to do with the character. Collision detection is also where you test if the character has bumped into obstacles.

- **Draw and move the background**—This is where you draw the game world, at least part of it that should be visible to the player.

- **Move the characters** as a response to the user input.

- **Play sound effects** as interesting events happen to the character or within the game world.

- **Play background music**—This isn't the same as playing sound effects. The background music persists throughout a level, so it needs to be continuous. This is where your knowledge of threads will come in handy.

- **Track the player's score**—As the game progresses, the player will accumulate points. You can store the game stats locally using a local storage. In case you need to update a leaderboard in the cloud, you need to use the networking APIs of Android. Tracking the player's score might also involve displaying a dedicated screen (an Activity or a Frame in Android) where the scores are tallied.

This isn't an exhaustive or definitive list of what you need to address in code, but it's a start. The number of things you need to do in the game loop and the game engine will increase or decrease depending on the complexity of the game.

Key Takeaways

- There is already a myriad of games. Your next game inspiration could come from existing games. Try playing the game analytically, clinically, and divorced from the entertainment aspect. Dissect them to get an idea of how they flow.

- Smoothness of the game experience is heavily affected by what you do inside the game loop. The faster the loop executes, the snappier your game is.

CHAPTER 6

Building the Crazy Eights Game

The best way to learn game programming is to start coding one. In this chapter, we'll build a simple card game, Crazy Eights. Crazy Eights is a popular game, both the actual card game and its electronic counterparts. If you search Google Play for Crazy Eights, it'll turn up quite a few selections.

We'll walk through the process of how to build a simple turn-based card game like Crazy Eights. The rules of this game are simple, and it doesn't involve a lot of moving parts; that's not to say it won't be challenging to build. There are plenty of challenges ahead, especially if this is the first time you'll build a game. In this chapter, we'll discuss the following:

- How to use Custom Views

- How to build a splash screen

- Drawing graphics

- Handling screen orientation

- Going full screen

- Drawing buttons from graphics

- Handling touch events

- Mechanics of the Crazy Eights game

- All the logic required for the Crazy Eights game

© Ted Hagos, Mario Zechner, J.F. DiMarzio and Robert Green 2020
T. Hagos et al., *Beginning Android Games Development*,
https://doi.org/10.1007/978-1-4842-6121-7_6

Throughout the chapter, I'll show the code snippets necessary to build the game and what the program looks like at specific stages of development. The best way to understand and learn the programming techniques in this chapter is to download the source code for the game and keep it open in Android Studio as you read through the chapter sections. If you want to follow along and build the project yourself, it's best to keep the source code for the chapter handy, so you can copy and paste particular snippets as necessary.

Basic Gameplay

Crazy Eights can be played by two up to five players with a deck of 52 cards; in our case, there will only be two players—a human player and a computer player. Of course, you can build this game to accommodate more players, but limiting the players to one human player makes the programming a lot simpler.

Seven cards are dealt to both players one card at a time; the top card of the remaining deck is placed face up to start the discard pile.

The object of the game is to be the first player to get rid of their cards. Cards with a matching suit or number can be played into the middle. Conventionally, the player to the left of the dealer goes first, but in our case, the human player will simply start. So, the human player (us) looks at our cards, and if we have a card that matches either the suit or the number of the top card in the discard pile, we can play that card. If we're unable to play any card, we will draw from the remaining deck (up to three cards); if we're still unable to play, we pass. In case we draw a card that can be played, that will be played. The eights (any suit) are wild, and it can be played on any card. The player of an eight will state or choose a suit, and the next player will have to play a card in the suit that was chosen. When one of the players is able to play the last card into the middle, the round is finished. The round can also finish if none of the players can play a hand.

The score is calculated by awarding players the point value of cards left in their hands at the end of the round; for example, if the computer bested us in the round, and we were left with the 9 of hearts and 3 of spades, our score will be 12.

The game ends when one of the players hits 100 or more points. The player with the lowest score wins.

Key Parts of the Program

To build the game, the key things to figure out are the following:

- **How to draw cards**—Android doesn't have a built-in View object that can display cards; we have to draw it for ourselves.

- **How to handle events**—There will be some parts of the program where we can use the traditional event handling of Android where we only have to attach a listener to the View object, but there will also be parts where we need to figure out if the user action falls on the region where we drew the button.

- Make the game full screen.

There are other technical challenges, but the preceding list is a good starting point.

We'll build the game app with mainly two Activities and two Views, two custom Views, to be precise. To illustrate the individual cards, the card deck, and the discard pile, we need to do 2D drawings. The Android SDK doesn't have a ready-made View object that will suit our needs. It's not like we can drag and drop a Card object from the palette and go from there; so, we have to build our own custom View object. The **android. view.View** is the basic class for drawing and handling input;

we will use this class to draw the cards, the deck, and other things we need for the game, like the scoreboard. We could use the SurfaceView class as our base class for our 2D drawings, and it would have been a better choice because of the performance benefits (it has to do with the way SurfaceView handles threads), but the SurfaceView requires a bit more effort in programming. So, let's go with the simpler View object. Our game doesn't need to go crazy on the animation anyway. We should be just fine with our choice.

Custom Views and Activities

In our past projects, you may recall that an Activity component is used to show the UI and that it has two parts—a Java program in code-behind and an XML file, which is essentially where the UI is structured as nested arrangements of the View object defined in XML. That was fine for apps, but we need to render custom drawings from image files, so that technique won't work. What we'll do is to create a Custom View object where we will draw everything we need, then we will set the content view of the Activity to that custom view. We can create the custom View by creating a Java class that extends **android.view.View**.

Assuming you've already created a project with an empty Activity, like how we did it in the previous chapters, you can add a class to your project by using the context menu in the Project tool window. Right-click the package name, then click New ➤ Java, as shown in Figure 6-1.

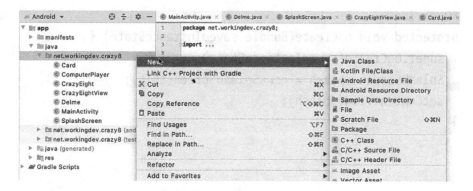

Figure 6-1. *Add a class to the project*

Type the name of the class, then hit ENTER. I named the class
SplashScreen, and its contents are shown in Listing 6-1.

Listing 6-1. SplashScreen.java

```
import android.content.Context;
import android.view.View;

public class SplashScreen extends View {
  public SplashScreen(Context context) {
    super(context);
  }
}
```

This is the starting point on how to create a custom View object. We
can associate this View to our MainActivity by setting the MainActivity's
View to SplashScreen, as shown in Listing 6-2.

Listing 6-2. MainActivity

```
import androidx.appcompat.app.AppCompatActivity;
import android.os.Bundle;

public class MainActivity extends AppCompatActivity {
```

71

```
@Override
protected void onCreate(Bundle savedInstanceState) {
    super.onCreate(savedInstanceState);
    SplashScreen splash = new SplashScreen(this);
    setContentView(splash);
  }
}
```

Drawing on the Screen

To draw on the screen, we can override the onDraw() method of the View object. Let's modify the SplashScreen class to draw a simple circle on the screen. The code is shown in Listing 6-3.

Listing 6-3. Drawing on the screen

```
import android.content.Context;
import android.graphics.Canvas;
import android.graphics.Paint;
import android.view.View;
import android.graphics.Color;

public class SplashScreen extends View {

    private Paint paint;
    private int cx;
    private int cy;
    private float radius;

    public SplashScreen(Context context) {
        super(context);
```

```
paint  = new Paint(); ❶
paint.setColor(Color.GREEN);
paint.setAntiAlias(true);

cx = 200; cy = 200; radius = 50; ❷❸❹
}

@Override
protected void onDraw(Canvas canvas) { ❺
  super.onDraw(canvas);
  canvas.drawCircle(cx,cy,radius,paint); ❻
}
}
```

---

❶	The Paint object determines how the circle will look like on the canvas.
❷❸❹	cx, cy, and radius variables hold the size and location where we'll paint the circle.
❺	When the Android runtime calls the **onDraw** method, a Canvas object is passed to the method, which we can use to draw something on the screen.
❻	The **drawCircle** is one of the drawing methods available from the Canvas object.

The important takeaway here is to remember that if you want to draw something on the screen, you need to do that on the onDraw() method of the View object. The parameter to onDraw() is a Canvas object that the View can use to draw itself. The Canvas defines methods for drawing lines, bitmaps, circles (as in our example here), and many other graphic primitives. Overriding the onDraw() is the key to creating a custom user interface.

You can run the example at this point. I won't take a screen capture anymore since it's just an unassuming circle.

Handling Events

The touchscreen is the most common type of input for game apps, so that's what we'll use. To handle touch events, we will override the onTouchEvent() callback of our SplashScreen class. Listing 6-4 shows the basic structure and a typical code for handling touch events. You can put the onTouchEvent() callback anywhere inside the SplashScreen program.

Listing 6-4. Handling touch events

```
public boolean onTouchEvent(MotionEvent evt) { ❶
  int action = evt.getAction(); ❷
  switch(action) {   ❸
    case MotionEvent.ACTION_DOWN:
      Log.d(TAG, "Down"); ❹
      break;
    case MotionEvent.ACTION_UP:
      Log.d(TAG, "Up");
      break;
    case MotionEvent.ACTION_MOVE:
      Log.d(TAG, "Move");
      cx = (int) evt.getX(); ❺
      cy = (int) evt.getY(); ❻
      break;
  }
  invalidate(); ❼
  return true;
}
```

❶   The Android runtime calls the **onTouchEvent** method when the screen is touched, dragged, or swiped.

❷   **evt.getAction()** returns an int value which tells us the action taken by the user, whether it was a swipe down, up, or just a touch. In our case, we're just watching for any movement.

❸   We can use a simple switch construct on the action to route the program logic.

❹   We don't need to handle the down action for now, but I'm logging it.

❺   This gets the x coordinate of where the touch happened.

❻   And this gets the y coordinate. We're updating the values of our **cx** and **cy** variables (the location of the circle).

❼   This will cause the Android runtime to call the **onDraw** method.

In Listing 6-4, all we did was capture the location where the touch happened. Once we extracted the x and y coordinates of the touch, we assigned those coordinates to our **cx** and **cy** member variables, then we called **invalidate()**, which forced a redraw of the View class. Each time a redraw is forced, the runtime will call the onDraw() method, which then draws the circle (again), but this time using the updated location of **cx** and **cy** (variables that hold the location of our small circle drawing). Listing 6-5 shows the completed code for SplashScreen.java.

Listing 6-5. SplashScreen completed code

```
import android.content.Context;
import android.graphics.Canvas;
import android.graphics.Paint;
import android.util.Log;
import android.view.MotionEvent;
import android.view.View;
import android.graphics.Color;
```

```java
public class SplashScreen extends View {

  private Paint paint;
  private int cx;
  private int cy;
  private float radius;
  private String TAG = getContext().getClass().getName();

  public SplashScreen(Context context) {
    super(context);

    paint  = new Paint();
    paint.setColor(Color.GREEN);
    paint.setAntiAlias(true);

    cx = 200;
    cy = 200;
    radius = 50;
  }

  @Override
  protected void onDraw(Canvas canvas) {
    super.onDraw(canvas);
    cx = cx + 50;
    cy = cy + 25;
    canvas.drawCircle(cx,cy,radius,paint);
  }

  public boolean onTouchEvent(MotionEvent evt) {

    int action = evt.getAction();
    switch(action) {
      case MotionEvent.ACTION_DOWN:
        Log.d(TAG, "Down");
        break;
```

```
      case MotionEvent.ACTION_UP:
        Log.d(TAG, "Up");
        break;
      case MotionEvent.ACTION_MOVE:
        Log.d(TAG, "Move");
        cx = (int) evt.getX();
        cy = (int) evt.getY();
        break;
    }
    invalidate();
    return true;
  }

}
```

If you run this code, all it will do is draw a small green circle on the screen, waiting for you to touch the screen. Every time you touch the screen, the circle will move to the location where you touched it.

This isn't part of our game. This is some sort of practice code so we can warm up to the actual game code. Now that we have some idea on how to paint something to the screen and how to handle basic touch event, let's proceed with the game code.

SplashScreen with a Title Graphic

We don't want to show just a small dot to the user when the game is launched; instead, we want to display some title graphic. Some games probably will show credits and some other info, but we'll keep ours simple. We'll display the title of the game using a simple bitmap. Before you can do this, you need to put the graphic file in the **app/res/drawable** folder of the project. A simple way to do that is to use the context menu; right-click the **app/res/drawable** ➤ **Reveal in Finder** (on macOS); if you're on Windows, this will read **Show in Explorer**. The dialog window in macOS is shown in Figure 6-2.

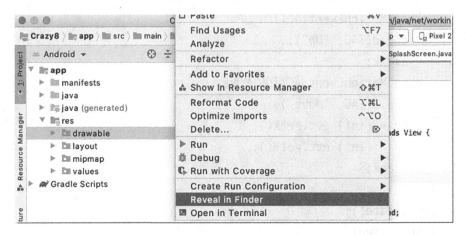

Figure 6-2. res ➤ drawable ➤ Reveal in Finder

When you launch the file manager, you can place the graphic file in there. The drawable folder is where graphical assets are usually stored.

To load the bitmap

Listing 6-6. Loading the bitmap

```
import android.graphics.Bitmap;
import android.graphics.BitmapFactory;
import android.content.Context;
import android.graphics.Canvas;
import android.view.View;

public class SplashScreen extends View {

  private Bitmap titleG;

  public SplashScreen(Context context) {
    super(context);
    titleG = BitmapFactory.decodeResource(getResources(),
            R.drawable.splash_graphic); ❶
  }
```

```
protected void onDraw(Canvas canvas) {
    super.onDraw(canvas);
    canvas.drawBitmap(titleG, 100, 100, null); ❷
}
}
```

---

❶ Use the BitmapFactory to decode the graphical resource from the drawable folder. This loads the bitmap onto memory which we will use later to draw the graphic onto the screen.

❷ The **drawBitmap** method of Canvas draws the bitmap to the screen.

Our splash screen is shown in Figure 6-3.

Figure 6-3. Splash screen

The screen doesn't look bad, but it's skewed to the left. That's because we hardcoded the drawing coordinates for the bitmap. We'll fix that in a little while; first, let's take care of that application title and the other widgets on top of the screen. Let's maximize the screen space for our game. Open *MainActivity.java* and make the changes shown in Listing 6-7.

Listing 6-7. Displaying the app full screen

```java
public class MainActivity extends AppCompatActivity {

  private View splash;

  @Override
  protected void onCreate(Bundle savedInstanceState) {
    super.onCreate(savedInstanceState);
    splash = new SplashScreen(this);
    splash.setKeepScreenOn(true);
    setContentView(splash);
  }

  private void setToFullScreen() {  ❶
    splash.setSystemUiVisibility(View.SYSTEM_UI_FLAG_LOW_
    PROFILE
        | View.SYSTEM_UI_FLAG_FULLSCREEN
        | View.SYSTEM_UI_FLAG_LAYOUT_STABLE
        | View.SYSTEM_UI_FLAG_IMMERSIVE_STICKY
        | View.SYSTEM_UI_FLAG_LAYOUT_HIDE_NAVIGATION
        | View.SYSTEM_UI_FLAG_HIDE_NAVIGATION);
  }
```

```
@Override
protected void onResume() {
  super.onResume();
  setToFullScreen(); ❷
 }
}
```

---

❶   Create a new method where we can put the necessary code to make the
      app full screen.

❷   Call the **setFullScreen** method on the **onResume** callback. onResume()
      is called just before the UI is visible to the user; so, this is a good place to
      put our fullscreen code. This lifecycle method may be called several times
      during the life of the app.

The **setSystemUiVisibility** method of the View object is the key to
display a more immersive screen experience to your users. There are
many combinations you can try for the system UI flags. You can read
more about them on the documentation page here: https://bit.ly/
androidfullscreen.

Next, we take care of the orientation. We can choose to let users play
the game either in portrait or landscape mode, but that means we need
to write more code to handle the orientation change; we won't do that
here. Instead, we will fix our game in portrait mode. This can be done in
the AndroidManifest file. You need to edit the manifest file to reflect the
modifications shown in Listing 6-8. To open the manifest file, double-click
the file from the Project tool window, as shown in Figure 6-4.

Figure 6-4. *AndroidManifest*

Listing 6-8. AndroidManifest

```
<?xml version="1.0" encoding="utf-8"?>
<manifest xmlns:android="http://schemas.android.com/apk/res/
android"
  package="net.workingdev.crazy8">

  <application
    android:allowBackup="true"
    android:icon="@mipmap/ic_launcher"
    android:label="@string/app_name"
    android:roundIcon="@mipmap/ic_launcher_round"
    android:supportsRtl="true"
    android:theme="@style/AppTheme">
    <activity android:name=".MainActivity"
            android:screenOrientation="portrait"   ❶
            android:configChanges="orientation|keyboard
            Hidden"   ❷
    >
      <intent-filter>
        <action android:name="android.intent.action.MAIN" />
```

```
        <category android:name="android.intent.category.
        LAUNCHER" />
        </intent-filter>
    </activity>
    </application>
</manifest>
```

---

❶   This fixes the screen orientation to portrait.

❷   This line prevents screen orientation changes when the software keyboard is toggled.

Now that we have the orientation fixed and full screen sorted out, we can work on centering the graphic.

To center the title graphic, we need the actual width of the screen and the actual width of the title graphic. The width of the screen minus the width of the title graphic divided by two should give us the location where we can start drawing the title graphic such that it's centered on the screen. Listing 6-9 shows the changes we need to make in SplashScreen to make all these happen.

Listing 6-9. Centering the title graphic

```
public class SplashScreen extends View {

  private Bitmap titleG;
  private int scrW; private int scrH; ❶

  public SplashScreen(Context context) {
    super(context);
    titleG = BitmapFactory.decodeResource(getResources(),
            R.drawable.splash_graphic);
  }
```

```
@Override
public void onSizeChanged (int w, int h, int oldw, int oldh){
  super.onSizeChanged(w, h, oldw, oldh);
  scrW = w; scrH = h; ❷

}

protected void onDraw(Canvas canvas) {
  super.onDraw(canvas);
  int titleGLeftPos =  (scrW - titleG.getWidth())/2; ❸
  canvas.drawBitmap(titleG, titleGLeftPos, 100, null); ❹
  }
}
```

❶   Let's declare some variables to hold the dimensions of the screen.

❷   As soon as the Android runtime is able to calculate the actual dimensions of
      the screen, the **onSizeChanged()** method is called. We can grab the actual
      width and height of the screen from here and assign them to our member
      variables which will hold screen-height and screen-width values.

❸   The **title.getWidth()** gets, well, the width of our title graphic, subtracts
      it from the screen width (which we grabbed during onSizeChanged), and
      divides it by two. That should center the graphic.

❹   Now we can draw the graphic with proper centering.

Figure 6-5 shows our app, as it currently stands.

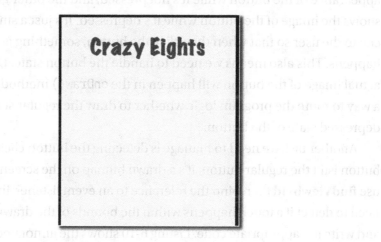

Figure 6-5. Centered graphic and full screen

Adding the Play Button

We will add a button to the splash screen so that we have a way for the user to actually start the game. We'll add just a "Play" button; we won't add a "Quit" button. We could add a Quit button, but we're not doing this because it's not consistent with Android app conventions. Our game is still, after all, an Android app. It needs to behave like most Android apps, and most Android apps don't have a Quit button. An app is typically launched, used, paused, and killed, and the Android OS already has a way to kill apps.

We can't drag and drop a Button View object from the Palette because we're using a custom view. We have to draw the button just like how we drew the title graphic. So, in the SplashScreen class, add the declaration statement for the button and then initialize it by loading the image using the BitmapFactory somewhere in the constructor of SplashScreen.

I prepared two graphics for the button; one graphic shows the regular appearance of the button while it's not pressed, and the other graphic shows the image of the button while it's depressed. It's just a small visual cue to the user so that when they click the button, something actually happens. This also means we need to handle the button state. Drawing the actual image of the button will happen in the onDraw() method; we need a way to route the program logic whether to draw the regular state or the depressed state of the button.

Another task we need to manage is detecting the button click. Our button isn't the regular button; it's a drawn bitmap on the screen. We cannot use **findViewbyId** then bind the reference to an event listener. Instead, we need to detect if a touch happens within the bounds of the drawn button and write the appropriate code. Listing 6-10 shows the annotated code for loading, drawing, and managing the state of the Play button. The other code related to the display and centering of the title graphic has been removed, so only the code relevant for the button is displayed.

Listing 6-10. Displaying and managing the Play button states

```
import android.view.MotionEvent;

public class SplashScreen extends View {

  private Bitmap playBtnUp; ❶
  private Bitmap playBtnDn;
  private boolean playBtnPressed; ❷

  public SplashScreen(Context context) {
    super(context);
    playBtnUp = BitmapFactory.decodeResource(getResources(),
    R.drawable.btn_up); ❸
    playBtnDn = BitmapFactory.decodeResource(getResources(),
    R.drawable.btn_down);
  }
```

```java
@Override
public void onSizeChanged (int w, int h, int oldw, int oldh){
  super.onSizeChanged(w, h, oldw, oldh);
  scrW = w;
  scrH = h;
}

public boolean onTouchEvent(MotionEvent event) {
  int evtAction = event.getAction();

  int X = (int)event.getX();
  int Y = (int)event.getY();

  switch (evtAction ) {

    case MotionEvent.ACTION_DOWN:

      int btnLeft = (scrW - playBtnUp.getWidth())/2; ❹
      int btnRight = btnLeft + playBtnUp.getWidth();
      int btnTop = (int) (scrH * 0.5);
      int btnBottom = btnTop + playBtnUp.getHeight();

      boolean withinBtnBounds = X > btnLeft && X
      < btnRight &&
                               Y > btnTop &&
                               Y < btnBottom; ❺

      if (withinBtnBounds) {
        playBtnPressed = true; ❻
      }
      break;

    case MotionEvent.ACTION_MOVE:
      break;
```

```
    case MotionEvent.ACTION_UP:
      if (playBtnPressed) {
        // Launch main game screen
      }
      playBtnPressed = false;
      break;
  }
  invalidate();
  return true;
}

protected void onDraw(Canvas canvas) {
  super.onDraw(canvas);

  int playBtnLeftPos = (scrW - playBtnUp.getWidth())/2;
  if (playBtnPressed) { ❼
    canvas.drawBitmap(playBtnDn, playBtnLeftPos, (int)
    (scrH *0.5), null);
  } else {
    canvas.drawBitmap(playBtnUp, playBtnLeftPos, (int)
    (scrH *0.5), null);
  }
 }
}
```

---

❶   It defines the variables to hold the bitmap for the button images.

❷   We'll use the **btnPressed** boolean variable as a switch; if this is false, it
      means the button isn't pressed, and we'll display the regular button graphic.
      If it's true, we'll display the button graphic for the depressed state.

❸   Let's load up the button bitmap from the graphical file, just like how we did it
      for the title graphic.

❹   The variables **btnLeft, btnTop, btnBottom**, and **btnRight** are screen
       coordinates for the bounds of the button.

❺   If the X and Y coordinates of the touch action are within the button bounds,
       this expression will return **true**.

❻   If the button is within the bounds, we set the **btnPressed** variable to true.

❼   During **onDraw**, we can display the appropriate button graphic depending on
       the value of the **btnPressed** variable.

Figure 6-6 shows our app with the centered title graphic and Play button.

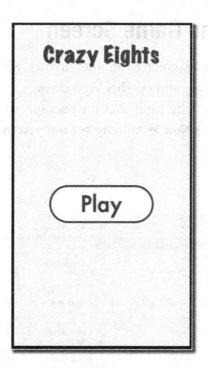

Figure 6-6. Splash screen with the Play button

The play button is centered vertically on the screen; if you want to adjust the vertical location of the button, you can change it in the **onDraw** method; it's the third parameter of the drawBitmap method, as shown in the following snippet.

```
canvas.drawBitmap(playBtnUp, playBtnLeftPos, (int)(scrH *0.5),
null);
```

The expression (int) (scrH *0.5) means to get the value of the midpoint of the detected screen height; multiplying the screen height by 50% gets you the midpoint.

Launching the Game Screen

We will launch the game screen as another Activity, which means we need to create another Activity and another View class.

To add another Activity, right-click the package name in the Project tool window, then click **New ➤ Activity ➤ Empty Activity**, as shown in Figure 6-7.

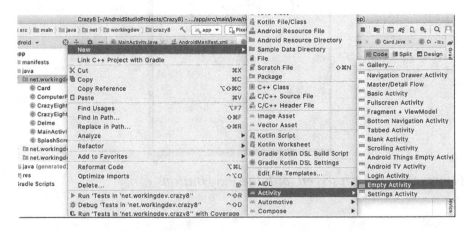

Figure 6-7. *New Empty Activity*

Then, fill up the Activity name, as shown in Figure 6-8.

Figure 6-8. *Configure Activity*

Next, add a new class to the project. You can do this by right-clicking the package name and choosing New ➤ Java Class, as shown in Figure 6-9.

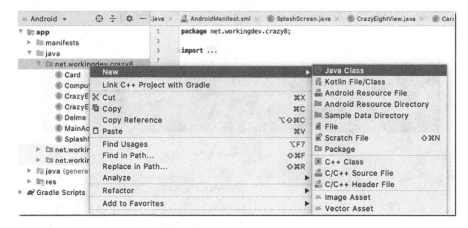

Figure 6-9. *New Java Class*

Name the class CrazyEightView, edit it, and make it extend the View class, just like our SplashScreen class. Listing 6-11 shows the code for CrazyEightView.

Listing 6-11. CrazyEightView.java

```java
import android.content.Context;
import android.graphics.Canvas;
import android.view.View;

public class CrazyEightView extends View {

  public CrazyEightView(Context context) {
    super(context);
  }

  protected void onDraw(Canvas canvas) {
    super.onDraw(canvas);
  }
}
```

Next, we fix the second Activity class (CrazyEight class) to occupy the whole screen, much like our MainActivity class. Listing 6-12 shows the code for CrazyEightActivity.

Listing 6-12. CrazyEightActivity

```
public class CrazyEight extends AppCompatActivity {

  private View gameView;

  @Override
  protected void onCreate(Bundle savedInstanceState) {
    super.onCreate(savedInstanceState);

    gameView = new CrazyEightView(this); ❶
    gameView.setKeepScreenOn(true);
    setContentView(gameView); ❷

  }

  private void setToFullScreen() { ❸
    gameView.setSystemUiVisibility(View.SYSTEM_UI_FLAG_LOW_
    PROFILE
        | View.SYSTEM_UI_FLAG_FULLSCREEN
        | View.SYSTEM_UI_FLAG_LAYOUT_STABLE
        | View.SYSTEM_UI_FLAG_IMMERSIVE_STICKY
        | View.SYSTEM_UI_FLAG_LAYOUT_HIDE_NAVIGATION
        | View.SYSTEM_UI_FLAG_HIDE_NAVIGATION);
  }

  @Override
  protected void onResume() {
    super.onResume();
    setToFullScreen(); ❹
  }
}
```

❶   Create an instance of the CrazyEightView class and pass the current context.

❷   Set the View of this Activity to our custom view (CrazyEightView).

❸   Here comes our code for getting the whole View to occupy the entire screen, same as we did before.

❹   We call the **setFullScreen** within the **onResume** callback because we want it to run just before the screen is visible to the user.

Now that we've got an Activity where the actual game will be played, we can put in the code in SplashScreen that will launch our second Activity (CrazyEight).

Android uses **Intent** objects for component Activation, and launching an Activity requires component Activation. There are many other uses for Intents, but we won't cover them here. We'll just put in the necessary code to launch our CrazyEight Activity.

Go back to SplashScreen's **onTouchEvent**, specifically the **MotionEvent.ACTION_UP** branch. In Listing 6-10, find the code where we made the comment // Launch main game screen, as shown in the snippet in Listing 6-13.

Listing 6-13. Code snippet MotionEvent.ACTION_UP

```
case MotionEvent.ACTION_UP:
  if (playBtnPressed) {
    // Launch main game screen
  }
  playBtnPressed = false;
  break;
```

94

We will replace that comment with the code that will actually launch the CrazyEight Activity, but first, we'll need to add a member variable to SplashScreen that will hold the current Context object. Just add a variable to the SplashScreen class like this:

```
private Context ctx;
```

Then, in SplashScreen's constructor, add this line:

```
ctx = context;
```

We need a reference to the current Context because we need to pass it as an argument to the Intent object.

Now, write the Intent code inside the ACTION_UP branch of SplashScreen's onTouchEvent handler so that it reads like Listing 6-14.

Listing 6-14. Intent to launch CrazyEight Activity

```
case MotionEvent.ACTION_UP:
  if (playBtnPressed) {
    Intent gameIntent = new Intent(ctx, CrazyEight.class);
    ctx.startActivity(gameIntent);

  }
  playBtnPressed = false;
  break;
```

Starting the Game

The game starts by shuffling a deck of cards, dealing seven cards to our opponent (the computer) and the user. After that, we place the top card of the remaining deck face up to start a discard pile.

To these things, we need something to represent a single card (we'll use a class for this); we need to represent the collection of cards in the human player's hand and in the computer's hand; we also need to represent the discard pile.

To represent a single card, let's create a new class and add it to the project. Right-click the project's package name in the Project tool window, as shown in Figure 6-10.

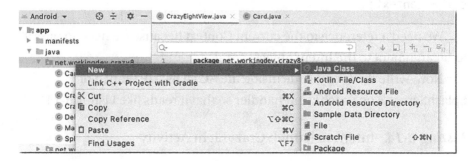

Figure 6-10. *Add a new class*

Name the new class "Card" and modify the contents, as shown in Listing 6-15.

Listing 6-15. Card class

```
import android.graphics.Bitmap;

public class Card {

  private int id;
  private int suit;
  private int rank;
  private Bitmap bmp;
  private int scoreValue;
```

```java
  public Card(int newId) {
    id = newId;
  }

  public void setBitmap(Bitmap newBitmap) {
    bmp = newBitmap;
  }
  public Bitmap getBitmap() {
    return bmp;
  }
  public int getId() {
    return id;
  }
}
```

Our Card class is a basic POJO. It's meant to represent a single card
in the deck. The constructor takes an int parameter, which represents
a unique id for the card. We've assigned an id to all the cards, from the
deuce of Diamonds to the Ace of Spades. The four suits (Diamonds, Clubs,
Hearts, and Spades) are given base values, as follows:

- Diamonds (100)

- Clubs (200)

- Hearts (300)

- Spades (400)

Each card in the suit has a rank, which is the number value of the card.
The lowest rank is 2 (the deuce), and the highest rank is 14 (the Ace). The
id of a Card object will be calculated as the base value of the suit plus the
rank of the card; so, the 2 of Diamonds is 102, the 3 of Clubs is 203, and so
on and so forth.

You can get your card images from a variety of places like www.
shutterstock.com and www.acbl.mybigcommerce.com (American
Contract Bridge League) or even create the images yourself if you're up
to it. No matter where you get your card image files, you have to name
them according to how we're assigning base values and rank. So, the 2
of Diamonds is "card102", Ace of Diamonds is "card114", and the Ace of
Spades is "card414".

The Card class also has get() and set() methods for the image files so
we can get and set the bitmap image for a particular card.

Now that we have a POJO for the Card, we need to build a deck of 52
cards; to do this, let's create a new method in the CrazyEightView class and
call it **initializeDeck()**; the annotated code is shown in Listing 6-16.

Listing 6-16. Initialize the deck

```
private void initializeDeck() {
  for (int i = 0; i < 4; i++) { ❶
    for (int j = 102; j < 115; j++) { ❷
      int tempId = j + (i*100); ❸
      Card tempCard = new Card(tempId); ❹
      int resourceId = getResources().
          getIdentifier("card" + tempId, "drawable",
                        ctx.getPackageName()); ❺
      Bitmap tempBitmap = BitmapFactory.decodeResource(ctx.
      getResources(),
                        resourceId);
      scaledCW = (int) (scrW /8); ❻
      scaledCH = (int) (scaledCW *1.28);
      Bitmap scaledBitmap = Bitmap.createScaledBitmap
      (tempBitmap,
                        scaledCW, scaledCH, false);
```

```
        tempCard.setBitmap(scaledBitmap);
        deck.add(tempCard);  ❼
      }
    }
}
```

❶   We loop through the suits (Diamonds, Clubs, Hearts, and Spades).

❷   Then, we loop through each rank in the current suit.

❸   Let's get a unique id. This id will now be what the current value of **j** + the current value of **i** multiplied by 100. Since we named our card images **card102.png** up until **card413.png**, we should be able to walk through all the image files using the j + (i * 100) expression.

❹   We create an instance of a Card object, passing in a unique id as an argument. This unique id is consistent with our naming convention for the card image files.

❺   Let's create a resource id for an image based on **tempId**.

❻   We're scaling the width of the card to 1/8th of the screen width so we can fit seven cards horizontally. The variables **scaledCW** and **scaledCH** should be declared as member variables in the Card class.

❼   Now, we add the Card object to the **dec** object, which is an ArrayList object that should be declared as a member variable. You can add a declaration for the deck like this: List<Card> deck = new ArrayList<Card>();

Now that we have a deck, we need to find a way to deal the cards to the players. We need to represent the hand of the human player and the hand of the computer player. Since we already used an ArrayList to represent the card deck, let's use ArrayLists as well to represent both hands (human player and the computer). We will also use an ArrayList to represent the discard pile.

Add the following member variable declarations to the CrazyEightView class:

```
private List<Card> playerHand = new ArrayList<>();
private List<Card> computerHand = new ArrayList<>();
private List<Card> discardPile = new ArrayList<>();
```

Now let's add the method to deal the cards to the human player and the computer player; Listing 6-17 shows the code for the method **dealCards()**.

Listing 6-17. Deal the cards to both players

```
private void dealCards() {
  Collections.shuffle(deck,new Random());
  for (int i = 0; i < 7; i++) {
    drawCard(playerHand);
    drawCard(computerHand);
  }
}
```

The first statement in the method is a Java utility function to randomize the order of elements in a List; this should satisfy our card shuffling requirement.

The for-loop comes around seven times (we want to give each hand seven cards), and inside the loop, we call the **drawCard()** method twice, once for each of the players; the code for this method is shown in Listing 6-18.

Listing 6-18. drawCard() method

```
  private void drawCard(List<Card> hand) { ❶
    hand.add(0, deck.get(0)); ❷
    deck.remove(0);  ❸
```

```
if (deck.isEmpty()) {  ❹
  for (int i = discardPile.size()-1; i > 0 ; i--) {
    deck.add(discardPile.get(i));
    discardPile.remove(i);
    Collections.shuffle(deck,new Random());
  }
 }
}
```

❶   The **drawCard()** method is called for both the human player and the computer. To call the method, we pass a List object as an argument; this argument represents which hand should we deal the card to.

❷   We get the card at the top of the **deck** and add it to the **hand** object.

❸   Next, getting the card at the top of the card doesn't automatically remove it; so, we remove it from the deck. When a card is dealt with a player, it should be removed from the deck.

❹   When the deck is empty, we bring cards from the discard pile back to the deck, and we give a fresh shuffle.

The methods for initializing the deck and dealing the cards should be placed inside the **onSizeChanged()** method. This method is called once the screen dimensions have been calculated by the runtime, and it may be called subsequently if, for some reason, the dimensions of the screen change. The orientation of the screen always starts as portrait, and since we made changes to the manifest file to always keep the orientation as portrait, there is a good chance that the **onSizeChanged()** method will be called only once (in the lifetime of the app at least). So, this seems like a good place to put game initialization methods like **initializeDeck()** and **drawCard()**.

Displaying the Cards

Our next tasks are to display the cards in the game, namely:

- The cards in our hand

- The computer's hand

- Discard pile

- Face up card

- The scores

Figure 6-11 shows the layout of cards in the game.

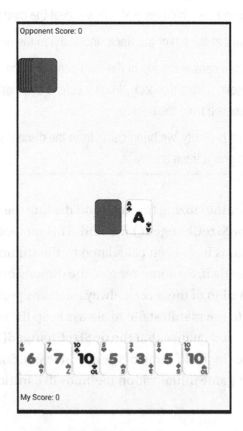

Figure 6-11. *How the game should look*

The computer's hand is faced down; we're not supposed to see them; so, all we need to do is to draw the back of the cards. We can do that by iterating through the computer's hand, and for each item in the List, we draw the back of the card. We have a graphic file for the back of the card. We'll simply draw this the same way we've drawn other graphics.

Before we do any further drawing, we'll need to establish some scale and get the density of the device's screen. We can do that with the following code:

```
scale = ctx.getResources().getDisplayMetrics().density;
```

We'll put that in the constructor of the CrazyEightView class. We need to define the scale as a member variable as well. So, somewhere in the top level of the class, define the scale as a variable, like this:

```
private float scale;
```

We will use the **scale** variable as a scaling factor for our drawings; this way, if the density of the mobile devices changes, our card graphics will still be in proportion.

Now we can draw the computer's hand. Listing 6-19 shows that code.

Listing 6-19. Draw the computer's hand

```
public void onSizeChanged (int w, int h, int oldw, int oldh){

// other statements

    scaledCW = (int) (scrW /8); ❶
    scaledCH = (int) (scaledCW *1.28); ❷

    Bitmap tempBitmap = BitmapFactory.decodeResource(ctx.
    getResources(),
                        R.drawable.card_back); ❸
```

```
cardBack = Bitmap.createScaledBitmap(tempBitmap, ❹
                        scaledCW, scaledCH, false);
}
protected void onDraw(Canvas canvas) {
  for (int i = 0; i < computerHand.size(); i++) {
    canvas.drawBitmap(cardBack, ❺
        i*(scale*5),
        paint.getTextSize()+(50*scale),
        null);
  }
}
```

---

❶ We won't use the actual size of card graphics; we want to draw them in proportion to the screen's density. The variables **scaledCW** and **scaledCH** (scaled Card height and width) will be used for drawing the scaled bitmaps. These are defined as member variables, because we need access to them outside the **onSizeChanged()** method.

❷ We'd like the scaled height to be 1.28 times longer than the scaled Card width.

❸ Load the bitmap like how we loaded bitmaps before.

❹ Now we create a scaled bitmap from the tempBitmap we've loaded.

❺ We're drawing all the cards in the computer's hand one graphic at a time and 5 pixels apart (horizontally) so that they overlap; we're also drawing the cards 50 scaling factors from the top of the screen plus the default text size of the Paint object.

In bullet number ❺, we referred to a Paint object. This variable is defined as a member variable, so if you're following, you need to add this variable right now, like this:

```
private Paint paint;
```

Then, somewhere in the constructor, add this statement:

```
paint = new Paint();
```

That should get us caught up already. We use the Paint object not only for determining sizes of the default text but also we use it (later) for writing some text to the screen.

Next, we draw the human player's hand. Listing 6-20 shows the annotated code.

Listing 6-20. Drawing the human player's hand

```
protected void onDraw(Canvas canvas) {

  // other statements

  for (int i = 0; i < playerHand.size(); i++) { ❶

    canvas.drawBitmap(playerHand.get(i).getBitmap(), ❷
        i*(scaledCW +5),
        scrH - scaledCH - paint.getTextSize()-(50*scale),
        null);

  }
}
```

---

❶   We walk through all cards in the hand.

❷   Then, we draw the bitmap using the scaled card height and width variables. The cards are drawn 5 pixels apart, and its **Y** position subtracts the (1) height of the card, (2) the text height (which we will use later for drawing the scores), and (3) 50 scaled pixels from the bottom of the screen.

Next, we show the draw pile; add the code in Listing 6-21 to the onDraw method so we can show the draw pile.

Listing 6-21. The draw pile

```
protected void onDraw(Canvas canvas) {

  // other statements

  float cbackLeft = (scrW/2) - cardBack.getWidth() - 10;
  float cbackTop = (scrH/2) - (cardBack.getHeight() / 2);
  canvas.drawBitmap(cardBack, cbackLeft, cbackTop, null);
}
```

The draw pile is represented by a single back of the card graphics. It's drawn approximately centered on the screen.

Next, we draw the discard pile. Remember that the discard pile is started as by getting the top card of what remains in the deck after the cards have been dealt with the players; so, before we draw them, we need to check if it's empty or not. Listing 6-22 shows the code for showing the discard pile.

Listing 6-22. Discard pile

```
if (!discardPile.isEmpty()) {
  canvas.drawBitmap(discardPile.get(0).getBitmap(),
      (scrW /2)+10,
      (scrH /2)-(cardBack.getHeight()/2),
      null);
}
```

Handling Turns

Crazy Eights is a turn-based game. We need to route the program logic based on whose turn it is, whether it's the computer or the human player. We can facilitate this by adding a boolean variable as a member of the CrazyEightView class, like this:

```
private boolean myTurn;
```

Throughout our code, we will enable or disable certain logic based on whose turn it is. In the onSizeChanged method, we add the following code:

```
myTurn = new Random().nextBoolean();
if (!myTurn) {
  computerPlay();
}
```

That should randomly choose who goes first. Naturally, the myTurn variable needs to be toggled every time either player plays a valid card, and also we need to add the **computerPlay()** method to our class; we'll do that in a little while.

Playing a Card

A valid play in Crazy Eights requires that a player matches the top card of the discard pile, which means we now need a way to get the rank and suit from a Card object. Let's modify the Card class to do just that. Listing 6-23 shows the revised Card class.

Listing 6-23. Revised Card class with rank and suit calculation

```
public class Card {

  private int id;
  private int suit;
  private int rank;
  private Bitmap bmp;
  private int scoreValue;

  public Card(int newId) {
    id = newId;
    suit = Math.round((id/100) * 100);
    rank = id - suit;

  }

  public int getScoreValue() {
    return scoreValue;
  }
  public void setBitmap(Bitmap newBitmap) {
    bmp = newBitmap;
  }
  public Bitmap getBitmap() {
    return bmp;
  }
  public int getId() {
    return id;
  }
  public int getSuit() {
    return suit;
  }
```

```
public int getRank() {
  return rank;
}
}
```

We added the **suit** and **rank** variables to hold the values of the suit and rank, respectively. We also added the logic necessary to calculate both values.

The suit variable is calculated by rounding it up to the nearest hundred; for example, if the id is 102 (2 of Diamonds), the suit value will be 100. The rank variable is calculated by subtracting the suit from the id; if the id is 102, we subtract 100 from 102; hence, we get 2 as the value of the rank.

Finally, we add a **getSuit()** and **getRank()** methods to provide getters for the suit and rank values, respectively.

Having a way to get the rank and the suit of the card, we can start writing the code for when it's the computer's turn to play. The code for **computerPlay()**, which must be added to the CrazyEightView class, is shown in Listing 6-24.

Listing 6-24. computerPlay()

```
private void computerPlay() {
  int tempPlay = 0;
  while (tempPlay == 0) {
    tempPlay = computerPlayer.playCard(computerHand, validSuit,
    validRank); ❶
    if (tempPlay == 0) {
      drawCard(computerHand); ❷
    }
  }
}
```

❶   The **computerPlay** variable should be a member variable; we haven't created the class for the ComputerPlayer yet, but we will shortly. For now, just imagine that the **playCard()** method should return a valid play. The playCard method should go through all the cards in the computer's hand if it has a valid play that will be returned to the **tempPlay** variable.

❷   If the computer doesn't have a play, it needs to draw a card from the deck.

Now, let's build the ComputerPlayer class. Add another class to the project and name it ComputerPlayer.java, as shown in Figure 6-12.

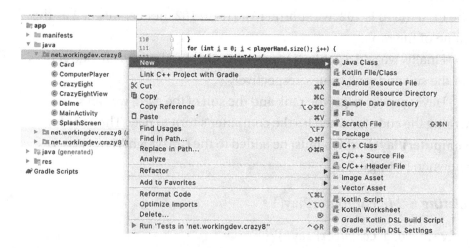

Figure 6-12. *Add another class to the project*

Code for ComputerPlayer.java is shown in Listing 6-25.

Listing 6-25. ComputerPlayer.java

```java
import java.util.List;

public class ComputerPlayer {

  public int playCard(List<Card> hand, int suit, int rank) {
    int play = 0;
    for (int i = 0; i < hand.size(); i++) {  ❶
      int tempId = hand.get(i).getId();        ❷
      int tempRank = hand.get(i).getRank();  ❸
      int tempSuit = hand.get(i).getSuit();  ❹
      if (tempRank != 8) {
        if (rank == 8) {  ❺
          if (suit == tempSuit) {
            play = tempId;
          }
        } else if (suit == tempSuit || rank == tempRank) {
          play = tempId;
        }
      }
    }
    if (play == 0) {  ❻
      for (int i = 0; i < hand.size(); i++) {  ❼
        int tempId = hand.get(i).getId();
        if (tempId == 108 || tempId == 208 || tempId == 308 ||
        tempId == 408) { // <>
          play = tempId;
        }
      }
    }
    return play;
  }
}
```

❶   The **playCard** method needs to go through all the cards in the computer's hand to see if we have a valid play.

❷   This gets the id of the current card.

❸   Let's get the rank of the current card.

❹   Let's also get the suit.

❺   If the top card is not an eight, let's see if we can match either the top card's rank or suit.

❻   After going through all our cards, we cannot match the top card; that's why **play** variable still equals to zero.

❼   Let's cycle through all our cards again and see if we have an eight.

Now we've got some simple logic for the opponent. Let's go back to the human player.

A play is made by dragging a valid card to the top card. We need to show some animation that the card is being dragged. We can do this on onTouchEvent. Listing 6-26 shows a snippet on how we can start doing exactly that.

Listing 6-26. Moving cards

```
public boolean onTouchEvent(MotionEvent event) {

    int eventaction = event.getAction();
    int X = (int)event.getX();
    int Y = (int)event.getY();

    switch (eventaction ) {

      case MotionEvent.ACTION_DOWN:
        if (myTurn) {   ❶
          for (int i = 0; i < 7; i++) {  ❷
```

```
        if (X > i*(scaledCW +5) && X < i*(scaledCW +5) +
        scaledCW &&
            Y > scrH - scaledCH - paint.getTextSize()-
            (50*scale)) {
            movingIdx = i;
            movingX = X;
            movingY = Y;
          }
        }
      }
      break;

    case MotionEvent.ACTION_MOVE:
      movingX = X;  ❸
      movingY = Y;
      break;

    case MotionEvent.ACTION_UP:
      movingIdx = -1;  ❹
      break;
  }
  invalidate();
  return true;
}
```

---

❶　　The human player can only move a card when it's their turn. The computer
　　　opponent plays very quickly, so this shouldn't be an issue. The game
　　　actually feels that it's always the human's turn.

❷　　Loop through all the cards in the human player's hand to see if they have
　　　touched on the area of the screen where any of the cards are drawn. If they
　　　have, we assign the index of that card to the **movingIdx** variable; this is the
　　　card that was moved by the player.

❸   As the player drags the card through the screen, we monitor the X and Y
        coordinates; we will use this to draw the card as it's being dragged across
        the screen.

❹   When the player lets up, we reset the value of **movingIdx**. A value of –1
        means no card is being moved.

The next thing we need to do is to reflect all these movements in the
onDraw method. Listing 6-27 shows the annotated code for drawing the
card as it's dragged across the screen.

Listing 6-27. Show the moving card

```
@Override
  protected void onDraw(Canvas canvas) {

    // some other statements

    for (int i = 0; i < playerHand.size(); i++) {
      if (i == movingIdx) { ❶
        canvas.drawBitmap(playerHand.get(i).getBitmap(),
            movingX,
            movingY,
            null);
      } else { ❷
        if (i < 7) {
          canvas.drawBitmap(playerHand.get(i).getBitmap(),
              i*(scaledCW +5),
              scrH - scaledCH - paint.getTextSize()-(50*scale),
              null);
        }
      }
    }
  }
```

```
  invalidate();
  setToFullScreen();
}
```

---

❶   Let's see if the current card matches the value of the **movingIdx** variable (the card being dragged by the user); if it's the right card, we draw it using the updated X and Y coordinates.

❷   If none of the cards are moving, we simply draw all the cards as we did before.

When you test the code as it stands now, you might notice that the position where the card is drawn (as you drag a card across the screen) isn't right. The card might be obscured by your finger. We can fix this by drawing the card with some offset values. Listing 6-28 shows the code.

Listing 6-28. Adding some offsets to X and Y coordinates

```
public boolean onTouchEvent(MotionEvent event) {
  int eventaction = event.getAction();
  int X = (int)event.getX();
  int Y = (int)event.getY();

  switch (eventaction ) {

    case MotionEvent.ACTION_DOWN:
      if (myTurn) {
        for (int i = 0; i < 7; i++) {
          if (X > i*(scaledCW +5) && X < i*(scaledCW +5) +
          scaledCW &&
              Y > scrH - scaledCH - paint.getTextSize()-
              (50*scale)) {
```

```
            movingIdx = i;
            movingX = X-(int)(30*scale);
            movingY = Y-(int)(70*scale);
          }
        }
      }
      break;

    case MotionEvent.ACTION_MOVE:
      movingX = X-(int)(30*scale);
      movingY = Y-(int)(70*scale);
      break;

  invalidate();
  return true;
}
```

The highlighted lines are the only changes we need; instead of following the original X and Y coordinates as it's passed to us by the event, we draw it 30 more pixels to the right and 70 more pixels offset up. This way, when the card is dragged, the player can see it.

Now that we can drag the card across the screen, we need to ensure that what's being dragged is a valid card for play. A valid card for play matches the top card either in rank or in suit; now, we need to keep track of the suit and rank of the top card. Listing 6-29 shows the onSizeChanged() method in the CrazyEightView class. The variables **validSuit** and **validRank** are added.

Listing 6-29. Keeping track of the valid card for play

```
@Override
public void onSizeChanged (int w, int h, int oldw, int oldh){
  super.onSizeChanged(w, h, oldw, oldh);
```

```
scrW = w;
scrH = h;

Bitmap tempBitmap = BitmapFactory.decodeResource(ctx.
getResources(),
                        R.drawable.card_back);
scaledCW = (int) (scrW /8);
scaledCH = (int) (scaledCW *1.28);
cardBack = Bitmap.createScaledBitmap(tempBitmap, scaledCW,
scaledCH, false);

initializeDeck();
dealCards();
drawCard(discardPile);
validSuit = discardPile.get(0).getSuit();
validRank = discardPile.get(0).getRank();

myTurn = new Random().nextBoolean();
if (!myTurn) {
  computerPlay();
}
}
```

When we draw a card from the deck and add it to the discard pile, the top card of the discard pile determines the suit and rank for a valid card.

So, when the human player tries to drag a card into the discard pile, we can determine if that card is a valid play; if it is, we add it to the discard pile; if not, we return it to the player's hand. With that, let's check for valid plays. Listing 6-30 shows the updated and annotated ACTION_UP of the onTouchEvent.

Listing 6-30. Check for valid play

```
case MotionEvent.ACTION_UP:
  if (movingIdx > -1 &&  ❶
     X > (scrW /2)-(100*scale) &&  ❷
     X < (scrW /2)+(100*scale) &&
     Y > (scrH /2)-(100*scale) &&
     Y < (scrH /2)+(100*scale) &&
     (playerHand.get(movingIdx).getRank() == 8 ||
         playerHand.get(movingIdx).getRank() == validRank ||  ❸
         playerHand.get(movingIdx).getSuit() == validSuit)) {  ❹

    validRank = playerHand.get(movingIdx).getRank();  ❺
    validSuit = playerHand.get(movingIdx).getSuit();
    discardPile.add(0, playerHand.get(movingIdx));      ❻
    playerHand.remove(movingIdx);  ❼

  }
break;
```

---

❶   Let's check if the card is being moved.

❷   These lines take care of the drop area, and we're basically dropping the card in the middle of the screen. There's no need to be precise on location.

❸   Let's check if it has a valid rank.

❹   Let's check if the card being dragged has a valid suit.

❺   If the play is valid, we update the value of **validRank** and **validSuit**. The card being offered by the player is now the card with valid suit and rank.

❻   We add the new card to the discard pile.

❼   We remove the card from the player's hand.

Next thing to handle is when the human player plays an eight.
Remember that eights are wild; they're always playable. When an eight
card is played (by the human player, let's handle that first; the computer
can also play an eight, remember?), we need a way for the player to choose
the suit for the next valid play.

To choose the next suit when an eight is played, we need a way to show
some options to the user. A dialog box is usually used for such tasks. We
can draw the dialog box just like we did the Play button, or we can use
Android's built-in dialogs. Figures 6-13 and 6-14 show the dialog in action.

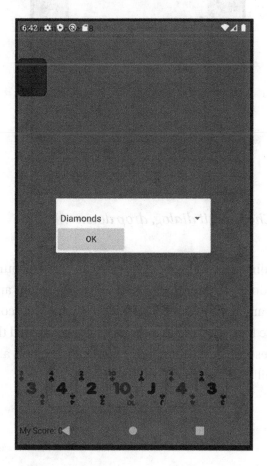

Figure 6-13. *Choose suit dialog*

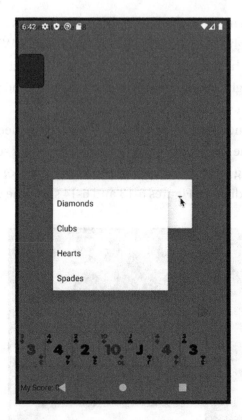

Figure 6-14. *Choose suit dialog, drop down*

To start building this dialog box, we need an array resource to the project. We can do this by adding an XML file to the folder app/res/values. Currently, there are already three XML files in that folder (colors, strings, and styles); these files were created for us when we created the project. Android uses these files as resources for application labels and color scheming. We will add another file to this folder.

Right-click the **app/res/values** folder as shown in Figure 6-15, then choose **New ➤ XML ➤ Values XML File**.

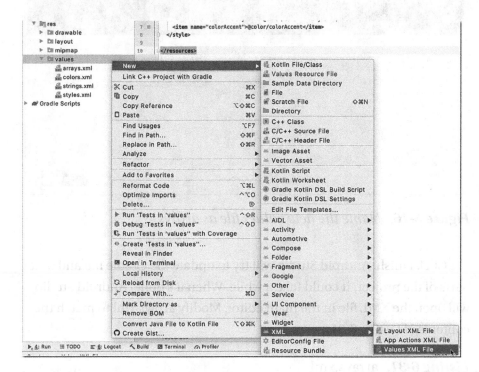

Figure 6-15. *Add Values XML File*

The next dialog window will ask for the name of the new resource file. Type **arrays**, as shown in Figure 6-16.

Figure 6-16. *Name the new values file as arrays*

Click Finish. Android Studio will try to update the Gradle file and other parts of the project; it could take a while. When it's done, Android Studio will open the XML file in the main editor. Modify arrays.xml to match the contents of Listing 6-31.

Listing 6-31. arrays.xml

```xml
<?xml version="1.0" encoding="utf-8"?>
<resources>
  <string-array name="suits">
    <item>Diamonds</item>
    <item>Clubs</item>
    <item>Hearts</item>
    <item>Spades</item>
  </string-array>
</resources>
```

We will use this array to load the option for our dialog. Next, let's create a layout file for the actual dialog. The layout file is also an XML file; to create it, right-click app/res/layout from the Project tool window, then choose New ➤ XML ➤ Layout XML File, as shown in Figure 6-17.

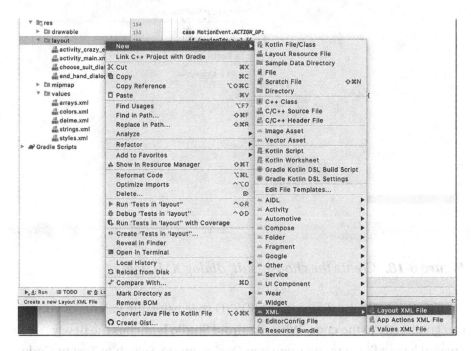

Figure 6-17. *Create a new Layout XML File*

Next, provide the layout file name, then type **choose_suit_dialog** (shown in Figure 6-18).

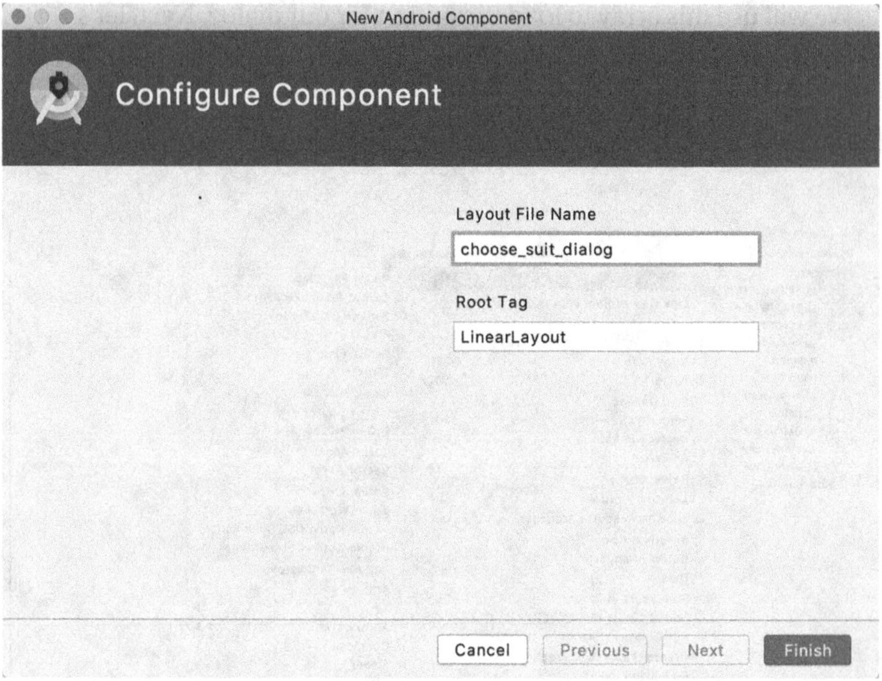

Figure 6-18. *Create the choose_suit_dialog XML File*

You can build the dialog in WYSIWYG style using the Palette, or you can go directly to the code. When Android Studio launches the newly created layout file, it might open it in Design mode. Switch to Text or Code mode, and modify the contents of choose_suit_dialog.xml to match the contents of Listing 6-32.

Listing 6-32. choose_suit.dialog.xml

```
<?xml version="1.0" encoding="utf-8"?>
<LinearLayout
android:id="@+id/chooseSuitLayout"
android:layout_width="275dp"
android:layout_height="wrap_content"
android:orientation="vertical"
```

```
android:layout_gravity="top"
xmlns:android="http://schemas.android.com/apk/res/android"
>
<TextView
android:id="@+id/chooseSuitText"
android:layout_width="wrap_content"
android:layout_height="wrap_content"
android:text="Choose a suit."
android:textSize="16sp"
android:layout_marginLeft="5dp"
android:textColor="#FFFFFF"
>
</TextView>
<Spinner
android:id="@+id/suitSpinner"
android:layout_width="fill_parent"
android:layout_height="wrap_content"
android:drawSelectorOnTop="true"
/>
<Button
android:id="@+id/okButton"
android:layout_width="125dp"
android:layout_height="wrap_content"
android:text="OK"
>
</Button>
</LinearLayout>
```

Figure 6-19 shows the dialog layout file in Design mode. You can click each constituent View object of the dialog file and inspect the individual properties in the properties window.

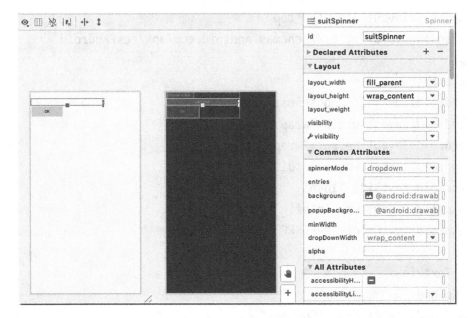

Figure 6-19.   choose_suit_dialog in Design mode

The layout file has three View objects as UI elements—a TextView, a Spinner, and a Button. The LinearLayout arranges these elements in a linear fashion (a straight line). The vertical orientation lays out the elements from top to bottom.

In the future, you can opt not to use the built-in View objects of Android to make the UI more visually appealing; but as you might have surmised from this chapter, drawing your own screen elements requires a lot of work.

The TextView, Spinner, and Button all have ids. We will refer to them later using these ids.

Now that we have the dialog sorted out, we can build the code to show the dialog. When the human player plays an eight for a card, we will show this dialog. Let's add a method to the CrazyEightView class and call this method changeSuit(). The contents of the changeSuit method are shown in Listing 6-33.

Listing 6-33. changeSuit method

```
private void changeSuit() {
  final Dialog changeSuitDlg = new Dialog(ctx);  ❶
  changeSuitDlg.requestWindowFeature(Window.FEATURE_NO_TITLE); ❷
  changeSuitDlg.setContentView(R.layout.choose_suit_dialog); ❸
  final Spinner spinner = (Spinner) changeSuitDlg.findViewById
  (R.id.suitSpinner); ❹
  ArrayAdapter<CharSequence> adapter = ArrayAdapter.createFrom
  Resource( ❺
      ctx, R.array.suits, android.R.layout.simple_spinner_item);
adapter.setDropDownViewResource(android.R.layout.
simple_spinner_dropdown_item);
  spinner.setAdapter(adapter);
  Button okButton = (Button) changeSuitDlg.findViewById
  (R.id.okButton); ❻

  okButton.setOnClickListener(new View.OnClickListener(){  ❼

    public void onClick(View view){
      validSuit = (spinner.getSelectedItemPosition()+1)*100;
      String suitText = "";
      if (validSuit == 100) {
        suitText = "Diamonds";
      } else if (validSuit == 200) {
        suitText = "Clubs";
      } else if (validSuit == 300) {
        suitText = "Hearts";
      } else if (validSuit == 400) {
        suitText = "Spades";
      }
```

```
        changeSuitDlg.dismiss();
        Toast.makeText(ctx, "You chose " + suitText, Toast.
        LENGTH_SHORT).show(); ❽
        myTurn = false;
        computerPlay();
      }
  });
  changeSuitDlg.show();
}
```

❶   This line creates a Dialog object; we pass the current context to its constructor.

❷   Remove the title of the dialog box. We'd like it as plain as possible.

❸   Then we set the contentView of the Dialog object to the layout resource file we created earlier.

❹   This line creates the Spinner object.

❺   The **ArrayAdapter** supplies data to the View and determines its format. This creates the ArrayAdapter using the **arrays.xml** we created earlier.

❻   Get a programmatic reference to the Button object using its id.

❼   Create an event handler for the Button. We use the onClickListener object here to handle the click event. Overriding the onClick method of this handler lets us code the logic necessary when the Button is clicked.

❽   A **Toast** is a small message displayed on the screen, like a tooltip. It's visible only for a few seconds. We use Toast here as feedback to show the user what suit was chosen.

The **changeSuit()** method must be called only when the human player plays an eight. We need to put this logic into the ACTION_UP branch of the onTouchEvent method. Listing 6-34 shows the annotated ACTION_UP branch.

Listing 6-34. Triggering the changeSuit() method

```
case MotionEvent.ACTION_UP:
  if (movingIdx > -1 &&
      X > (scrW /2)-(100*scale) &&
      X < (scrW /2)+(100*scale) &&
      Y > (scrH /2)-(100*scale) &&
      Y < (scrH /2)+(100*scale) &&
      (playerHand.get(movingIdx).getRank() == 8 ||
          playerHand.get(movingIdx).getRank() == validRank ||
          playerHand.get(movingIdx).getSuit() == validSuit)) {
    validRank = playerHand.get(movingIdx).getRank();
    validSuit = playerHand.get(movingIdx).getSuit();
    discardPile.add(0, playerHand.get(movingIdx));
    playerHand.remove(movingIdx);
    if (playerHand.isEmpty()) {
      endHand();
    } else {
      if (validRank == 8) { ❶
        changeSuit();
      } else {
        myTurn = false;
        computerPlay();
      }
    }
  }
break;
```

❶   When the human player plays an eight, we call the **changeSuit** method,
     which lets the player choose the suit. At this point, it's still the turn of the
     human player; presumably, they play another card.

When there is no Valid Play

It is possible to run out of valid cards to play. When that happens, the human player must draw a card from the pile; and they must continue to do so until there is a card to play. This means a player may have more than seven cards. Remember in the onDraw method that we scaled the cards on the player deck to display just seven? We may exceed that number now.

To solve this, we can draw an arrow icon to signify to the user that there are more than seven cards on their deck. By clicking the arrow icon, we should be able to pan the player's View of the cards. To do this, we need to draw the arrow.

Add the following Bitmap object to the member variables of the CrazyEightView class.

```
private Bitmap nextCardBtn;
```

We can load the Bitmap on the onSizeChanged method, just like the other Bitmaps we drew earlier.

```
nextCardBtn = BitmapFactory.decodeResource(getResources(),
              R.drawable.arrow_next);
```

We need to draw the arrow when the player's cards exceed seven. We can do this in the onDraw method. Listing 6-35 shows that code.

Listing 6-35. Draw the next arrow

```
if (playerHand.size() > 7) { ❶
  canvas.drawBitmap(nextCardBtn, ❷
      scrW - nextCardBtn.getWidth()-(30*scale),
      scrH - nextCardBtn.getHeight()- scaledCH -(90*scale),
      null);
}
```

```
for (int i = 0; i < playerHand.size(); i++) {
  if (i == movingIdx) {
    canvas.drawBitmap(playerHand.get(i).getBitmap(),
        movingX,
        movingY,
        null);
  } else {
    if (i < 7) {
      canvas.drawBitmap(playerHand.get(i).getBitmap(),
          i*(scaledCW +5),
          scrH - scaledCH - paint.getTextSize()-(50*scale),
          null);
    }
  }
}
```

---

❶   Determine if the player has more than seven cards.

❷   If it's more than seven, draw the next arrow.

Drawing the arrow is simply groundwork for our next task. Of course, before we allow the player to draw a card from the pile, we need to determine if they truly need to draw a card. If the player has a valid card to play (if they have cards with matching suit and rank or they've got an eight), then we should not let them draw. We need to provide that logic; so, we add another method to the CrazyEightView class named **isValidDraw()**. This method goes through all the cards in the player's deck and checks if there are cards with matching suit or rank (or if there's an eight card). Listing 6-36 shows the code for **isValidDraw()**.

Listing 6-36. isValidDraw()

```
private boolean isValidDraw() {
  boolean canDraw = true;
  for (int i = 0; i < playerHand.size(); i++) {
    int tempId = playerHand.get(i).getId();
    int tempRank = playerHand.get(i).getRank();
    int tempSuit = playerHand.get(i).getSuit();
    if (validSuit == tempSuit || validRank == tempRank ||
        tempId == 108 || tempId == 208 || tempId == 308 ||
        tempId == 408) {
      canDraw = false;
    }
  }
  return canDraw;
}
```

We loop through all the cards; check if we can match either the suit or the rank or if there's an eight among the cards; if there is, we return false (because the player has a valid play); otherwise, we return true.

When the human player tries to draw a card from the deck despite having a valid play, let's display a Toast message to remind them that they can't draw a card because they've got a valid play. This can be done on the **ACTION_UP** branch of the **onTouchEvent** method (code shown in Listing 6-37).

Listing 6-37. Toast message when the player has a valid play

```
if (movingIdx == -1 && myTurn &&
    X > (scrW /2)-(100*scale) &&
    X < (scrW /2)+(100*scale) &&
    Y > (scrH /2)-(100*scale) &&
    Y < (scrH /2)+(100*scale)) {
```

```
if (isValidDraw()) { ❶
  drawCard(playerHand); ❷
} else {
  Toast.makeText(ctx, "You have a valid play.",
            Toast.LENGTH_SHORT).show(); ❸
}
}
```

❶   Before we allow them to draw a card from the deck, check if the player has a
       valid play. If they have, **isValidDraw()** will return false.

❷   Otherwise, let the player draw a card.

❸   If the player has a valid play, display a Toast message.

When it's the Computer's Turn

Earlier in the chapter, we created a method named **computerPlay()**; this
method is invoked when the human player finishes their turn; we only
coded the stub of that method. Now, we need to put the additional logic so
that we can have a really playable opponent.

Let's modify the computerPlay() method in the CrazyEightView class
to reflect the code in Listing 6-38.

Listing 6-38. computerPlay() method

```
private void computerPlay() {
  int tempPlay = 0; ❶
  while (tempPlay == 0) { ❷
    tempPlay = computerPlayer.playCard(computerHand, validSuit,
    validRank);
```

```java
      if (tempPlay == 0) {
        drawCard(computerHand);
      }
    }
    if (tempPlay == 108 ||
        tempPlay == 208 ||
        tempPlay == 308 ||
        tempPlay == 408) {

      validRank = 8;
      validSuit = computerPlayer.chooseSuit(computerHand); ❸
      String suitText = "";
      if (validSuit == 100) {
        suitText = "Diamonds";
      } else if (validSuit == 200) {
        suitText = "Clubs";
      } else if (validSuit == 300) {
        suitText = "Hearts";
      } else if (validSuit == 400) {
        suitText = "Spades";
      }
      Toast.makeText(ctx, "Computer chose " + suitText, Toast.
      LENGTH_SHORT).show();
    } else {
      validSuit = Math.round((tempPlay/100) * 100); ❹
      validRank = tempPlay - validSuit;
    }
    for (int i = 0; i < computerHand.size(); i++) { ❺
      Card tempCard = computerHand.get(i);
```

```
  if (tempPlay == tempCard.getId()) {
    discardPile.add(0, computerHand.get(i));
    computerHand.remove(i);
  }
}
if (computerHand.isEmpty()) {
  endHand();
}
myTurn = true; ❻
}
```

---

❶   **tempPlay** variable holds the id of the played card.

❷   A value of zero means there is no valid play for the computer's hand. When we call the **playCard()** method of the **ComputerPlayer** class, it will return the id of the card that is a valid play. If the computer's hand doesn't have a valid play, let the computer draw a card from the pile; keep drawing until there is a valid card for play.

❸   If the computer chooses to play an eight, we need to change the suit; we've done this already for the human player, but we haven't done it yet for the computer player. We will now. The **chooseSuit()** method doesn't exist yet, and we will implement it shortly. For now, just imagine that the **chooseSuit()** method will return an integer value which will let us set the new **validSuit** for the next play.

❹   If the computer doesn't play an eight, we simply reset the **validRank** and **validSuit** to whatever the played cards' value were.

❺   We loop through the computer's hand, adding the played card to the discard pile.

❻   Finally, the human will take the next turn.

Ending a Hand

When either the computer or the human player plays the last card, the hand ends. When this happens, we need to

1. Display a dialog to signify that the current hand has ended

2. Show and update the scores for both the human and the computer player

3. Start a new hand

We'll display the scores on the top and bottom parts of the screen, as shown in Figure 6-20.

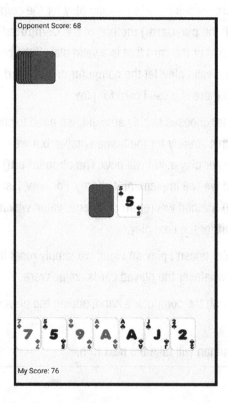

Figure 6-20. Displaying the scores

To display the scores, we first need to calculate it. When a hand ends, all the remaining cards (either the computer's or the human player's) must be totaled. To facilitate this, we need to update the Card class. Listing 6-39 shows the updated Card class.

Listing 6-39. Card.java

```java
public class Card {

  private int id;
  private int suit;
  private int rank;
  private Bitmap bmp;
  private int scoreValue; ❶

  public Card(int newId) {
    id = newId;
    suit = Math.round((id/100) * 100);
    rank = id - suit;
    if (rank == 8) {  ❷
      scoreValue = 50;
    } else if (rank == 14) {
      scoreValue = 1;
    } else if (rank > 9 && rank < 14) {
      scoreValue = 10;
    } else {
      scoreValue = rank;
    }
  }

  public int getScoreValue() {
    return scoreValue;
  }
```

```
    public void setBitmap(Bitmap newBitmap) {
      bmp = newBitmap;
    }
    public Bitmap getBitmap() {
      return bmp;
    }
    public int getId() {
      return id;
    }
    public int getSuit() {
      return suit;
    }
    public int getRank() {
      return rank;
    }
}
```

❶   Create a variable to hold the score for the card.

❷   Check the rank of the card and assign a score value. If an eight card is
         left on the player's hand, it's worth 50 points to the opponent. Face cards
         are worth 10 points, aces 1 point, and the rest of the cards are worth their
         face values.

Next, we need a method to update the scores of both the computer
and the human player. Let's add a new method to CrazyEightView named
updateScores(); the code for this method is shown in Listing 6-40.

Listing 6-40. updateScores() method

```java
private void updateScores() {
  for (int i = 0; i < playerHand.size(); i++) {
    computerScore += playerHand.get(i).getScoreValue();
    currScore += playerHand.get(i).getScoreValue();
  }
  for (int i = 0; i < computerHand.size(); i++) {
    myScore += computerHand.get(i).getScoreValue();
    currScore += computerHand.get(i).getScoreValue();
  }
}
```

The variables **currScore**, **computerScore**, and **myScore** need to be declared as member variables in CrazyEightView.

If the computer's hand is empty, we go through all the cards in the human player's hand, sum it up, and credit it to the computer's score. If the human player's hand is empty, we go through all the remaining cards in the computer's hand, sum it up, and credit that score to the human player.

Now that the scores are calculated, we can display them.

To display the scores, we will use the Paint object we defined earlier in the chapter. We need to set some attributes of the Paint object before we can draw some text with it. Listing 6-41 shows the constructor of CrazyEightView, which contains the code we need for the Paint object.

Listing 6-41. Paint object

```java
import android.graphics.Color;

public CrazyEightView(Context context) {
  super(context);
  ctx = context;
  scale = ctx.getResources().getDisplayMetrics().density;
  paint = new Paint();
```

```
paint.setAntiAlias(true);
paint.setColor(Color.BLACK);
paint.setStyle(Paint.Style.FILL);
paint.setTextAlign(Paint.Align.LEFT);
paint.setTextSize(scale*15);
}
```

To draw the scores, modify the onDraw() method and add the two drawText() methods, as shown in Listing 6-42.

Listing 6-42. Drawing the scores

```
protected void onDraw(Canvas canvas) {

  canvas.drawText("Opponent Score: " + Integer.
toString(computerScore), 10,
                  paint.getTextSize()+10, paint);
  canvas.drawText("My Score: " + Integer.toString(myScore),
  10, scrH -
                  paint.getTextSize()-10, paint);

  // ...

}
```

Next, we need to take care of the dialog for starting a new hand. This will be similar to the change suit dialog. This is a new dialog, so we need to create it. Right-click the **res/layout** folder in the Project tool window, as shown in Figure 6-21.

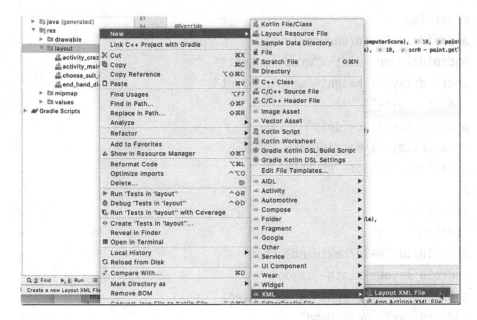

Figure 6-21. *New Layout XML File*

In the next window, enter **end_hand_dialog** for the layout file name.
When Android Studio opens the newly created layout file in the main
editor window, modify it to reflect the code, as shown in Listing 6-43.

Listing 6-43. end_hand_dialog.xml

```xml
<?xml version="1.0" encoding="utf-8"?>
<LinearLayout
android:id="@+id/endHandLayout"
android:layout_width="275dp"
android:layout_height="wrap_content"
android:orientation="vertical"
android:layout_gravity="top"
xmlns:android="http://schemas.android.com/apk/res/android"
>
```

```
<TextView
android:id="@+id/endHandText"
android:layout_width="wrap_content"
android:layout_height="wrap_content"
android:text=""
android:textSize="16sp"
android:layout_marginLeft="5dp"
android:textColor="#FFFFFF"
>
</TextView>
<Button
android:id="@+id/nextHandButton"
android:layout_width="125dp"
android:layout_height="wrap_content"
android:text="Next Hand"
>
</Button>
</LinearLayout>
```

This layout file is much simpler than the change suit dialog. This one only has a TextView and a Button.

Next, we add another method to CrazyEightView to handle the logic when a given hand ends. Listing 6-44 shows the code for the **endHand()** method.

Listing 6-44. endHand() method

```
private void endHand() {
    String endHandMsg = "";
    final Dialog endHandDlg = new Dialog(ctx);   ❶
    endHandDlg.requestWindowFeature(Window.FEATURE_NO_TITLE);
    endHandDlg.setContentView(R.layout.end_hand_dialog);
    updateScores();   ❷
```

```
TextView endHandText = (TextView) endHandDlg.
findViewById(R.id.endHandText); ❸
if (playerHand.isEmpty()) {
  if (myScore >= 300) {
    endHandMsg = String.format("You won. You have %d
    points. Play again?",
                myScore);
  } else {
    endHandMsg = String.format("You lost, you only got %d",
    currScore);
  }
} else if (computerHand.isEmpty()) {
  if (computerScore >= 300) {
    endHandMsg = String.format("Opponent scored %d. You
    lost. Play again?",
                computerScore);
  } else {
    endHandMsg = String.format("Opponent has lost. He
    scored %d points.",
                currScore);
  }
  endHandText.setText(endHandMsg);
}

Button nextHandBtn = (Button) endHandDlg.findViewById(R.
id.nextHandButton); ❹

if (computerScore >= 300 || myScore >= 300) { ❺
  nextHandBtn.setText("New Game");
}
```

```
    nextHandBtn.setOnClickListener(new View.OnClickListener(){ ❻
      public void onClick(View view){
        if (computerScore >= 300 || myScore >= 300) {
          myScore = 0;
          computerScore = 0;
        }
        initNewHand();
        endHandDlg.dismiss();
      }
    });
    endHandDlg.show();
  }
```

---

❶   Same as the previous dialog we created. Create an instance of a Dialog
     and make sure it doesn't display any titles. Then set the content view to the
     layout file we created.

❷   When a hand ends, we call the **updateScore()** methods to display the
     score information.

❸   Get a programmatic reference to the TextView object, and in the statements
     that follow, depending on who ran out of cards, we display how many
     points were earned.

❹   Get a programmatic reference to the Button.

❺   Let's check if the game is already over. When one of the players reaches
     300 points, the game is over. If it is, we change the text on the Button to
     read "New Game" instead of "New Hand."

❻   Create a listener object for the Button to handle the click event. In the
     onClick method of the click handler, we call the **initNewHand()** method to
     start a new hand; the code for this method is shown in Listing 6-45.

Listing 6-45. initNewHand() method

```
private void initNewHand() {
  currScore = 0;  ❶
  if (playerHand.isEmpty()) {  ❷
    myTurn = true;
  } else if (computerHand.isEmpty()) {
    myTurn = false;
  }
  deck.addAll(discardPile);  ❸
  deck.addAll(playerHand);
  deck.addAll(computerHand);
  discardPile.clear();
  playerHand.clear();
  computerHand.clear();
  dealCards();  ❹
  drawCard(discardPile);
  validSuit = discardPile.get(0).getSuit();
  validRank = discardPile.get(0).getRank();
  if (!myTurn) {
    computerPlay();
  }
}
```

❶ Let's reset the points earned for the hand.

❷ If the human player won the previous hand, then it's their turn to play first.

❸ Add the discard pile and both players' cards back to the deck, then clear the lists and the discard pile. We're basically putting all the cards back to the deck.

❹ Deal the cards, like at the beginning of the game.

Now that we have all the required logic and assets for ending a hand, it's time to put the code for checking if the hand has ended. We can do this on the ACTION_UP case of the onTouchEvent method; Listing 6-46 shows this code. The pertinent code is in bold.

Listing 6-46. Check if the hand has ended

```
case MotionEvent.ACTION_UP:
  if (movingIdx > -1 &&
      X > (scrW /2)-(100*scale) &&
      X < (scrW /2)+(100*scale) &&
      Y > (scrH /2)-(100*scale) &&
      Y < (scrH /2)+(100*scale) &&
      (playerHand.get(movingIdx).getRank() == 8 ||
          playerHand.get(movingIdx).getRank() == validRank ||
          playerHand.get(movingIdx).getSuit() == validSuit)) {
    validRank = playerHand.get(movingIdx).getRank();
    validSuit = playerHand.get(movingIdx).getSuit();
    discardPile.add(0, playerHand.get(movingIdx));
    playerHand.remove(movingIdx);
    if (playerHand.isEmpty()) {
      endHand();
    } else {
      if (validRank == 8) {
        changeSuit();
      } else {
        myTurn = false;
        computerPlay();
      }
    }
  }
```

We simply need to check if the player's hand is empty; if it is, the hand has ended. The next thing we need to do is to check on the computer's side if the hand has ended. Listing 6-47 shows that code.

Listing 6-47. Complete listing of the computerPlay() method

```
private void computerPlay() {
  int tempPlay = 0;
  while (tempPlay == 0) {
    tempPlay = computerPlayer.playCard(computerHand, validSuit,
    validRank);
    if (tempPlay == 0) {
      drawCard(computerHand);
    }
  }
  if (tempPlay == 108 || tempPlay == 208 || tempPlay == 308 ||
  tempPlay == 408) {
    validRank = 8;
    validSuit = computerPlayer.chooseSuit(computerHand);
    String suitText = "";
    if (validSuit == 100) {
      suitText = "Diamonds";
    } else if (validSuit == 200) {
      suitText = "Clubs";
    } else if (validSuit == 300) {
      suitText = "Hearts";
    } else if (validSuit == 400) {
      suitText = "Spades";
    }
```

```
    Toast.makeText(ctx, "Computer chose " + suitText, Toast.
    LENGTH_SHORT).show();
  } else {
    validSuit = Math.round((tempPlay/100) * 100);
    validRank = tempPlay - validSuit;
  }
  for (int i = 0; i < computerHand.size(); i++) {
    Card tempCard = computerHand.get(i);
    if (tempPlay == tempCard.getId()) {
      discardPile.add(0, computerHand.get(i));
      computerHand.remove(i);
    }
  }
  if (computerHand.isEmpty()) { ❶
    endHand();
  }
  myTurn = true;
}
```

---

❶   We simply check if the computer's hand is empty; if it is, the hand has ended.

And that's all the logic we need to write for the Crazy Eights game. The logic for ending the game is already shown in Listing 6-44 (bullet 5); when either one of the players reaches 300, the game ends.

CHAPTER 7

Building the Balloon Popper Game

Let's jump into the next game. This game will be simpler than the previous one we built, both in mechanics and technique, but this one will incorporate the use of audio and some sound effects. In this chapter, we'll discuss the following:

- How to use ImageView as a graphic object in the game

- Use the ValueAnimator in animating movements of game objects

- Use AudioManager, MediaPlayer, and the SoundPool classes to add audio effects and music to your game

- Use Java threads to run things in the background

Like in the previous chapter, I'll show the code snippets necessary to build the game; at times, even full code listings of some classes will be provided. The best way to understand and learn the programming techniques in this chapter is to download the source code for the game and keep it open in Android Studio as you read through the chapter sections. If you want to follow along and build the project yourself, it's best to keep the source code for the chapter handy, so you can copy and paste particular snippets as necessary.

© Ted Hagos, Mario Zechner, J.F. DiMarzio and Robert Green 2020
T. Hagos et al., *Beginning Android Games Development*,
https://doi.org/10.1007/978-1-4842-6121-7_7

Game Mechanics

We will make balloons float from the bottom of the screen, rising to the top. The players' goal is to pop as many balloons as they can before the balloons reach the top of the screen. If a balloon reaches the top without being popped, that will be a point against the user. The player will have five lives (pins, in this case); each time the player misses a balloon, they lose a pin. When the pins run out, it's game over.

We'll introduce the concept of levels. In each level, there will be several balloons. As the player progresses in levels, the time it takes for the balloon to float from the bottom to the top becomes less and less; the balloons float faster as the level increases. It's that simple. Figure 7-1 shows a screenshot of Balloon Popper game.

Figure 7-1. Pop balloons

The balloons will show up on random locations from the bottom of the screen.

We will devote the lower strip of the screen to game statistics. We will use this to display the score and the level. On the lower left side, we'll place a Button view which the user can use to start the game and to start a new level.

The game will be played in full screen (like our previous game), and it will be done so exclusively in landscape mode.

Creating the Project

Create a new project with an empty Activity, as shown in Figure 7-2.

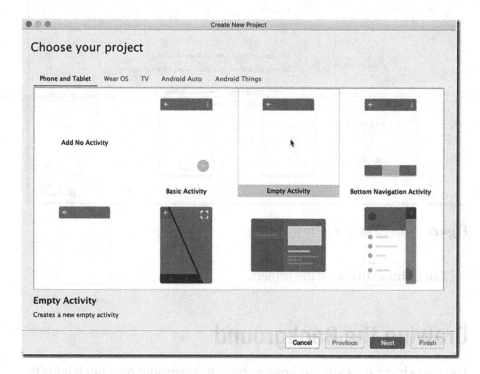

Figure 7-2. New project with an empty Activity

In the window that follows, fill out the project details, as shown in Figure 7-3.

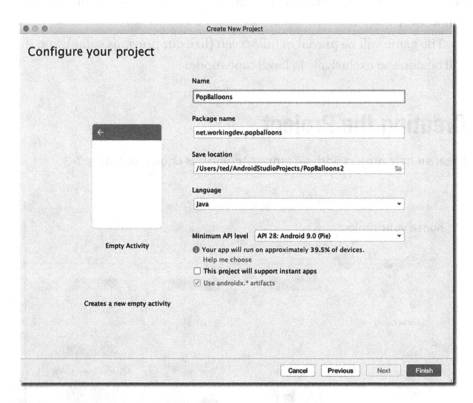

Figure 7-3. Create a new project

Click **Finish** to create the project.

Drawing the Background

The game has a background image; you can do without one, but it adds to the user experience. Surely, if you'll release a commercial game, you'll use an image that has more professional polish. I grabbed this image from one of the public domain sites; feel free to use any image you prefer.

When I got the background image, I downloaded only one file and named it "background.jpg." I could have used this image and dropped it in the **app/res/drawable** folder and be done with it. Had I done that, the runtime will use this same image file as background for different display densities, and it will try to make that adjustment while the game is playing, which may result in a jittery game experience. So, it's very important to provide a background image for different screen densities. If you're quite handy with Photoshop or GIMP, you can try to generate the images for different screens; or, you can use just one background image and then use an application called **Android Resizer** (https://github.com/asystat/Final-Android-Resizer) to generate the images for you. You can download the application from its GitHub repo and use it right away. It's an executable Java archive (JAR) file.

Once downloaded, you can open the zipped file and double-click the file **Final Android Resizer.jar** in the Executable Jar folder (shown in Figure 7-4).

Name	^	Date Modified
🖼 Android Final Resizer.jar		Oct 6, 2017 at 2:09 AM
▼ 📁 Executable Jar		Oct 6, 2017 at 2:09 AM
🖼 Final Android Resizer.jar		Oct 6, 2017 at 2:09 AM
🗋 Final-Android-Resizer.iml		Oct 6, 2017 at 2:09 AM
▶ 📁 libs		Oct 6, 2017 at 2:09 AM
🗋 miglayout-src.zip		Oct 6, 2017 at 2:09 AM
🖼 miglayout15-swing.jar		Oct 6, 2017 at 2:09 AM
🗋 README.md		Oct 6, 2017 at 2:09 AM
▶ 📁 src		Oct 6, 2017 at 2:09 AM

Figure 7-4. *Android Resizer app*

In the window that follows (Figure 7-5), modify the settings of the "export" section; the various screen density targets are in the Export section. I ticked off ldpi because we don't have to support the low-density screens. I also ticked off the tvdpi because our targets don't include Android TVs.

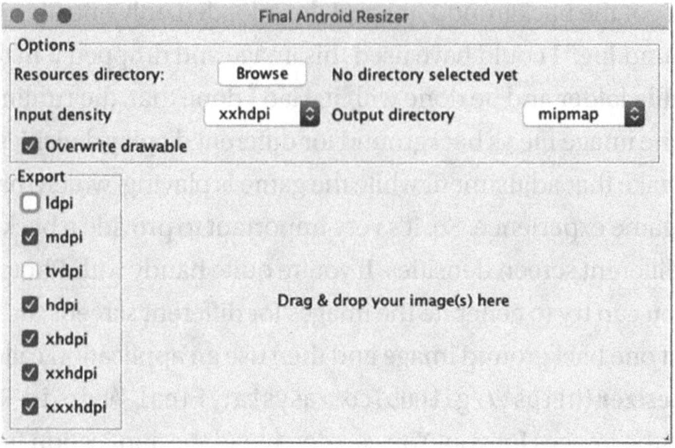

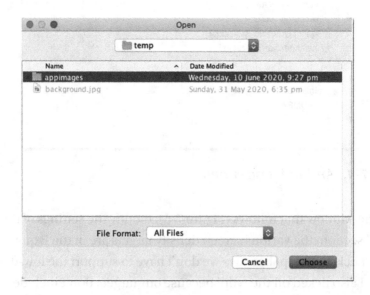

Figure 7-5. *Android Resizer*

Click the browse button of the Android Resizer to set the target folder where you would like to generate the images, as shown in Figure 7-6; then click **Choose**.

Figure 7-6. *Target folder for generated images*

The target directory (resources directory) should now be set. Remember this directory because you will fetch the images from here and transfer them to the Android project. In the window that follows (Figure 7-7), you will set the target directory.

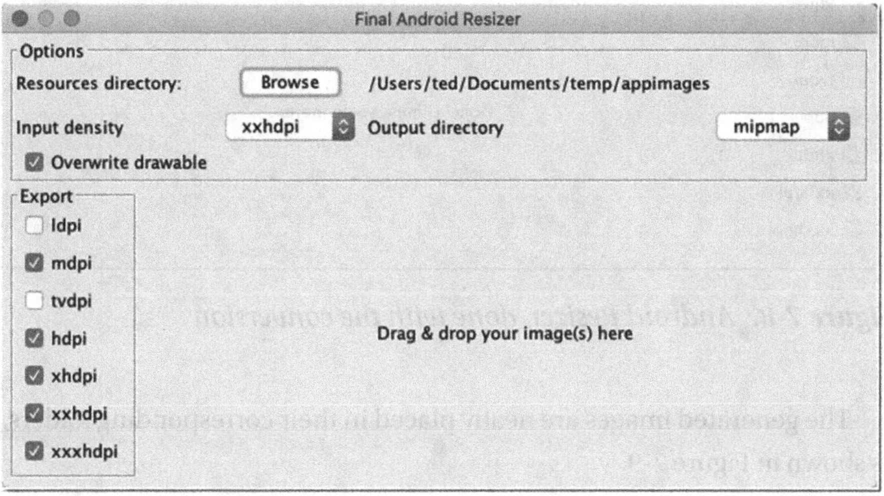

Figure 7-7. *Android Resizer, target directory set*

Next, drag the image you'd like to resize in the center area of the Resizer app. As soon as you drop the image, the conversion begins. When the conversion finishes, you'll see a message "Done! Gimme some more...", as shown in Figure 7-8.

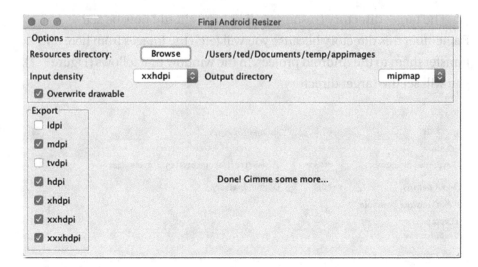

Figure 7-8. *Android Resizer, done with the conversion*

The generated images are neatly placed in their corresponding folders, as shown in Figure 7-9.

Name	^	Date Modified
▼ 📁 mipmap-hdpi		Today at 9:30 PM
🖼 background.jpg		Today at 9:30 PM
▼ 📁 mipmap-mdpi		Today at 9:31 PM
🖼 background.jpg		Today at 9:30 PM
▼ 📁 mipmap-xhdpi		Today at 9:30 PM
🖼 background.jpg		Today at 9:30 PM
▼ 📁 mipmap-xxhdpi		Today at 9:30 PM
🖼 background.jpg		Today at 9:30 PM
▼ 📁 mipmap-xxxhdpi		Today at 9:30 PM
🖼 background.jpg		Today at 9:30 PM

Figure 7-9. *Generated images*

The background image file isn't the only thing we need to resize. We also need to do this for the balloon image. We will use a graphic image to represent the balloons in the game. The balloon file is just a grayscale image (shown in Figure 7-10); we'll add the colors in the program later.

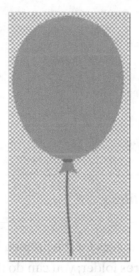

Figure 7-10. *Grayscale image of the balloon*

Drag and drop the balloon image in the Resizer app, as you did with the background file. When it's done, the Android Resizer would have generated the files **balloons.png** and **background.jpg** in the appropriate folders (as shown in Figure 7-11).

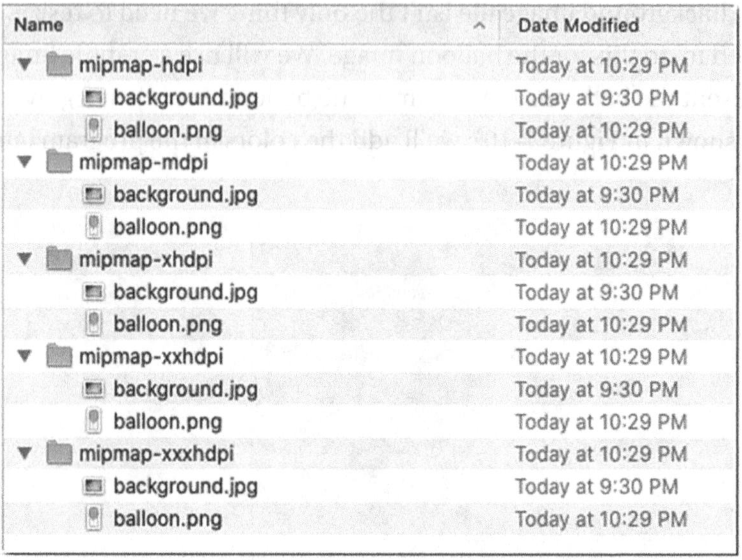

Name	^	Date Modified
▼ 📁 mipmap-hdpi		Today at 10:29 PM
🖼 background.jpg		Today at 9:30 PM
📱 balloon.png		Today at 10:29 PM
▼ 📁 mipmap-mdpi		Today at 10:29 PM
🖼 background.jpg		Today at 9:30 PM
📱 balloon.png		Today at 10:29 PM
▼ 📁 mipmap-xhdpi		Today at 10:29 PM
🖼 background.jpg		Today at 9:30 PM
📱 balloon.png		Today at 10:29 PM
▼ 📁 mipmap-xxhdpi		Today at 10:29 PM
🖼 background.jpg		Today at 9:30 PM
📱 balloon.png		Today at 10:29 PM
▼ 📁 mipmap-xxxhdpi		Today at 10:29 PM
🖼 background.jpg		Today at 9:30 PM
📱 balloon.png		Today at 10:29 PM

Figure 7-11. *Generated files*

We can now use these images for the project. To move the images to the project, open the **app/res** folder; you can do this by using a context action; right-click **app/res**, then choose **Reveal in Finder** (if you're on macOS); if you're on Windows, it will be **Show in Explorer** (as shown in Figure 7-12).

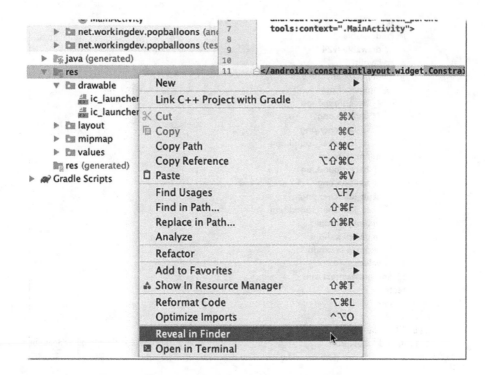

Figure 7-12. Reveal in Finder

Now, you can simply drag and drop the generated image folders (and files) into the correct folders in **app/res/** directory.

Figure 7-13 shows an updated **app/res** directory of the project. I switched the scope of the Project tool from *Android scope* to *Project scope* to see the physical layout of the files. I usually change scopes, depending on what I need.

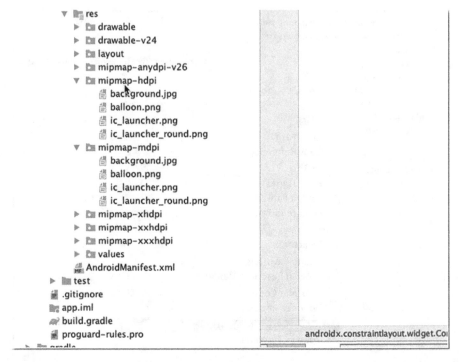

Figure 7-13. *app/res folder with the appropriate image files*

Before we draw the background image, let's take care of the
screen orientation. It's best to play this game in landscape mode;
that's why we'll fix the orientation to landscape. We can do this in the
AndroidManifest file. Edit the project's AndroidManifest to match
Listing 7-1; Figure 7-14 shows the location of the AndroidManifest file
in the Project tool window.

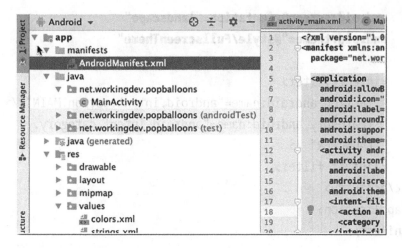

Figure 7-14. *AndroidManifest.xml*

Listing 7-1. AndroidManifest.xml

```
<?xml version="1.0" encoding="utf-8"?>
<manifest xmlns:android="http://schemas.android.com/apk/res/
android"
  package="net.workingdev.popballoons">

  <application
    android:allowBackup="true"
    android:icon="@mipmap/ic_launcher"
    android:label="@string/app_name"
    android:roundIcon="@mipmap/ic_launcher_round"
    android:supportsRtl="true"
    android:theme="@style/AppTheme">
    <activity android:name=".MainActivity"
    android:configChanges="orientation|keyboardHidden|
    screenSize"
    android:label="@string/app_name"
```

```
    android:screenOrientation="landscape"
    android:theme="@style/FullscreenTheme"
    >
    <intent-filter>
      <action android:name="android.intent.action.MAIN" />
      <category android:name="android.intent.category.
      LAUNCHER" />
    </intent-filter>
  </activity>
 </application>
</manifest>
```

The entries responsible for fixing the orientation to landscape are found on the attributes of the <activity> node in the manifest file. At this point, the project would have an error because the **Android:theme=" style/FullScreenTheme"** attribute doesn't exist as of yet. We'll fix that shortly.

Edit the **/app/res/styles.xml** file and add another style, as shown in Listing 7-2.

Listing 7-2. /app/res/styles.xml

```
<resources>
  <!-- Base application theme. -->
  <style name="AppTheme" parent="Theme.AppCompat.Light.
  DarkActionBar">
    <!-- Customize your theme here. -->
    <item name="colorPrimary">@color/colorPrimary</item>
    <item name="colorPrimaryDark">@color/colorPrimaryDark
    </item>
    <item name="colorAccent">@color/colorAccent</item>
  </style>
```

```
<style name="FullscreenTheme" parent="AppTheme">
  <item name="android:windowBackground">@android:color/white
  </item>
</style>
</resources>
```

That should fix it. Figure 7-15 shows the app in its current state.

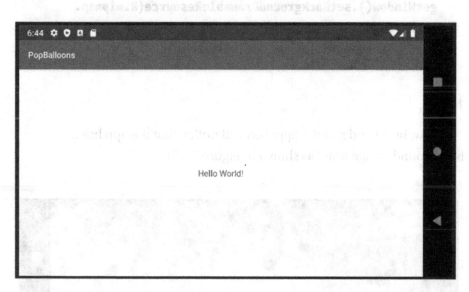

Figure 7-15. *PopBalloons*

To load the background image from the **app/res/mipmap** folders, we will use the following code:

```
getWindow().setBackgroundDrawableResource(R.mipmap.background);
```

We need to call this statement in the **onCreate()** method of MainActivity, just before we call **setContentView()**. Listing 7-3 shows our (still) minimal MainActivity.

Listing 7-3. MainActivity

```
public class MainActivity extends AppCompatActivity {

  @Override
  protected void onCreate(Bundle savedInstanceState) {
    super.onCreate(savedInstanceState);

    getWindow().setBackgroundDrawableResource(R.mipmap.
    background);
    setContentView(R.layout.activity_main);

  }
}
```

Now, build and run the app. You will notice that the app has a background image now (as shown in Figure 7-16).

Figure 7-16. *With background image*

Game Controls and Pin Icons

We will use the bottom part of the screen to show the score and the level. We'll also use this portion of the screen to place a button that triggers the start of the game and the start of the level.

Let's fix the **activity_main** layout file first. Currently, this layout file is set to ConstraintLayout (this is the default), but we don't need this layout, so we'll replace it with the RelativeLayout. We'll set the **layout_width** and **layout_height** of this container to **match_parent** so that it expands to the available space. Listing 7-4 shows our refactored main layout.

Listing 7-4. activity_main

```
<RelativeLayout xmlns:android="http://schemas.android.com/apk/
res/android"
  xmlns:tools="http://schemas.android.com/tools"
  android:layout_width="match_parent"
  android:layout_height="match_parent"
  tools:context=".MainActivity">

</RelativeLayout>
```

Next, we will add the Button and the TextView objects, which we'll use to start the game and to display game statistics. The idea is to nest the TextViews inside a LinearLayout container, which is oriented horizontally, and then put it side by side with a Button control; then, we'll enclose the Button and the LinearLayout container within another RelativeLayout container. Listing 7-5 shows the complete activity_main layout, with the game controls added.

Listing 7-5. activity_main.xml

```
<RelativeLayout xmlns:android="http://schemas.android.com/apk/
res/android"
  xmlns:tools="http://schemas.android.com/tools"
  android:layout_width="match_parent"
  android:layout_height="match_parent"
  tools:context=".MainActivity">

<!-- Buttons and status displays -->
<RelativeLayout
  android:layout_width="match_parent"
  android:layout_height="wrap_content"
  android:layout_alignParentBottom="true"
  android:background="@color/lightGrey">

  < Button
    android:id="@+id/go_button"
    style="?android:borderlessButtonStyle"
    android:layout_width="wrap_content"
    android:layout_height="wrap_content"
    android:layout_alignParentStart="true"
    android:layout_centerVertical="true"
    android:text="@string/play_game"
    android:layout_alignParentLeft="true"/>

  <LinearLayout
    android:id="@+id/status_display"
    android:layout_width="wrap_content"
    android:layout_height="wrap_content"
    android:layout_alignParentEnd="true"
    android:layout_centerVertical="true"
    android:layout_marginEnd="8dp"
```

```
android:orientation="horizontal"
tools:ignore="RelativeOverlap">

<TextView
  android:layout_width="wrap_content"
  android:layout_height="wrap_content"
  android:text="@string/level_label"
  android:textSize="20sp"
  android:textStyle="bold"
  tools:ignore="RelativeOverlap" />

<TextView
  android:id="@+id/level_display"
  android:layout_width="40dp"
  android:layout_height="wrap_content"
  android:layout_marginEnd="32dp"
  android:gravity="end"
  android:text="@string/maxNumber"
  android:textSize="20sp"
  android:textStyle="bold" />

<TextView
  android:id="@+id/score_label"
  android:layout_width="wrap_content"
  android:layout_height="wrap_content"
  android:text="@string/score_label"
  android:textSize="20sp"
  android:textStyle="bold"
  tools:ignore="RelativeOverlap" />

<TextView
  android:id="@+id/score_display"
  android:layout_width="40dp"
```

```
    android:layout_height="wrap_content"
    android:layout_marginEnd="16dp"
    android:gravity="end"
    android:text="@string/maxNumber"
    android:textSize="20sp"
    android:textStyle="bold" />
  </LinearLayout>

</RelativeLayout>

</RelativeLayout>
```

We referenced a couple of string and color resources in **activity_main. xml**, and we need to add them to **strings.xml** and **colors.xml** in the resources folder.

Open **colors.xml** and edit it to match Listing 7-6.

Listing 7-6. app/res/values/colors.xml

```
<?xml version="1.0" encoding="utf-8"?>
<resources>
  <color name="colorPrimary">#008577</color>
  <color name="colorPrimaryDark">#00574B</color>
  <color name="colorAccent">#D81B60</color>

  <color name="lightGrey">#DDDDDD</color>
  <color name="pinColor">@color/black_overlay</color>
  <color name="black_overlay">#66000000</color>
</resources>
```

Open **strings.xml** and edit it to match Listing 7-7.

Listing 7-7. app/res/values/strings.xml

```
<resources>
    <string name="app_name">PopBalloons</string>
    <string name="play_game">Play</string>
    <string name="stop_game">Stop</string>
    <string name="score_label">Score:</string>
    <string name="maxNumber">999</string>
    <string name="level_label">Level:</string>
    <string name="wow_that_was_awesome">Wow, that was awesome
    </string>
    <string name="more_levels_than_ever">More Levels than Ever!
    </string>
    <string name="new_top_score">New Top Score!</string>
    <string name="your_top_score_is">Top score: %s</string>
    <string name="you_completed_n_levels">Levels completed:
    %s</string>
    <string name="game_over">Game over!</string>
    <string name="missed_that_one">Missed that one!</string>
    <string name="you_finished_level_n">You finished level
    %s!</string>
    <string name="popping_pin">Popping Pin</string>
</resources>
```

String literals are stored in strings.xml to avoid hardcoding the String literals in our program. This approach of using a resources file for String literals makes it easier to change the Strings later on—say, when you release the game to non-English speaking countries.

Figure 7-17 shows the app with game controls.

Figure 7-17. *With game controls*

Next, let's draw the pins. You can get the pins from Google's material icons. These are SVG icons, so we don't have to create multiple copies for different screen resolutions; they scale just fine. The vector definitions of the pins will be in the drawable folder. We'll create two vector definitions for the pin; one image represents a whole pin (an unused game life) and the other a broken pin (a used game life).

We need to create these files inside the drawable folder; we can do this with the context menu actions. Right-click the **app/res/drawable** folder of the project, as shown in Figure 7-18.

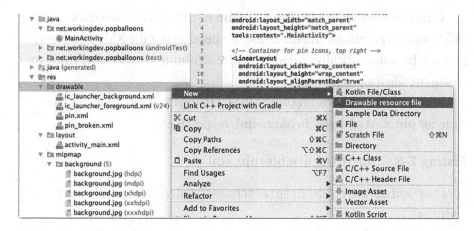

Figure 7-18. *New drawable resource file*

In the window that follows, type the name of the file (as shown in Figure 7-19).

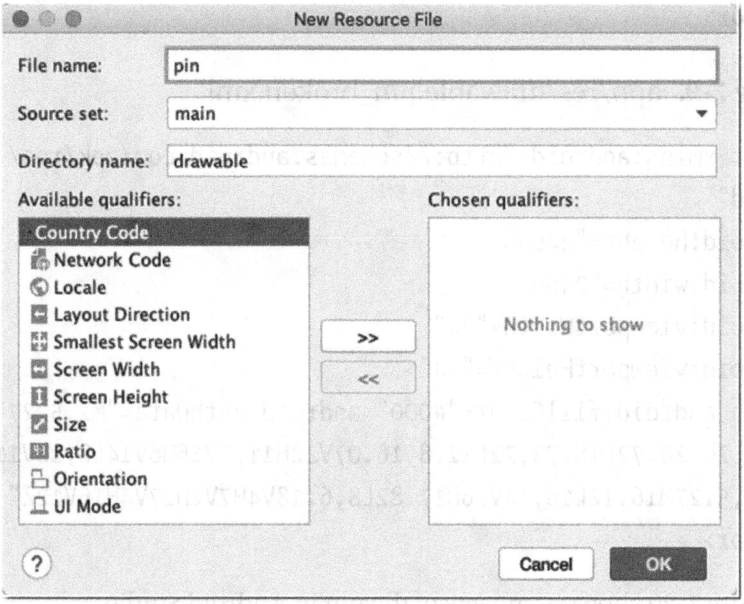

Figure 7-19. *New Resource File*

Check to see that the **Directory name** is "drawable," then click
OK. Simply type **pin** for the file name; no need to put the XML extension,
that will be automatically added by Android Studio. Do the same thing to
create the file for **pin_broken**.

Edit the newly created resource files. Listings 7-8 and 7-9 show the
code for **pin.xml** and **pin_broken.xml**, respectively.

Listing 7-8. app/res/drawable/pin.xml

```
<vector xmlns:android="http://schemas.android.com/apk/res/
android"
  android:height="24dp"
  android:width="24dp"
  android:viewportWidth="24"
  android:viewportHeight="24">
  <path android:fillColor="#000" android:pathData="M16,
  12V4H17V2H7V4H8V12L6,14V16H11.2V22H12.8V16H18V14L16,12Z" />
</vector>
```

Listing 7-9. app/res/drawable.pin_broken.xml

```
<vector xmlns:android="http://schemas.android.com/apk/res/
android"
  android:height="24dp"
  android:width="24dp"
  android:viewportWidth="24"
  android:viewportHeight="24">
  <path android:fillColor="#000" android:pathData="M2,5.27L3.
  28,4L20,20.72L18.73,22L12.8,16.07V22H11.2V16H6V14L8,12V11.
  27L2,5.27M16,12L18,14V16H17.82L8,6.18V4H7V2H17V4H16V12Z" />
</vector>
```

Figure 7-20 shows a preview of the pin in Android Studio.

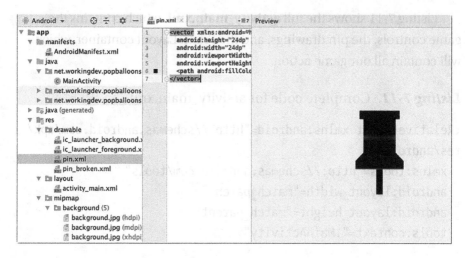

Figure 7-20. *Preview of the pin image*

Now that we have images for the pins, we can add them to the **activity_main** layout file. We'll place five ImageView objects at the top part of the screen, and then we will point each ImageView to the pin images we recently created. Listing 7-10 shows a snippet of the pin definitions in XML.

Listing 7-10. Pin definitions in XML

```
<ImageView
    android:id="@+id/pushpin1"
    android:layout_width="40dp"
    android:layout_height="40dp"
    android:contentDescription="@string/popping_pin"
    android:src="@drawable/pin"
    android:tint="@color/pinColor" />
```

The **android:src** attribute points the ImageView to our vector drawing in the drawable folder.

Listing 7-11 shows the full **activity_main.xml**, which contains the
game controls, the pin drawings, and the FrameLayout container, which
will contain all our game action.

Listing 7-11. Complete code for activity_main.xml

```
<RelativeLayout xmlns:android="http://schemas.android.com/apk/
res/android"
  xmlns:tools="http://schemas.android.com/tools"
  android:layout_width="match_parent"
  android:layout_height="match_parent"
  tools:context=".MainActivity">

  <FrameLayout
    android:id="@+id/content_view"
    android:layout_width="match_parent"
    android:layout_height="match_parent" />

  <!-- Container for pin icons -->
  <LinearLayout
    android:layout_width="wrap_content"
    android:layout_height="wrap_content"
    android:layout_alignParentEnd="true"
    android:layout_alignParentTop="true"
    android:layout_marginEnd="16dp"
    android:layout_marginTop="16dp"
    android:orientation="horizontal">

    <ImageView
      android:id="@+id/pushpin1"
      android:layout_width="40dp"
      android:layout_height="40dp"
      android:contentDescription="@string/popping_pin"
      android:src="@drawable/pin"
      android:tint="@color/pinColor" />
```

```xml
<ImageView
    android:id="@+id/pushpin2"
    android:layout_width="40dp"
    android:layout_height="40dp"
    android:contentDescription="@string/popping_pin"
    android:src="@drawable/pin"
    android:tint="@color/pinColor" />

<ImageView
    android:id="@+id/pushpin3"
    android:layout_width="40dp"
    android:layout_height="40dp"
    android:contentDescription="@string/popping_pin"
    android:src="@drawable/pin"
    android:tint="@color/pinColor" />

<ImageView
    android:id="@+id/pushpin4"
    android:layout_width="40dp"
    android:layout_height="40dp"
    android:contentDescription="@string/popping_pin"
    android:src="@drawable/pin"
    android:tint="@color/pinColor" />

<ImageView
    android:id="@+id/pushpin5"
    android:layout_width="40dp"
    android:layout_height="40dp"
    android:contentDescription="@string/popping_pin"
    android:src="@drawable/pin"
    android:tint="@color/pinColor" />

</LinearLayout>
```

```xml
<!-- Buttons and game statistics -->
<RelativeLayout
  android:layout_width="match_parent"
  android:layout_height="wrap_content"
  android:layout_alignParentBottom="true"
  android:background="@color/lightGrey">

  < Button
    android:id="n"
    style="?android:borderlessButtonStyle"
    android:layout_width="wrap_content"
    android:layout_height="wrap_content"
    android:layout_alignParentStart="true"
    android:layout_centerVertical="true"
    android:text="@string/play_game" />

  <LinearLayout
    android:id="@+id/status_display"
    android:layout_width="wrap_content"
    android:layout_height="wrap_content"
    android:layout_alignParentEnd="true"
    android:layout_centerVertical="true"
    android:layout_marginEnd="8dp"
    android:orientation="horizontal"
    tools:ignore="RelativeOverlap">

    <TextView
      android:layout_width="wrap_content"
      android:layout_height="wrap_content"
      android:text="@string/level_label"
      android:textSize="20sp"
      android:textStyle="bold"
      tools:ignore="RelativeOverlap" />
```

```
    <TextView
        android:id="@+id/level_display"
        android:layout_width="40dp"
        android:layout_height="wrap_content"
        android:layout_marginEnd="32dp"
        android:gravity="end"
        android:text="@string/maxNumber"
        android:textSize="20sp"
        android:textStyle="bold" />

    <TextView
        android:id="@+id/score_label"
        android:layout_width="wrap_content"
        android:layout_height="wrap_content"
        android:text="@string/score_label"
        android:textSize="20sp"
        android:textStyle="bold"
        tools:ignore="RelativeOverlap" />

    <TextView
        android:id="@+id/score_display"
        android:layout_width="40dp"
        android:layout_height="wrap_content"
        android:layout_marginEnd="16dp"
        android:gravity="end"
        android:text="@string/maxNumber"
        android:textSize="20sp"
        android:textStyle="bold" />
    </LinearLayout>
  </RelativeLayout>
</RelativeLayout>
```

At this point, you should have something that looks like Figure 7-21.

Figure 7-21. *The app with game controls and pins*

It's starting to shape up, but we still need to fix that toolbar and the other widgets displayed on the top strip of the screen. We've already done this in the previous chapter so that this technique will be familiar. Listing 7-12 shows the code for the **setToFullScreen()** method.

Listing 7-12. setToFullScreen()

```
private void setToFullScreen() {

  contentView.setSystemUiVisibility(View.SYSTEM_UI_FLAG_
  LOW_PROFILE
      | View.SYSTEM_UI_FLAG_FULLSCREEN
      | View.SYSTEM_UI_FLAG_LAYOUT_STABLE
      | View.SYSTEM_UI_FLAG_IMMERSIVE_STICKY
      | View.SYSTEM_UI_FLAG_LAYOUT_HIDE_NAVIGATION
      | View.SYSTEM_UI_FLAG_HIDE_NAVIGATION);
}
```

Enabling fullscreen mode is well documented in the Android Developer website; here's the link for more information: https://developer. android.com/training/system-ui/immersive.

Listing 7-13 shows the annotated listing of MainActivity.

Listing 7-13. Annotated MainActivity

```java
import androidx.appcompat.app.AppCompatActivity;

import android.os.Bundle;
import android.view.MotionEvent;
import android.view.View;
import android.view.ViewGroup;

public class MainActivity extends AppCompatActivity {

  ViewGroup contentView; ❶

  @Override
  protected void onCreate(Bundle savedInstanceState) {
    super.onCreate(savedInstanceState);

    getWindow().setBackgroundDrawableResource(R.mipmap.
    background);
    setContentView(R.layout.activity_main);
    contentView = (ViewGroup) findViewById
    (R.id.content_view); ❷
    contentView.setOnTouchListener(new View.OnTouchListener() {
      @Override
      public boolean onTouch(View v, MotionEvent event) { ❸
        if (event.getAction() == MotionEvent.ACTION_DOWN) {
          setToFullScreen();
        }
        return false;
      }
```

```
  });

}

@Override
protected void onResume() {
  super.onResume();
  setToFullScreen();  ❹
}

private void setToFullScreen() {

  contentView.setSystemUiVisibility(View.SYSTEM_UI_FLAG_
  OW_PROFILE
      | View.SYSTEM_UI_FLAG_FULLSCREEN
      | View.SYSTEM_UI_FLAG_LAYOUT_STABLE
      | View.SYSTEM_UI_FLAG_IMMERSIVE_STICKY
      | View.SYSTEM_UI_FLAG_LAYOUT_HIDE_NAVIGATION
      | View.SYSTEM_UI_FLAG_HIDE_NAVIGATION);
  }
}
```

❶   Declare the **contentView** variable as a member; we'll use this on a couple of methods, so we need it available class-wide.

❷   Get a reference to the FrameLayout container we defined earlier in **activity_main**. Store the returned value to the **containerView** variable.

❸   The fullscreen setting is temporary. The screen may revert to displaying the toolbar later (e.g., when dialog windows are shown). We're binding the **setOnTouchListener()** to the FrameLayout to allow the user to simply tap anywhere on the screen once to restore the full screen.

❹   We're calling the **setToFullScreen()** here in the **onResume()** lifecycle method. We want to set the screen to full when all of the View objects are already visible to the user.

Figure 7-22 shows the app in fullscreen mode.

Figure 7-22. *The app in full screen*

Drawing the Balloons

The idea is to create a lot of balloons that will rise from the bottom to the top of the screen. We need to create the balloons programmatically. We can do this by creating a class that represents the balloon. We'll write some logic that will create instances of the Balloon class and make them appear at random places at the bottom of the screen, but first things first, let's create that Balloon class.

Right-click the project's package, then choose **New ➤ Java Class**, as shown in Figure 7-23.

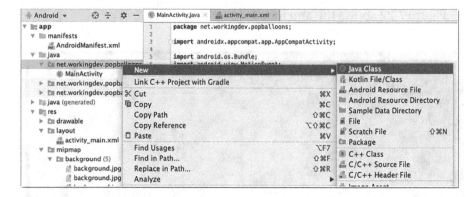

Figure 7-23. *New Java class*

In the window that follows, type the name of the class (Balloon) and type its superclass (AppCompatImageView), as shown in Figure 7-24.

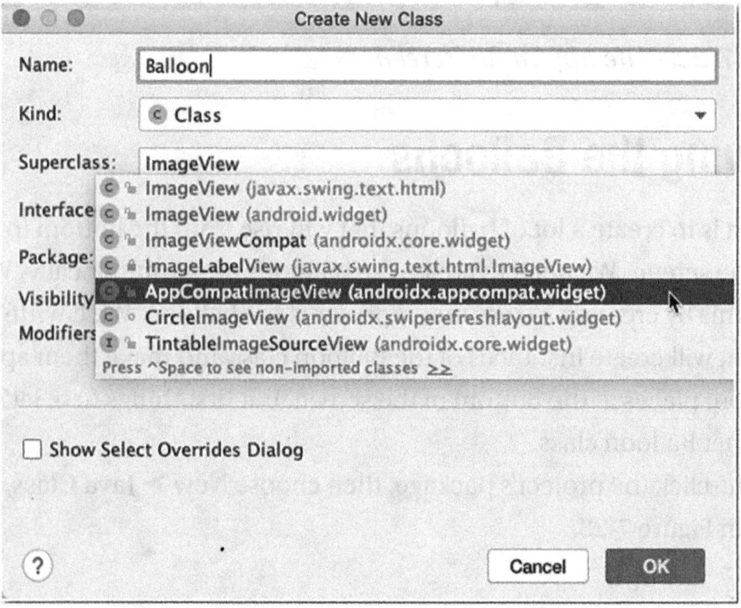

Figure 7-24. *Create a new class*

Listing 7-14 shows the code for the Balloon class.

Listing 7-14. Balloon class

```java
import androidx.appcompat.widget.AppCompatImageView;
import android.content.Context;
import android.util.TypedValue;
import android.view.ViewGroup;
public class Balloon extends AppCompatImageView {

    public Balloon(Context context) { ❶
        super(context);
    }

    public Balloon(Context context, int color, int height, int
    level ) { ❷
        super(context);

        setImageResource(R.mipmap.balloon); ❸
        setColorFilter(color); ❹
        int width = height / 2;  ❺

        int dpHeight = pixelsToDp(height, context); ❻
        int dpWidth = pixelsToDp(width, context);

        ViewGroup.LayoutParams params =
            new ViewGroup.LayoutParams(dpWidth, dpHeight);
        setLayoutParams(params);

    }

    public static int pixelsToDp(int px, Context context) {
        return (int) TypedValue.applyDimension(
            TypedValue.COMPLEX_UNIT_DIP, px,
            context.getResources().getDisplayMetrics());
    }
}
```

❶   This is the default constructor of the AppCompatImageView. We'll leave this alone

❷   We need a new constructor, one that takes in some parameters that we'll need for the game. Overload the constructor and create one that takes in parameters for the balloon's color, height and game level

❸   Set the source for the image. Point it to the balloon image in the mipmap folders

❹   The balloon image is just monochromatic gray. The **setColorFilter()** tints the image with any color you like. This is the reason why we want to parameterize the color

❺   The image file of the balloon is set so that it's twice as long as its width. To calculate the width of the balloon, we divide the height by 2

❻   We want to calculate the device-independent pixels for the image; so, we created a static method in the Balloon class that does exactly that (see the implementation of **pixelsToDp()**)

If you want to see this in action, you can modify the **onTouch()** listener of the contentView container in MainActivity such that, every time you touch the screen, a red balloon pops up exactly where you touched the screen. The code for that is shown in Listing 7-15.

Listing 7-15. MainActivity's onTouchListener

```
contentView.setOnTouchListener(new View.OnTouchListener() {
  @Override
  public boolean onTouch(View v, MotionEvent event) {
    Balloon btemp = new Balloon(MainActivity.this,
    0xFFFF0000, 100, 1); ❶
    btemp.setY(event.getY());   ❷
    btemp.setX(event.getX());   ❸
    contentView.addView(btemp); ❹
```

```
  if (event.getAction() == MotionEvent.ACTION_DOWN) {
    setToFullScreen();
  }
  return false;
 }
});
```

---

❶   Create an instance of the Balloon class; pass the context, the color RED, an arbitrary height, and 1 (for the level, this isn't important right now).

❷   Set the Y coordinate where we want the Balloon object to show up.

❸   Set the X coordinate.

❹   Add the new Balloon object as a child to the View object; this is important because this makes the Balloon visible to us.

At this point, every time you click the screen, a red balloon shows up. We need to mix up the colors of the balloons to make it more interesting. Let's use at least three colors: red, green, and blue. We can look up the hex values of these colors, or we can use the Color class in Android. To get the red color, we can write something like this:

```
Color.argb(255, 255, 0, 0);
```

For blue and green, it would be as follows:

```
Color.argb(255, 0, 255, 0);
Color.argb(255, 0, 0, 255);
```

A simple solution to rotate the colors is to set up an array of three elements, where each element contains a color value. Listing 7-16 shows the partial code for this task.

Listing 7-16. Array of colors (this goes into the MainActivity)

```
private int[] colors = new int[3];

@Override
protected void onCreate(Bundle savedInstanceState) {
  super.onCreate(savedInstanceState);
  // ...
  colors[0] = Color.argb(255, 255, 0, 0);
  colors[1] = Color.argb(255, 0, 255, 0);
  colors[2] = Color.argb(255, 0, 0, 255);
}
```

Next, we set up a method that returns a random number between 0 and 2. We'll make this our random selector for color. Listing 7-17 shows this code.

Listing 7-17. nextColor() method

```
private static int nextColor() {
  int max = 2;
  int min = 0;
  int retval = 0;

  Random random = new Random();
  retval = random.nextInt((max - min) + 1) + min;

  return retval;
}
```

Next, we modify that part of our code in MainActivity when we create the Balloon (inside the **onTouch()** method) and assign it a color; now, we will assign it a random color. Listing 7-18 shows that code.

Listing 7-18. Assigning a random color

```
int curColor = colors[nextColor()];
Balloon btemp = new Balloon(MainActivity.this, curColor, 100, 1);
btemp.setY(event.getY());
btemp.setX(event.getX());

contentView.addView(btemp);
```

Figure 7-25 shows the app randomizing the colors of the balloons.

Figure 7-25. *Random colors*

Making the Balloons Float

To make the balloons float from the bottom to the top, we will use a built-in class in Android SDK. We won't micromanage the position of the balloon as it rises to the top of the screen.

The ValueAnimator class (**Android .animation.ValueAnimator**) is essentially a timing engine for running animations. It calculates animated values and then sets them on the target objects.

Since we want to animate each balloon, we'll put the animation logic inside the Balloon class; let's add a new method named **release()** where we will put the necessary code to make the balloon float. Listing 7-19 shows the code.

Listing 7-19. release() method in the Balloon class

```
private BalloonListener listener;

// some other statements  ...

listener = new BalloonListener(this);

// some other statements ...

public void release(int scrHeight, int duration) { ❶
    animator = new ValueAnimator();  ❷
    animator.setDuration(duration);  ❸
    animator.setFloatValues(scrHeight, 0f);  ❹
    animator.setInterpolator(new LinearInterpolator()); ❺
    animator.setTarget(this);  ❻

    animator.addListener(listener);
    animator.addUpdateListener(listener); ❼
    animator.start(); ❽
}
```

❶   The **release()** method takes two arguments; the first one is the height of the screen (we need this for the animation), and the second one is *duration*; we need this later for the levels. As the level increases, the faster the balloon will rise.

❷   Create the Animator object.

❸   This sets the duration of the animation. The higher this value is, the longer the animation.

❹   This sets the float values that will be animated between. We want to animate from the bottom of the screen to the top; hence, we pass **0f** and the screen height.

❺   We set the time interpolator used in calculating the elapsed fraction of this animation. The interpolator determines whether the animation runs with linear or nonlinear motion, such as acceleration and deceleration. In our case, we want a linear acceleration, so we pass an instance of the LinearInterpolator.

❻   The target of the animation is the specific instance of a Balloon, hence **this**.

❼   The animation has a life cycle. We can listen to these updates by adding some Listener objects. We will implement these listeners in a little while.

❽   Start the animation.

Create a new class (on the same package) and name it **BalloonListener.java**; Listing 7-20 shows the code for the BalloonListener.

Listing 7-20. BalloonListener.java

```java
import android.animation.Animator;
import android.animation.ValueAnimator;

public class BalloonListener implements ❶
    Animator.AnimatorListener,
    ValueAnimator.AnimatorUpdateListener{

  Balloon balloon;

  public BalloonListener(Balloon balloon) {
    this.balloon = balloon;   ❷
  }
```

```
@Override
public void onAnimationUpdate(ValueAnimator valueAnimator) {
  balloon.setY((float) valueAnimator.getAnimatedValue()); ❸
}
// some other lifecycle methods ...
}
```

---

❶ We're interested in the lifecycle methods of the Animation; hence, we implement **Animator.AnimatorListener** and **ValueAnimator. AnimatorUpdateListener**.

❷ We need a reference to the Balloon object; hence, we take it in as a parameter when this listener object gets created.

❸ When the ValueAnimator updates its values, we will set the Y position of the balloon instance to this value.

In MainActivity (where we create an instance of the Balloon), we need to calculate the screen height. Listing 7-21 shows the annotated code that will accomplish that.

Listing 7-21. Calculate the screen's height and width

```
ViewTreeObserver viewTreeObserver = contentView.
getViewTreeObserver(); ❶
if (viewTreeObserver.isAlive()) { ❷
  viewTreeObserver.addOnGlobalLayoutListener(new ViewTree
  Observer.OnGlobalLayoutListener() {  ❸
    @Override
    public void onGlobalLayout() {
      contentView.getViewTreeObserver().removeOnGlobalLayout
      Listener(this); ❹
```

```
    scrWidth = contentView.getWidth(); ❺
    scrHeight = contentView.getHeight();
  }
});
}
```

---

❶	Get an instance of the ViewTreeObserver.
❷	We can only work with this observer when it's alive; so, we wrap the whole logic inside an **if-statement**.
❸	We want to be notified when the global layout state or the visibility of views within the view tree changes.
❹	We want to get notified only once; so, once the **onGlobalLayout()** method is called, we remove the listener.
❺	Now, we can get the screen's height and width.

Listing 7-22 shows MainActivity with the code to calculate the screen's height and width.

Listing 7-22. MainActivity

```
public class MainActivity extends AppCompatActivity {

  ViewGroup contentView;
  private static  String TAG;

  private int[] colors = new int[3];
  private int scrWidth; ❶
  private int scrHeight;

  @Override
  protected void onCreate(Bundle savedInstanceState) {
    super.onCreate(savedInstanceState);
```

```
    TAG = getClass().getName();

    // other statements ...

    contentView = (ViewGroup) findViewById(R.id.content_view);
    contentView.setOnTouchListener(new View.OnTouchListener() {
      @Override
      public boolean onTouch(View v, MotionEvent event) {
        Log.d(TAG, "onTouch");

        int curColor = colors[nextColor()];
        Balloon btemp = new Balloon(MainActivity.this,
        curColor, 100, 1);
        btemp.setY(scrHeight); ❷
        btemp.setX(event.getX());

        contentView.addView(btemp);
        btemp.release(scrHeight, 4000); ❸

        Log.d(TAG, "Balloon created");

        if (event.getAction() == MotionEvent.ACTION_DOWN) {
          setToFullScreen();
        }
        return false;
      }
    });

  }

  @Override
  protected void onResume() {
    super.onResume();

    setToFullScreen(); ❹
```

```
ViewTreeObserver viewTreeObserver = contentView.
getViewTreeObserver(); ❺
if (viewTreeObserver.isAlive()) {
  viewTreeObserver.addOnGlobalLayoutListener(new
                  ViewTreeObserver.OnGlobalLayoutListener() {
    @Override
    public void onGlobalLayout() {
      contentView.getViewTreeObserver().removeOnGlobal
      LayoutListener(this);
      scrWidth = contentView.getWidth();
      scrHeight = contentView.getHeight();
    }
  });
}


}
}
```

❶   Create member variables **scrHeight** and **scrWidth**.

❷   Change the value of Y coordinate for the Balloon instance. Instead of showing the Y position of the Balloon where the click occurred, let's start the Y position of the Balloon at the bottom of the screen.

❸   Call the **release()** method of the Balloon. We would have calculated the screen height by the time we make this call. The second argument is hardcoded for now (duration), which means the Balloon will take about 4 seconds to rise to the top of the screen.

❹   Before we calculate the screen height and width, it's very important that we already called **setToFullScreen()**; that way, we've got an accurate set of dimensions.

❺   Put the code to calculate the screen's height and width on the callback when all the View objects are already visible to the user; that's the **onResume()** method.

At this point, if you run the app, a Balloon object will rise from the bottom to the top of the screen whenever you click anywhere on the screen (Figure 7-26).

Figure 7-26. Balloons rising to the top

Launching the Balloons

Now that we can make balloons rise to the top one at a time, we need to figure out how to launch a couple of balloons that resembles a level of a game. Right now, the balloons appear on the screen in response to the user's click; this isn't how we want to play the game. We need to make some changes.

What we want is for the player to click a button, then start the gameplay. When the button is first clicked, that automatically gets the user into the first level. The levels of the game aren't complicated; as the levels rise, we'll simply increase the speed of the balloons.

To launch the balloons, we need to do the following:

1. Make the Button in **activity_main.xml** respond to click events.

2. Create a new method in MainActivity that will contain all the code needed to start a level.

3. Write a loop that will launch several balloons.

4. Randomize the X position of the Balloons as they are created.

To make the Button respond to click events, we need to bind it to an OnClickListener object, as shown in Listing 7-23.

Listing 7-23. Binding the Button to an onClickListener

```
Button btn = (Button) findViewById(R.id.btn);
btn.setOnClickListener(new View.OnClickListener() {
  @Override
  public void onClick(View view) {
    // start the level
    // when this is clicked
  }
});
```

The code to start a level is shown in Listing 7-24.

Listing 7-24. startLevel() in MainActivity

```
private void startLevel() {
  // we'll fill this codes later
}
```

We need to refactor the code to launch a single balloon. Right now, we're doing it inside the onTouchListener. We want to enclose this logic in a method. Listing 7-25 shows the **launchBalloon()** method in MainActivity.

Listing 7-25. launchBalloon()

```
public void launchBalloon(int xPos) { ❶

    int curColor = colors[nextColor()];
    Balloon btemp = new Balloon(MainActivity.this, curColor, 100, 1);
    btemp.setY(scrHeight);
    btemp.setX(xPos); ❷

    contentView.addView(btemp);
    btemp.release(scrHeight, 3000);

    Log.d(TAG, "Balloon created");
}
```

---

❶   The method takes an int parameter. This will be the X position of the Balloon on the screen.

❷   Set the horizontal position of the Balloon.

We want to launch the balloons in the background; you don't want to do these things in the main UI thread because that will affect the game's responsiveness. We don't want the game to feel janky. So, we'll write the looping logic in a Thread. Listing 7-26 shows the code for this Thread class.

Listing 7-26. LevelLoop (implemented as an inner class in MainActivity)

```
class LevelLoop extends Thread { ❶

  int balloonsLaunched = 0;

  public void run() {
    while (balloonsLaunched <= 15) { ❷
      balloonsLaunched++;
      Random random = new Random(new Date().getTime());
      final int xPosition = random.nextInt(scrWidth - 200); ❸

      try {
        Thread.sleep(1000);  ❹
      }
      catch(InterruptedException e) {
        Log.e(TAG, e.getMessage());
      }

      // need to wrap this on runOnUiThread

      runOnUiThread(new Thread() {
        public void run() {
          launchBalloon(xPosition);  ❺
        }
      });

    }
  }
}
```

❶   LevelLoop is an inner class in MainActivity. Implementing it as an inner class lets us access the outer class' (MainActivity) member variables and methods (which will be handy).

❷   The loop will stop when we've launched 15 balloons. The number of balloons to launch is hardcoded right now, but we'll refactor this later.

❸   Get a random number to pick an X coordinate for the Balloon.

❹   Let's introduce a delay; if you don't introduce the delay, all 15 balloons can appear and rise to the top at the same time. Right now, the delay is hardcoded; we'll refactor this later. We need to vary this according to the level. By the way, **Thread.sleep()** throws the **InterruptedException**; that's why we need to wrap this in a try-catch block.

❺   Finally, call the **launchBalloon()** method of the outer class. We need to wrap this call in a **runOnUiThread()** method because it's illegal for a background process to make calls on UI elements; UI elements are rendered on the main thread (otherwise known as the UI thread). If you need to make a call on objects that are on the UI thread while you are running in the background, you'll need to wrap that call on a **runOnUiThread()** method like what we did here.

At this point, every time you click the "Play" button, the game will launch a series of 15 balloons that will rise to the top of the screen; however, the game has no concept of levels yet. No matter how many times you click "Play," the speed of the rising balloons remains constant. Let's fix that in the next section.

Handling Game Levels

To introduce levels, let's create a member variable in MainActivity to hold the value of the levels, and every time we call the **startLevel()** method, we increment that variable by 1. Listing 7-27 shows the code for these changes.

Listing 7-27. Preparing the levels

```
private int level; ❶

// other statements ...

@Override
protected void onCreate(Bundle savedInstanceState) {
  super.onCreate(savedInstanceState);

  // other statements ...

  levelDisplay = (TextView) findViewById(R.id.level_display); ❷
  scoreDisplay = (TextView) findViewById(R.id.score_display); ❸
}

private void startLevel() {

  level++; ❹
  new LevelLoop(level).start(); ❺
  levelDisplay.setText(String.format("%s", level)); ❻
}
```

---

❶   Declare **level** as a member variable.

❷   Get a reference to the TextView object that displays the current level.

❸   While we're at it, also get a reference to the TextView object that displays the current score.

❹   Increment the **level** variable every time the **startLevel()** method is called.

❺   Let's pass the **level** variable to the **LevelLoop** object (we need to refactor the LevelLoop class, so it becomes aware of the game level).

❻   Let's display the current level.

Next, let's refactor the LevelLoop class to make it sensitive to the current game level. Listing 7-28 shows these changes.

Listing 7-28. LevelLoop

```
class LevelLoop extends Thread {

  private int shortDelay = 500;  ❶
  private int longDelay = 1_500;
  private int maxDelay;
  private int minDelay;
  private int delay;
  private int looplevel;

  int balloonsLaunched = 0;

  public LevelLoop(int argLevel) { ❷
    looplevel = argLevel;
  }

  public void run() {

    while (balloonsLaunched < 15) {

      balloonsLaunched++;
      Random random = new Random(new Date().getTime());
      final int xPosition = random.nextInt(scrWidth - 200);

      maxDelay = Math.max(shortDelay,
      (longDelay - ((looplevel -1)) * 500)); ❸
      minDelay = maxDelay / 2;
      delay = random.nextInt(minDelay) + minDelay;

      Log.i(TAG, String.format("Thread delay = %d", delay));
```

```
    try {
      Thread.sleep(delay); ❹
    }
    catch(InterruptedException e) {
      Log.e(TAG, e.getMessage());
    }

    // need to wrap this on runOnUiThread

    runOnUiThread(new Thread() {
      public void run() {
        launchBalloon(xPosition);
      }
    });

  }
 }
}
```

---

❶   Let's introduce the variables **longDelay** and **shortDelay**, which hold the
     integer values for the longest possible delay (in milliseconds) and the
     shortest possible delay, respectively.

❷   Refactor the constructor to accept a level parameter. Assign this parameter
     to the member variable **looplevel**.

❸   This bit of math calculates the delay (which is now affected by the level).
     The delay won't be lower than **shortDelay** nor will it be higher than
     longDelay.

❹   Use the calculated **delay** in the Thread.sleep() method.

Pop the Balloons

To score points, the player has to touch the balloons, thereby popping them before they get to the top of the screen. When a balloon gets to the top of the screen, it also pops, but the player doesn't score a point; in fact, the player loses a pin when that happens.

To pop a balloon, we need to set up a touch listener for the Balloon, then inform MainActivity that the player popped the balloon; we need to inform MainActivity because

1. In MainActivity, we will update the score and the status of how many pins are left.

2. Also in MainActivity, we will remove the Balloon from the ViewGroup, regardless of how it got popped, whether the player popped it or the balloon got away.

To do this, we need to set up an interface between the Balloon class and MainActivity. Let's create an interface and add it to the project. Creating an interface in Android Studio is very similar to how we create classes. Use the context menu; right-click the project's package, then choose **New ➤ Java Class**, as shown in Figure 7-27.

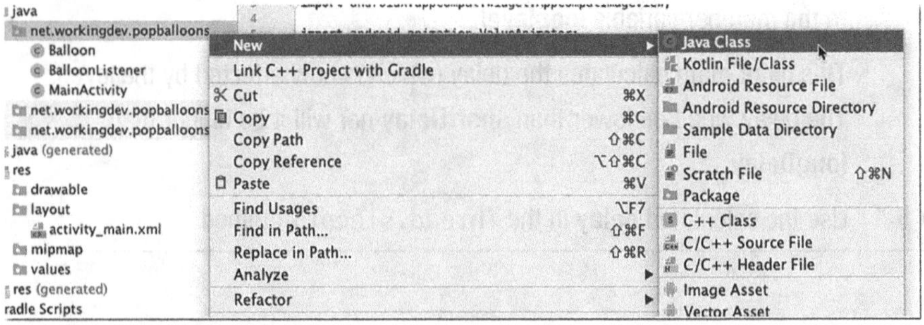

Figure 7-27. *New Java class*

In the window that follows, type the name of the interface (PopListener) and choose **Interface** as the kind (shown in Figure 7-28).

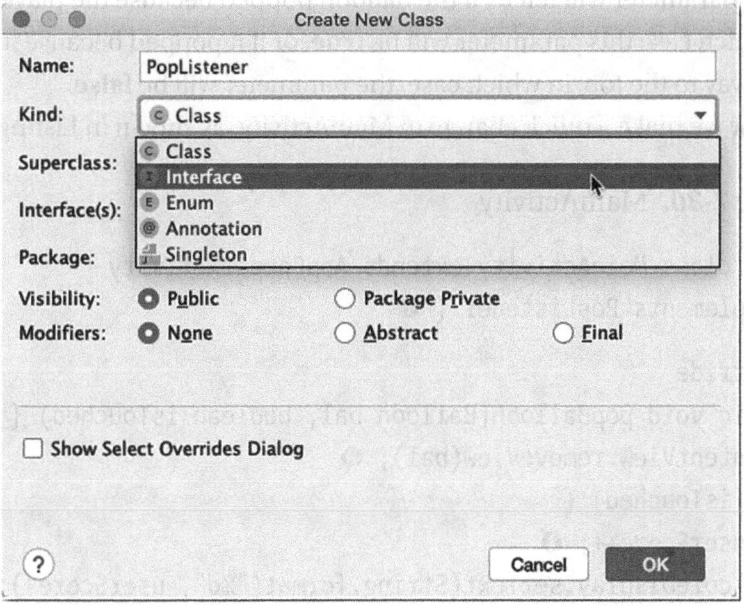

Figure 7-28. *New interface*

The PopListener interface will only have one method (shown in Listing 7-29).

Listing 7-29. PopListener interface

```
public interface PopListener {
 void popBalloon(Balloon bal, boolean isTouched);
}
```

The first parameter (**bal**) refers to a specific instance of a Balloon. We need this reference because this is what we'll remove from the ViewGroup. Removing it from the ViewGroup makes it disappear from the screen. The second parameter will tell us if the balloon popped because the player got it, in which case this parameter will be **true**, or if it popped because it went all the way to the top, in which case, the parameter will be **false**.

Now we make a quick change to MainActivity, as shown in Listing 7-30.

Listing 7-30. MainActivity

```
public class MainActivity extends AppCompatActivity
    implements PopListener { ❶

  @Override
  public void popBalloon(Balloon bal, boolean isTouched) { ❷
    contentView.removeView(bal); ❸
    if(isTouched) {
      userScore++; ❹
      scoreDisplay.setText(String.format("%d", userScore)); ❺
    }
  }
}
```

❶	Implement the PopListener interface.
❷	Implement the actual **popBalloon()** method.
❸	This code removes a specific instance of a Balloon in the ViewGroup.
❹	Now we can increment the player's score.
❺	This will display the score of the player.

Then we make adjustments on the Balloon class; Listing 7-31 shows these changes.

Listing 7-31. Balloon class

```
public class Balloon extends AppCompatImageView
    implements View.OnTouchListener { ❶

  private ValueAnimator animator;
  private BalloonListener listener;
  private boolean isPopped; ❷

  private PopListener mainactivity; ❸
  private final String TAG = getClass().getName();

  public Balloon(Context context) {
    super(context);
  }

  public Balloon(Context context, int color, int height,
  int level ) {
    super(context);

    mainactivity = (PopListener) context; ❹
    // other statements ...
    setOnTouchListener(this);  ❺

  }

  // other methods ...

  @Override
  public boolean onTouch(View view, MotionEvent motionEvent) {
    Log.d(TAG, "TOUCHED");
    if(!isPopped) {
      mainactivity.popBalloon(this, true);
      isPopped = true;
      animator.cancel();
    }
```

```
    return true;
  }

  public void pop(boolean isTouched) { ❻
    mainactivity.popBalloon(this, isTouched); ❼
  }

  public boolean isPopped() {  ❽
    return isPopped;
  }

}
```

---

❶   Implement the **View.OnTouchListener** on the Balloon class. We'll make this class the listener for touch events.

❷   The **isPopped** variable holds the state of any particular balloon, whether popped or not.

❸   Create a reference to MainActivity (which implements the PopListener interface).

❹   In the Balloon's constructor, cast the Context object to PopListener and assign it to the **mainactivity** variable.

❺   Set the onTouchListener for this Balloon instance.

❻   Create a utility function named **pop()**. We're making it public because we'll need to call this method from the **BalloonListener** class later on.

❼   Create a utility function named **isPopped()**; we will also call this method from the **BalloonListener** class.

At this point, you can play the game with limited functionality. When you click "Play," a set of Balloons floats to the top; clicking a balloon removes it from the ViewGroup. When a balloon reaches the top, it also gets removed from the ViewGroup.

Managing the Pins

When a balloon gets away from the player, we want to update the pushpin images on top of the screen. For every missed balloon, we want to display a broken pushpin image. The code we need to change is in MainActivity; so, let's implement that change.

We can start by declaring two member variables on MainActivity.

- **numberOfPins = 5;**—The number of pins in our layout.

- **pinsUsed;**—Each time a balloon gets away, we increment this variable.

Let's also create an ArrayList to hold the pushpin images. We want to put them in an ArrayList so we can reference the pushpin images programmatically. Creating and populating the ArrayList with the pushpin images can be done with the code in Listing 7-32. This code can be written inside the **onCreate()** method of MainActivity.

Listing 7-32. Pushpin images in an ArrayList

```
private ArrayList<ImageView> pinImages = new ArrayList<>();

pinImages.add((ImageView) findViewById(R.id.pushpin1));
pinImages.add((ImageView) findViewById(R.id.pushpin2));
pinImages.add((ImageView) findViewById(R.id.pushpin3));
pinImages.add((ImageView) findViewById(R.id.pushpin4));
pinImages.add((ImageView) findViewById(R.id.pushpin5));
```

We've already got the logic to handle the missed balloons inside the **popBalloon()** method. We already know how to handle the case when the player pops the Balloon; all we need to do is add some more logic to the existing *if-else* condition. Listing 7-33 shows us that code.

Listing 7-33. popBalloon()

```
public void popBalloon(Balloon bal, boolean isTouched) {
  contentView.removeView(bal);
  if(isTouched) {
    userScore++;
    scoreDisplay.setText(String.format("%d", userScore));
  }
  else { ❶
    pinsUsed++; ❷
    if (pinsUsed <= pinImages.size() ) { ❸
      pinImages.get(pinsUsed -1).setImageResource
      (R.drawable.pin_broken); ❹
      Toast.makeText(this, "Ouch!",Toast.LENGTH_SHORT).
      show(); ❺
    }
    if(pinsUsed == numberOfPins) { ❻
      gameOver();
    }
  }
}

private void gameOver() {
  // TODO: implement GameOver method
  Toast.makeText(this, "Game Over", Toast.LENGTH_LONG).show();
}
```

❶   If **isTouched** is *false*, that means the balloon got away from the player.

❷   Increment the **pinsUsed** variable. For every missed balloon, we increment this variable.

❸   Let's check if **pinsUsed** is less than or equal to the size of the ArrayList which contains the pushpin images (which has five elements); if this expression is *true*, that means it isn't game over yet, the player still has some pins to spare, and we can continue the gameplay.

❹   This code replaces the image of the pushpin; it sets the image to that of the broken pin.

❺   We display a simple Toast message to the player. A Toast message is a small pop-up that appears at the bottom of the screen, then fades away from view.

❻   Let's check if the player has used up all five pins. If they have, we call the **gameOver()** method, which we still have to implement.

When the Game is Over

When the game is over, we need to do some cleanup; at the very least, we have to reset the pushpin images—which is easy enough to do. Listing 7-34 should accomplish that job.

Listing 7-34. Resetting the pushpin images

```
for (ImageView pin: pinImages) {
  pin.setImageResource(R.drawable.pin);
}
```

We also need to reset a couple of counters. To do these cleanups, let's reorganize MainActivity a little bit. Start with implementing the **gameOver()** method, as shown in Listing 7-35.

Listing 7-35. gameOver()

```
private void gameOver() {

  isGameStopped = true;
  Toast.makeText(this, "Game Over", Toast.LENGTH_LONG).show();
  btn.setText("Play game");
}
```

We're simply displaying a Toast to the player, announcing the game over message. We're also resetting the text of the Button. You might have noticed the **isGameStopped** variable; that's another member variable we need to create to help us manage some rudimentary game states.

Next, let's add another method called **finishLevel()**, so we can group some actions we need to take when the player finishes a level; the code for that is in Listing 7-36.

Listing 7-36. finishLevel()

```
private void finishLevel() {

  Log.d(TAG, "FINISH LEVEL");

  String message = String.format("Level %d finished!", level);
  Toast.makeText(this, message, Toast.LENGTH_LONG).
  show(); // ❶
  level++; ❷
  updateGameStats(); ❸
  btn.setText(String.format("Start level %d", level)); ❹

  Log.d(TAG, String.format("balloonsLaunched = %d",
  balloonsLaunched));
  balloonsPopped = 0; ❺

}
```

❶　Tell the player that the level is finished.

❷　Increment the level variable.

❸　We haven't implemented this method yet, but you could probably guess what it will do. It will simply display the current score and the current level.

❹　Change the text of the Button to one that reflects the next level.

❺　We're resetting the **balloonsPopped** variable to zero. We also need to create this member variable. It will keep track of all the Balloons that got popped. We will use this to determine if the level is already finished.

Listing 7-37 shows the code for the updateGameStats() method.

Listing 7-37. updateGameStats()

```
private void updateGameStats() {
  levelDisplay.setText(String.format("%s", level));
  scoreDisplay.setText(String.format("%s", userScore));
}
```

Now, we need to know when the level is finished. We never bothered with this before because we simply let the LevelLoop thread do its work of launching the balloons, but now we need to manage some game states. There are a couple of places in MainActivity where we can signal the end of the level. We can do it inside the LevelLoop thread. As soon as the while loop ends, that should signal the end of the level; but the game might feel out of sync if we put it there. The Toast messages might appear while some balloons are still being animated. We will call the **finishLevel()** inside the **popBalloon()** method instead.

If we simply count the number of Balloons that gets popped—which is everything, because every balloon gets popped one way or another—compare it with the number of balloons we launch per level; when the two variables are equal, that should signal the end of the level. Listing 7-38 shows that implementation.

Listing 7-38. popBalloon()

```
@Override
public void popBalloon(Balloon bal, boolean isTouched) {

  balloonsPopped++;
  contentView.removeView(bal);
  if(isTouched) {
    userScore++;
    scoreDisplay.setText(String.format("%d", userScore));
  }
  else {
    pinsUsed++;
    if (pinsUsed <= pinImages.size() ) {
      pinImages.get(pinsUsed -1).setImageResource(R.drawable.
      pin_broken);
      Toast.makeText(this, "Ouch!",Toast.LENGTH_SHORT).show();
    }
    if(pinsUsed == numberOfPins) {
      gameOver();
    }
  }
  if (balloonsPopped == balloonsPerLevel) {
    finishLevel();
  }
}
```

Next, let's move to the **startLevel()** method. The refactored code is shown in Listing 7-39.

Listing 7-39. startLevel()

```
private void startLevel() {

  if (isGameStopped) { ❶

    isGameStopped = false; ❷
    startGame(); ❸
  }

  updateGameStats(); ❹
  new LevelLoop(level).start();

}
```

---

❶   Let's check for some game state. This will be false the very first time a player starts the game. This gets reset in the **gameOver()** method. If this condition is true, it means we're starting a new game.

❷   Let's set the value of **isGameStopped** to false since we have started a new game.

❸   Call the **startGame()** method. We will implement this shortly.

❹   Update the game statistics.

Next, implement the **startGame()** method; Listing 7-40 shows us how.

Listing 7-40. startGame() method

```
private void startGame() {

  // reset the scores
  userScore = 0;
  level = 1;
  updateGameStats();

  //reset the pushpin images
  for (ImageView pin: pinImages) {
    pin.setImageResource(R.drawable.pin);
  }
}
```

That should take care of some basic housekeeping.

Audio

Most games use music in the background to enhance the player's experience. These games also use sound effects for a more immersive feel. Our little game will use both. We will play a background music when the game starts, and we'll also play a sound effect when a Balloon gets popped.

I got the background music and the popping sound effect from YouTube Audio Library; feel free to source your preferred background music.

Once you've procured the audio files, you need to add them to the project; firstly, you need to create a raw folder in the **app/res** directory. You can do that with the context menu. Right-click **app/res**, then choose **New ➤ Folder ➤ Raw Resources Folder**, as shown in Figure 7-29.

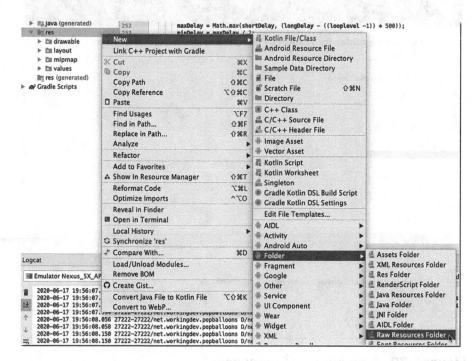

Figure 7-29. *New Resources Folder*

In the window that follows, click Finish, as shown in Figure 7-30.

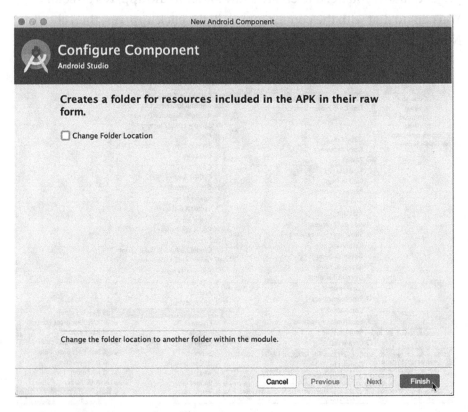

Figure 7-30. *New Android Component*

Next, right-click the raw folder. Depending on what OS you're using, choose either **Reveal in Finder** or **Show in Explorer**.

You can now drag and drop the audio files in the **raw** folder.

To play the background music, we will need a MediaPlayer object. This object is built-in in Android SDK. We simply need to import it to our Java source file. The following are the key method calls for the MediaPlayer object. Listing 7-41 shows the important APIs we will use.

Listing 7-41. Key method calls on the MediaPlayer object

```
import android.media.MediaPlayer

MediaPlayer mplayer;

mplayer = MediaPlayer.create(ctx.getApplicationContext(),
R.raw.ngoni); ❶
mplayer.setVolume(07.f, 0.7f); ❷
mplayer.setLooping(true); ❸
mplayer.start(); ❹
mplayer.pause() ❺
```

❶   This statement creates an instance of MediaPlayer. It takes two arguments;
       the first one is a Context object, and the second argument is the name of the
       resource file in the raw folder (ngoni.mp3). We are specifying a resource file
       here, so there is no need to add the **.mp3** extension.

❷   The **setVolume()** method takes two arguments. The first one is a float value
       to specify the left channel volume, and the second one is for the volume of
       the right channel. The range of these values is from 0.0 to 1.0. As you can
       see, I specified a 70% volume. In an actual game, you might want to store
       these values in a preferences file and let the user control it.

❸   I'd like the music to keep on playing. I'm setting it on auto-repeat here.

❹   This will start playing the music.

❺   This will pause the music.

To play the popping sound for the Balloon, we'll use the SoundPool
object. The popping sound is provided as a very short audio file that will be
used over and over (every time we pop a balloon). These kinds of sounds
are best managed using the SoundPool object.

There's a bit of setup required before you can use a SoundPool object; Listing 7-42 shows this setup.

Listing 7-42. SoundPool

```
public Audio(Activity activity) { ❶

  AudioManager audioManager = (AudioManager)
        activity.getSystemService(Context.AUDIO_SERVICE);
  float actVolume = (float)
        audioManager.getStreamVolume(AudioManager.
        STREAM_MUSIC); ❷
  float maxVolume = (float)
        audioManager.getStreamMaxVolume(AudioManager.
        STREAM_MUSIC);
  volume = actVolume / maxVolume;

  activity.setVolumeControlStream(AudioManager.STREAM_MUSIC); ❸

  AudioAttributes audioAttrib = new AudioAttributes.Builder() ❹
      .setUsage(AudioAttributes.USAGE_GAME)
      .setContentType(AudioAttributes.CONTENT_TYPE_SONIFICATION)
      .build();

  soundPool = new SoundPool.Builder()
              .setAudioAttributes(audioAttrib)
              .setMaxStreams(6)
              .build();

  soundPool.setOnLoadCompleteListener(new SoundPool.OnLoad
  CompleteListener() { ❺
```

```
  @Override
  public void onLoadComplete(SoundPool soundPool, int
  sampleId, int status) {
    Log.d(TAG, "SoundPool is loaded");
    isLoaded = true;
  }
});
soundId = soundPool.load(activity, R.raw.pop, 1); ❻

}

public void playSound() {

  if (isLoaded) {
    soundPool.play(soundId, volume, volume, 1, 0, 1f); ❼
  }
  Log.d(TAG, "playSound");
}
```

---

❶   Setting up the SoundPool and the AudioManager is usually done on the
    constructor. We need to pass an Activity instance (which will be MainActivity),
    so we can get a reference to the audio service.

❷   We will use the **getStreamVolume()** and **getStreamMaxVolume()** to
    determine how loud we want our sound effect to be.

❸   This binds the volume control to MainActivity.

❹   We need to set some attributes to build the sound pool. This method of
    building the sound pool is for Android versions 5.0 and up (Lollipop).

❺   The sound is loaded asynchronously. We need to set up a listener, so we get
    notified when it's loaded.

❻   Now we get to load the sound file from our raw folder.

❼   This line plays the sound. This is what we will call in the **popBalloon()** method.

We're going to put all of this code in a separate class; we'll name it the **Audio** class. Create a new Java class named Audio. You can do that by right-clicking the project's package, then choosing **New ➤ Java Class**, as we did before. Listing 7-43 shows the full code for the Audio class.

Listing 7-43. Audio class

```java
import android.app.Activity;
import android.content.Context;
import android.media.AudioAttributes;
import android.media.AudioManager;
import android.media.MediaPlayer;
import android.media.SoundPool;
import android.util.Log;

public class Audio {

  private final int soundId;
  private MediaPlayer mplayer;
  private float volume;
  private SoundPool soundPool;
  private boolean isLoaded;

  private final String TAG = getClass().getName();

  public Audio(Activity activity) {
    AudioManager audioManager = (AudioManager) activity.get
    SystemService(Context.AUDIO_SERVICE);
    float actVolume = (float) audioManager.getStream
    Volume(AudioManager.STREAM_MUSIC);
    float maxVolume = (float) audioManager.getStream
    MaxVolume(AudioManager.STREAM_MUSIC);
    volume = actVolume / maxVolume;

    activity.setVolumeControlStream(AudioManager.STREAM_MUSIC);
```

```
AudioAttributes audioAttrib = new AudioAttributes.Builder()
    .setUsage(AudioAttributes.USAGE_GAME)
    .setContentType(AudioAttributes.CONTENT_TYPE_
    SONIFICATION)
    .build();

soundPool = new SoundPool.Builder()
                .setAudioAttributes(audioAttrib)
                .setMaxStreams(6)
                .build();

soundPool.setOnLoadCompleteListener(new SoundPool.OnLoad
CompleteListener() {

  @Override
  public void onLoadComplete(SoundPool soundPool,
  int sampleId, int status) {
    Log.d(TAG, "SoundPool is loaded");
    isLoaded = true;
  }
});
  soundId = soundPool.load(activity, R.raw.pop, 1);

}

public void playSound() {

  if (isLoaded) {
    soundPool.play(soundId, volume, volume, 1, 0, 1f);
  }
  Log.d(TAG, "playSound");
}
```

```
public void prepareMediaPlayer(Context ctx) {
  mplayer = MediaPlayer.create(ctx.getApplicationContext(),
  R.raw.ngoni);
  mplayer.setVolume(05.f, 0.5f);
  mplayer.setLooping(true);
}

public void playMusic() {
  mplayer.start();
}

public void stopMusic() {
  mplayer.stop();
}

public void pauseMusic() {
  mplayer.pause();
}
}
```

Now we can add some sounds to the app. In the MainActivity class, we need to create a member variable of type Audio, like this:

```
Audio audio;
```

Then, in the **onCreate()** method, we instantiate the Audio class and call the prepareMediaPlayer() method, as shown in the following:

```
audio = new Audio(this);
audio.prepareMediaPlayer(this);
```

We want to play the music only when the game is in play; so, in MainActivity's **startGame()** method, we add the following statement:

```
audio.playMusic();
```

When the game is not at play anymore, we want the music to stop; so, in the **gameOver()** method, we add this statement:

```
audio.pauseMusic();
```

Finally, in the **popBalloon()** method, add the following statement:

```
audio.playSound();
```

Final Touches

If you've been following the coding exercise (and running the game), you may have noticed that even after the game is over, you can still see some balloons flying around; you can thank the background thread for that. Even when all the five pins have been used up, the level is still active, and we still see some balloons being launched. To handle that, we can do the following:

1. Keep track of all the balloons being released per level. We can do this using an ArrayList. Every time we launch a balloon, we add it to the list.

2. As soon as a Balloon is popped, we take it out of the list.

3. If we reach game over, we go through all the remaining Balloon objects in the ArrayList and set their status to popped.

4. Lastly, remove all the remaining Balloon objects from the ViewGroup.

First, let's declare an ArrayList (as a member variable on MainActivity) to hold all the references to all Balloons that will be launched per level. The following code accomplishes that:

```
private ArrayList<Balloon> balloons = new ArrayList<>();
```

Next, in the **launchBalloon()** method, we insert a statement that adds a Balloon object to the ArrayList, like this:

```
balloons.add(btemp);
```

Next, in the **gameOver()** method, we add a logic that will loop through all the remaining Balloons in the ArrayList, set their popped status to true, and also remove the Balloon instance from the ViewGroup (the code is shown in Listing 7-44).

Listing 7-44. gameOver() method

```
private void gameOver() {

  isGameStopped = true;
  Toast.makeText(this, "Game Over", Toast.LENGTH_LONG).show();
  btn.setText("Play game");

  for (Balloon bal : balloons) {
    bal.setPopped(true);
    contentView.removeView(bal);
  }

  balloons.clear();
  audio.pauseMusic();
}
```

Finally, we need to add the **setPopped()** method to the Balloon class, as shown in Listing 7-45.

Listing 7-45. setPopped() method in the Balloon class

```
public void setPopped(boolean b) {
  isPopped = true;
}
```

That should do it. The final code listing we will see in this chapter is the complete code for MainActivity. It may be difficult to keep things straight after all the changes we made to MainActivity; so, to provide as a reference, Listing 7-46 shows MainActivity's complete code.

Listing 7-46. MainActivity

```
import android.graphics.Color;
import android.os.Bundle;
import android.util.Log;
import android.view.MotionEvent;
import android.view.View;
import android.view.ViewGroup;
import android.view.ViewTreeObserver;
import android.widget.Button;
import android.widget.ImageView;
import android.widget.TextView;
import android.widget.Toast;

import java.util.ArrayList;
import java.util.Date;
import java.util.Random;

public class MainActivity extends AppCompatActivity
    implements PopListener {

  ViewGroup contentView;
  private static  String TAG;

  private int[] colors = new int[3];
  private int scrWidth;
  private int scrHeight;
  private int level = 1;
```

```
private TextView levelDisplay;
private TextView scoreDisplay;
private int numberOfPins = 5;
private int pinsUsed;

private int balloonsLaunched;
private int balloonsPerLevel = 8;
private int balloonsPopped = 0;

private boolean isGameStopped = true;

private ArrayList<ImageView> pinImages = new ArrayList<>();
private ArrayList<Balloon> balloons = new ArrayList<>();

private int userScore;
Button btn;

Audio audio;

@Override
protected void onCreate(Bundle savedInstanceState) {
    super.onCreate(savedInstanceState);

    TAG = getClass().getName();

    getWindow().setBackgroundDrawableResource
    (R.mipmap.background);
    setContentView(R.layout.activity_main);

    colors[0] = Color.argb(255, 255, 0, 0);
    colors[1] = Color.argb(255, 0, 255, 0);
    colors[2] = Color.argb(255, 0, 0, 255);

    contentView = (ViewGroup) findViewById(R.id.content_view);
    levelDisplay = (TextView) findViewById(R.id.level_display);
    scoreDisplay = (TextView) findViewById(R.id.score_display);
```

```java
pinImages.add((ImageView) findViewById(R.id.pushpin1));
pinImages.add((ImageView) findViewById(R.id.pushpin2));
pinImages.add((ImageView) findViewById(R.id.pushpin3));
pinImages.add((ImageView) findViewById(R.id.pushpin4));
pinImages.add((ImageView) findViewById(R.id.pushpin5));

btn = (Button) findViewById(R.id.btn);
btn.setOnClickListener(new View.OnClickListener() {
  @Override
  public void onClick(View view) {
    startLevel();
  }
});

contentView.setOnTouchListener(new View.OnTouchListener() {
  @Override
  public boolean onTouch(View v, MotionEvent event) {
    if (event.getAction() == MotionEvent.ACTION_DOWN) {
      setToFullScreen();
    }
    return false;
  }
});

audio = new Audio(this);
audio.prepareMediaPlayer(this);

}

@Override
protected void onResume() {
  super.onResume();

  updateGameStats();
  setToFullScreen();
```

```java
    ViewTreeObserver viewTreeObserver = contentView.getView
    TreeObserver();
    if (viewTreeObserver.isAlive()) {
      viewTreeObserver.addOnGlobalLayoutListener(new ViewTree
      Observer.OnGlobalLayoutListener() {
        @Override
        public void onGlobalLayout() {
          contentView.getViewTreeObserver().removeOnGlobal
          LayoutListener(this);
          scrWidth = contentView.getWidth();
          scrHeight = contentView.getHeight();
        }
      });
    }

}

public void launchBalloon(int xPos) {

  balloonsLaunched++;

  int curColor = colors[nextColor()];
  Balloon btemp = new Balloon(MainActivity.this,
  curColor, 100,  level);
  btemp.setY(scrHeight);
  btemp.setX(xPos);

  balloons.add(btemp);

  contentView.addView(btemp);
  btemp.release(scrHeight, 5000);

  Log.d(TAG, "Balloon created");

}
```

```java
private void startLevel() {

  if (isGameStopped) {

    isGameStopped = false;
    startGame();
  }

  updateGameStats();
  new LevelLoop(level).start();

}

private void finishLevel() {

  Log.d(TAG, "FINISH LEVEL");

  String message = String.format("Level %d finished!",
  level);
  Toast.makeText(this, message, Toast.LENGTH_LONG).show();
  level++;
  updateGameStats();
  btn.setText(String.format("Start level %d", level));

  Log.d(TAG, String.format("balloonsLaunched = %d",
  balloonsLaunched));
  balloonsPopped = 0;

}

private void updateGameStats() {
  levelDisplay.setText(String.format("%s", level));
  scoreDisplay.setText(String.format("%s", userScore));
}

private void setToFullScreen() {
```

```java
    contentView.setSystemUiVisibility(View.SYSTEM_UI_FLAG_LOW_
    PROFILE
        | View.SYSTEM_UI_FLAG_FULLSCREEN
        | View.SYSTEM_UI_FLAG_LAYOUT_STABLE
        | View.SYSTEM_UI_FLAG_IMMERSIVE_STICKY
        | View.SYSTEM_UI_FLAG_LAYOUT_HIDE_NAVIGATION
        | View.SYSTEM_UI_FLAG_HIDE_NAVIGATION);
}

private static int nextColor() {

    int max = 2;
    int min = 0;
    int retval = 0;

    Random random = new Random();
    retval = random.nextInt((max - min) + 1) + min;

    Log.d(TAG, String.format("retval = %d", retval));
    return retval;
}

@Override
public void popBalloon(Balloon bal, boolean isTouched) {

    balloonsPopped++;
    balloons.remove(bal);
    contentView.removeView(bal);

    audio.playSound();

    if(isTouched) {
      userScore++;
      scoreDisplay.setText(String.format("%d", userScore));
    }
```

```java
  else {
    pinsUsed++;
    if (pinsUsed <= pinImages.size() ) {
      pinImages.get(pinsUsed -1).setImageResource
      (R.drawable.pin_broken);
      Toast.makeText(this, "Ouch!",Toast.LENGTH_SHORT).show();
    }
    if(pinsUsed == numberOfPins) {
      gameOver();
    }
  }

  if (balloonsPopped == balloonsPerLevel) {
    finishLevel();
  }
}

private void startGame() {

  // reset the scores
  userScore = 0;
  level = 1;

  updateGameStats();

  //reset the pushpin images
  for (ImageView pin: pinImages) {
    pin.setImageResource(R.drawable.pin);
  }

  audio.playMusic();
}

private void gameOver() {
```

```
  isGameStopped = true;
  Toast.makeText(this, "Game Over", Toast.LENGTH_LONG).show();
  btn.setText("Play game");

  for (Balloon bal : balloons) {
    bal.setPopped(true);
    contentView.removeView(bal);
  }

  balloons.clear();
  audio.pauseMusic();
}

class LevelLoop extends Thread {

  private int shortDelay = 500;
  private int longDelay = 1_500;
  private int maxDelay;
  private int minDelay;
  private int delay;
  private int looplevel;

  int balloonsLaunched = 0;

  public LevelLoop(int argLevel) {
    looplevel = argLevel;
  }

  public void run() {

    while (balloonsLaunched <= balloonsPerLevel) {

      balloonsLaunched++;
      Random random = new Random(new Date().getTime());
      final int xPosition = random.nextInt(scrWidth - 200);
```

```java
maxDelay = Math.max(shortDelay, (longDelay -
((looplevel -1)) * 500));
minDelay = maxDelay / 2;
delay = random.nextInt(minDelay) + minDelay;

Log.i(TAG, String.format("Thread delay = %d", delay));

try {
  Thread.sleep(delay);
}
catch(InterruptedException e) {
  Log.e(TAG, e.getMessage());
}

// need to wrap this on runOnUiThread

runOnUiThread(new Thread() {
  public void run() {
    launchBalloon(xPosition);
  }
});
    }

  }
 }

}
```

CHAPTER 8

Testing and Debugging

What we'll cover:

- Types of game testing

- Unit testing

- Debugging

- Android Profiler

We've gone through the programming phase of our project; next, we go through testing and debugging. It's in this stage that we must find all errors and inconsistencies in the code. A polished game doesn't have rough edges; we need to test it, debug it, and make sure it doesn't hog computing resources.

Types of Game Testing

Functional testing. A game is basically an app. Functional testing is a standard way of testing an app. It's called *functional* because we're testing the app's features (also known as functions) as they are specified in the requirement specification—the requirement specification is something you (or the game designer) would have written during the planning stages of the game. This would have been written in a document (usually called

© Ted Hagos, Mario Zechner, J.F. DiMarzio and Robert Green 2020
T. Hagos et al., *Beginning Android Games Development*,
https://doi.org/10.1007/978-1-4842-6121-7_8

functional requirements specification). Examples of what you might find in a functional specification are "user must log in to the game server before entering the game" and "user may be able to select or go back to levels which have been completed; user cannot select a level which has not been completed." The testers, usually called QA or QC (short for quality assurance and quality control, respectively), are the ones who carry out these tests. They will create test assets, craft a test strategy, execute them, and eventually report on the results of the executions. Failing tests are usually assigned back to the developer (you) to fix and resubmit. What I'm describing here is a typical practice for a development team that has a separate or dedicated testing team; if you're a one-person team, the QA will most likely be you as well. Testing is an entirely different skill; I strongly encourage you to enlist the help of other people, preferably those who have experience in testing.

Performance testing. You could probably guess what this type of testing does just from its name. It pushes the game to its limit and sees it performs under stress. What you want to see here is how the game responds when subjected to above-normal conditions. **Soak testing or endurance testing** is a kind of performance testing; usually, you leave the game running for a long long time and in various modes of operation, for example, leave the game for a really long time while it's paused or at the title screen. What you're trying to find here is how the game responds to these conditions and how it utilizes system resources like the memory, CPU, network bandwidth, and so on; you will use tools like the *Android Profiler* to carry out these measurements.

Another form of performance testing is **volume testing**; if your game uses a database, you might want to find out how the game will respond when data is loaded to the database. What you're checking is how the system responds under various loads of data.

Spike testing or scalability testing is also another kind of performance test. If your game depends on a central server, this test will usually raise the number of users (device endpoints) connected to the central server. You'd want to observe how a spike in number of users affects player experience; is the game still responsive, was there an effect on frames per second, are there lags, and so on?

Compatibility testing is where you check how the game behaves on different devices and configurations of hardware/software. This is where AVDs (Android Virtual Devices) will come in handy; because AVDs are simply software emulators, you don't have to buy different devices. Use the AVDs whenever you can. There will be some games that will be difficult to test reliably on emulators; when you're in that situation, you really have to fork over money for testing devices.

Compliance or conformance testing. This is where you check the game against Google Play guidelines on apps or games; make sure you read Google Play's Developer Policy Center at https://bit.ly/developerpolicycenter. Make sure you are also acquainted with PEGI (Pan European Game Information) and ESRB (Entertainment Software Rating Board). If the game has objectionable content that's not aligned with a specific rating, they need to be identified and reported. Violations could be a cause for rejection, which may result in costly rework and resubmission.

Localization testing is important especially if the game is intended for global markets. Game titles, contents, and texts need to be translated and tested in the supported languages.

Recovery testing. This is taking edge case testing to another level. Here, the app is forced to fail, and you're observing how the application behaves as it fails and how it comes back after it fails. It should give you insight whether you've written enough **try-catch-finally** blocks or not. Apps should fail gracefully, not abruptly. Whenever possible, runtime errors should be guarded by try-catch blocks; and when the exception happens, try to write a log and save the state of the game.

Penetration or security testing. This kind of testing tries to discover the weaknesses of the game. It simulates the activities that a would-be attacker will do in order to circumvent all the security features of the game; for example, if the game uses a database to store data, especially user data, a pen tester (a professional who practices penetration testing) might play through the game while Wireshark is running—Wireshark is a tool that inspects packets; it's a network protocol analyzer. If you stored passwords in clear text, it will show up in these tests.

Sound testing. Check if there are any errors loading the files; also, listen to the sound files if there's a cracking sound or others.

Developer testing. This is the kind of testing you (the programmer) do as you add layers and layers of code to the game. This involves writing test code (in Java as well) to test your actual program. This is known as unit testing. Android developers usually perform JVM testing and instrumented testing; we'll discuss these some more in the following sections.

Unit Testing

Unit testing is actually functional testing that a developer performs, not the QA or QC. A unit test is simple; it's a particular thing that a method might do or produce. An application typically has many unit tests because each test is a very narrowly defined set of behavior. So, you'll need lots of tests to cover the whole functionality. Android developers usually use JUnit to write unit tests.

JUnit is a regression testing framework written by Kent Beck and Erich Gamma; you might remember them as the one who created extreme programming and the other one from Gang of Four (GoF, Design Patterns), respectively, among other things.

Java developers have long used JUnit for unit testing. Android Studio comes with JUnit and is very well integrated in it. We don't have to do much by way of setup. We only need to write our tests.

JVM Test vs. Instrumented Test

If you look at any Android application, you'll see that it has two parts: a Java-based behavior and an Android-based behavior.

The Java part is where we code business logic, calculations, and data transformations. The Android part is where we actually interact with the Android platform. This is where we get input from users or show results to them. It makes perfect sense if we can test the Java-based behavior separate from the Android part because it's much quicker to execute. Fortunately, this is already the way it's done in Android Studio. When you create a project, Android Studio creates two separate folders—one for the JVM tests and another for the instrumented tests. Figure 8-1 shows the two test folders in Android view, and Figure 8-2 shows the same two folders in Project view.

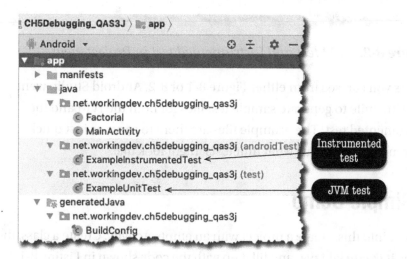

Figure 8-1. JVM test and instrumented test in Android view

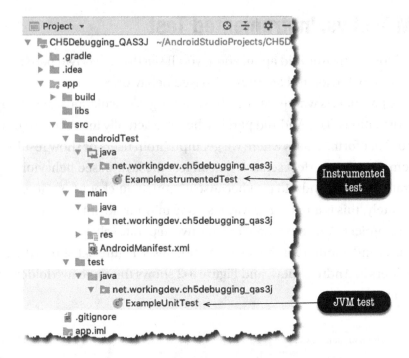

Figure 8-2. *JVM test and instrumented test in Project view*

As you can see from either Figure 8-1 or 8-2, Android Studio went the extra mile to generate sample test files for both the JVM and the instrumented test. The example files are there to serve as just quick references; it shows us what unit tests might look like.

A Simple Demo

To dive into this, create a project with an empty Activity. Create a class, then name it **Factorial.java**, and fill it up with the code shown in Listing 8-1.

Listing 8-1. Factorial.java

```java
public class Factorial {
  public static double factorial(int arg) {
    if (arg == 0) {
```

```
    return 1.0;
  }
  else {
    return arg + factorial(arg - 1);
  }
  }
}
```

Make sure that *Factorial.java* is open in the main editor, as shown in Figure 8-3; then, from the main menu bar, go to **Navigate ➤ Test**. Similarly, you can also create a test using the keyboard shortcut (Shift+Command+T on macOS and Ctrl+Shift+T for Linux and Windows).

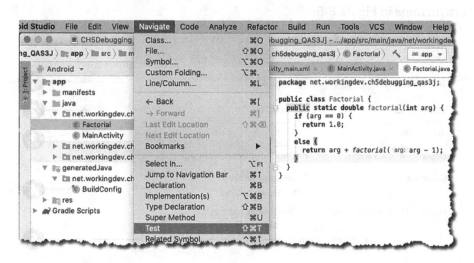

Figure 8-3. *Create a test for Factorial.java*

Right after you click "Test," a pop-up dialog (Figure 8-4) will prompt you to click another link—click "Create New Test" as shown in Figure 8-4.

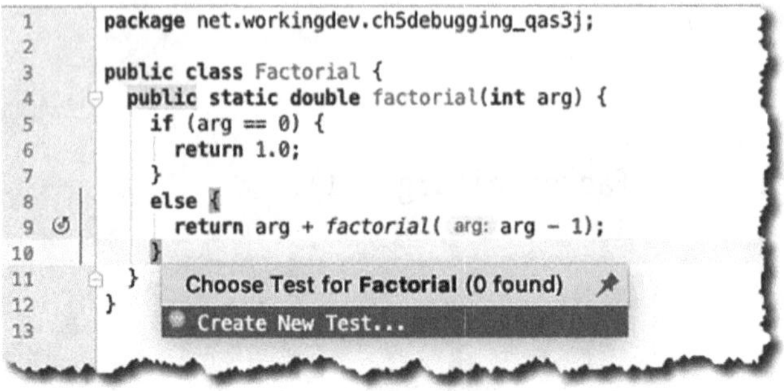

```
 1    package net.workingdev.ch5debugging_qas3j;
 2
 3    public class Factorial {
 4        public static double factorial(int arg) {
 5            if (arg == 0) {
 6                return 1.0;
 7            }
 8            else {
 9                return arg + factorial( arg: arg - 1);
10            }
11        }           Choose Test for Factorial (0 found)  📌
12    }              Create New Test...
13
```

Figure 8-4. *Create New Test pop-up*

Right after creating a new test, you'll see another pop-up dialog, shown
in Figure 8-5, which I've annotated. Please follow the annotations and
instructions in Figure 8-5.

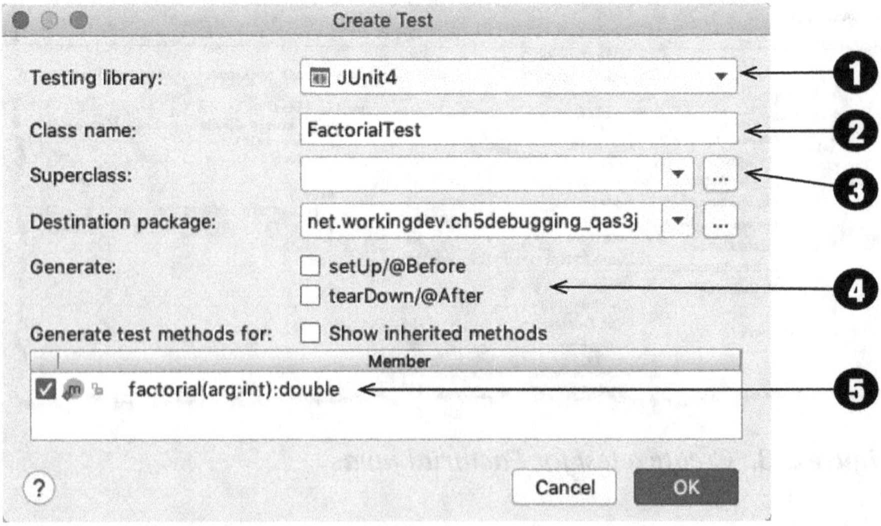

Figure 8-5. *Create FactorialTest*

❶   You can choose which testing library you want to use. You can choose JUnit 3, 4, or 5. You can even choose Groovy JUnit, Spock, or TestNG. I used JUnit4 because it comes installed with Android Studio.

❷   The convention for naming a test class is "name of the class to test" + "Test". Android Studio populates this field using that convention.

❸   Leave this blank; we don't need to inherit from anything.

❹   We don't need `setUp()` and `tearDown()` routines for now, so leave these unchecked.

❺   Let's check the `factorial()` method because we want to generate a test for this.

When you click the **OK** button, Android Studio will ask where you want to save the test file. This is a JVM test, so we want to save it in the "test" folder (not in androidTest). See Figure 8-6. Click "OK."

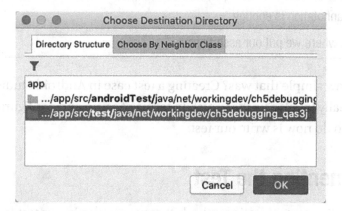

***Figure 8-6.** Choose Destination Directory*

Android Studio will now create the test file for us. If you open **FactorialTest.java**, you'll see the generated skeleton code—shown in Figure 8-7.

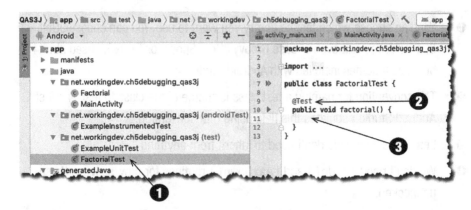

Figure 8-7. *FactorialTest.java in Project view and the main editor*

---

❶   The file *Factorial.java* was created under the *test* folder.

❷   A `factorial()` method was created, and it's annotated as `@Test`. This is how JUnit will know that this method is a unit test. You can prepend your method names with "test", for example, testFactorial(), but that is not necessary, the @ Test annotation is enough.

❸   This is where we put our assertions.

See how simple that was? Creating a test case in Android Studio doesn't really involve us that much in terms of setup and configuration. All we need to do now is write our test.

Implementing the Test

JUnit supplies several static methods that we can use in our test to make assertions about our code's behavior. We use assertions to show an expected result which is our control data. It's usually calculated independently and is known to be true or correct—that's why you use it as a control data. When the expected data is returned from the assertion, the test passes; otherwise, the test fails. Table 8-1 shows the common assert methods you might need for your code.

Table 8-1. *Common assert methods*

Method	Description
assertEquals()	Returns true if two objects or primitives have the same value
assertNotEquals()	The reverse of assertEquals()
assertSame()	Returns true if two references point to the same object
assertNotSame()	Reverse of assertSame()
assertTrue()	Tests a Boolean expression
assertFalse()	Reverse of assertTrue()
assertNull()	Tests for a null object
assertNotNull()	Reverse of assertNull()

Now that we know a couple of assert methods, we're ready to write some test. Listing 8-2 shows the code for FactorialTest.java.

Listing 8-2. FactorialTest.java

```java
import org.junit.Test;
import static org.junit.Assert.*;

public class FactorialTest {

  @Test
  public void factorial() {
    assertEquals(1.0, Factorial.factorial(1),0.0);
    assertEquals(120.0, Factorial.factorial(5), 0.0);
  }
}
```

Our FactorialTest class has only one method because it's for illustration purposes only. Real-world code would have many more methods than this, to be sure.

Notice that each test (method) is annotated by **@Test**. This is how JUnit knows that factorial() is a test case. Notice also that assertEquals() is a method of the Assert class, but we're not writing the fully qualified name here because we've got a static import on Assert—it certainly makes life easier.

The assertEquals() method takes three parameters; they're illustrated in Figure 8-8.

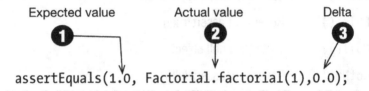

Figure 8-8. *assertEquals method*

---

❶   The **Expected** value is your control data; this is usually hardcoded in the test.

❷   The **Actual** value is what your method returns. If the expected value is the same as the actual value, the assertEquals() passes—your code is behaving as expected.

❸   **Delta** is intended to reflect how close the *actual* and *expected* values can be and still be considered equal. Some developers call this parameter the "fuzz" factor. When the difference between the expected and actual values is greater than the "fuzz factor," then assertEquals() will fail. I used 0.0 here because I don't want to tolerate any kind of deviation. You can use other values like 0.001, 0.002, and so on; it depends on your use case and how much fuzz your app is willing to tolerate.

Now, our code is complete. You can insert a couple more asserts in the code so you can get into the groove of things, if you prefer.

There are a couple of things I did not include in this sample code. I did not override the setUp() and tearDown() methods because I didn't need it. You would normally use the setUp() method if you need to set up database connections, network connections, and so on. Use the tearDown() method to close whatever it is you opened in the setUp().

Now, we're ready to run the test.

Running a Unit Test

You can run just one test or all the tests in the class. The little green arrows in the gutter of the main editor are clickable. When you click the little arrow beside the name of the class, that will run all the tests in the class. When you click the one beside the name of the test method, that will run only that test case. See Figure 8-9.

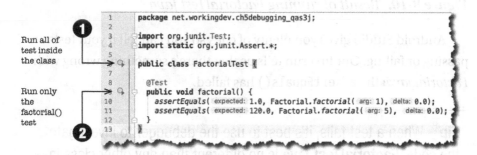

Figure 8-9. *FactorialTest.java in the main editor*

Similarly, you can also run the test from the main menu bar; go to **Run ➤ Run**.

Figure 8-10 shows the result of the text execution.

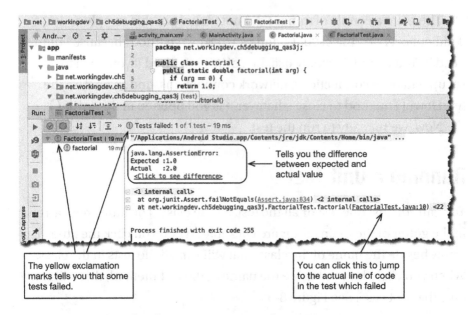

Figure 8-10. *Result of running FactorialTest.java*

Android Studio gives you plenty of cues so you can tell if your tests are passing or failing. Our first run tells us that there's something wrong with *Factorial.java*; the `assertEquals()` has failed.

Tip   When a test fails, it's best to use the debugger to investigate the code. **FactorialTest.java** is no different than any other class in our project; it's just another Java file, we can definitely debug it. Put some breakpoints on strategic places of your test code, then instead of "running" it, run the "debugger" so you can walk through it.

Our test failed because the factorial of 1 isn't 2, it's 1. If you look closer at *Factorial.java*, you'll notice that the factorial value isn't calculated properly.

Edit the *Factorial.java* file, then change this line:

```
return arg + factorial(arg - 1);
```

to this line

```
return arg * factorial(arg - 1);
```

If we run the test again, we see successful results, as shown in Figure 8-11.

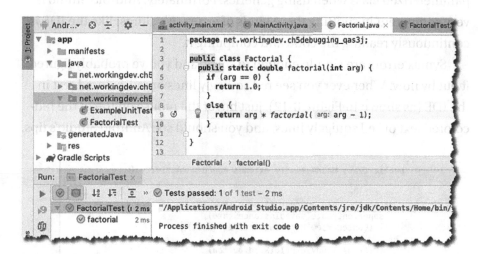

Figure 8-11. *Successful test*

Instead of yellow exclamation marks, we now see green check marks. Instead of seeing "Test failed," we now see "Test passed." Now we know that our code works as expected.

Debugging

We've been writing code for a while now; I'm sure you've had some mishaps with your code by now and have seen the various ways that Android Studio prompted your attention about these errors.

Syntax Errors

One of the errors you'll encounter with annoying frequency is syntax errors. They happen because you wrote something in the code that's not supposed to be there; or you forgot to write something (like a semicolon). These errors can be as benign as forgetting a closing curly brace or can be as complex as passing the wrong type of argument to a method or a parameterized class when using generics. Fortunately, Android Studio is very competent in spotting these kinds of errors. It's almost like the IDE is continuously reading the code and compiling it.

Syntax errors are simple enough to solve, and you've probably figured it out by now. Whenever you see red squiggly lines or red-colored text in the IDE (as shown in Figure 8-12), just hover the mouse on top of the red-colored text or red squiggly lines, and you should see Android Studio's tips.

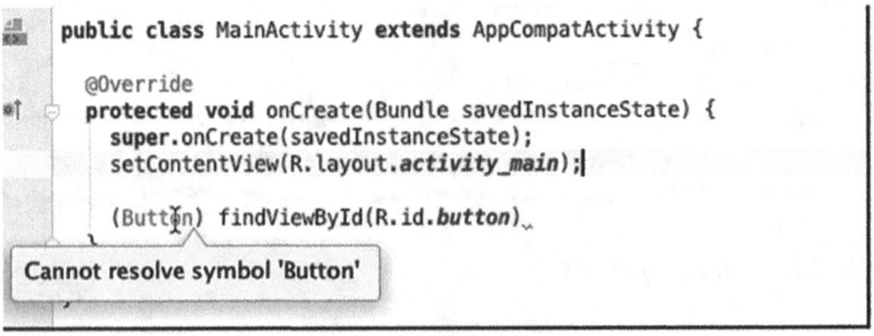

Figure 8-12. *Syntax errors shown in the editor*

The tips typically tell you what's wrong with the code. In Figure 8-12, the error is **Cannot resolve symbol 'Button'**, which means you haven't imported the Button class just yet. To resolve this, position the mouse cursor on the offending word (Button, in this case), then use the Quick Fix feature (**Option+Enter** in Mac, **Alt+Enter** in Windows). Quick Fix in action is shown in Figure 8-13.

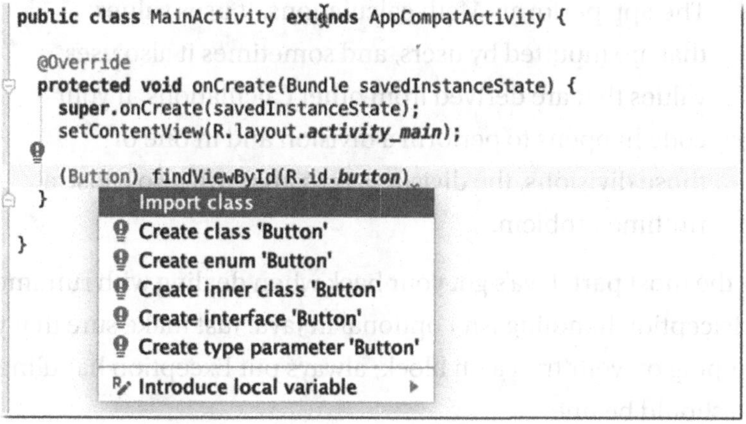

```
public class MainActivity extends AppCompatActivity {

  @Override
  protected void onCreate(Bundle savedInstanceState) {
    super.onCreate(savedInstanceState);
    setContentView(R.layout.activity_main);

    (Button) findViewById(R.id.button)
  }                Import class
                ♀ Create class 'Button'
}               ♀ Create enum 'Button'
                ♀ Create inner class 'Button'
                ♀ Create interface 'Button'
                ♀ Create type parameter 'Button'
                ᴿ⁄ Introduce local variable      ▸
```

Figure 8-13. Quick Fix

Runtime Errors

Runtime errors happen when your code encounters a situation it doesn't expect; and as its name implies, that errant condition is something that appears only when the program is running—it's not something you or the compiler can see at the time of compilation. Your code will compile without problems, but it may stop running when something in the runtime environment doesn't agree with what your code wants to do. There are many examples of these things; here are some of them:

- The app gets something from the Internet, a picture or a file and so on, so it assumes that the Internet is available and there is a network connection. Always. Experience should tell you that isn't always the case. Network connections go down sometimes, and if you don't factor this in your code, it may crash.

- The app needs to read from a file. Just like our first case earlier, your code assumes that the file will always be there. Sometimes, files get corrupted and may become unreadable. This should also be factored in the code.

251

- The app performs Math calculations. It uses values
  that are inputted by users, and sometimes it also uses
  values that are derived from other calculations. If your
  code happens to perform a division and in one of
  those divisions, the divisor is zero, that will also cause a
  runtime problem.

For the most part, Java's got your back when dealing with runtime
errors. Exception handling isn't optional in Java. Just make sure that you're
not skimping on your try-catch block; always put Exception handling code,
and you should be fine.

Logic Errors

Logic errors are the hardest to find. As its name suggests, it's an error on
your logic. When your code is not doing what you thought it should be
doing, that's logic error. There are many ways to cope with it, but the most
common methods are (1) using log statements and (2) using breakpoints
and walking/stepping through the code.

Printing log messages is a simple way of marking the footprints of the
program; you can do it with the simple System.out.println() statement,
but I'd encourage you to use the Log class instead. Listing 8-3 shows a
basic usage of the Log class.

Listing 8-3. Basic use of the Log class

```
public class MainActivity extends AppCompatActivity {

  final String TAG = getClass().getName();

  @Override
  protected void onCreate(Bundle savedInstanceState) {
    super.onCreate(savedInstanceState);
```

```java
    setContentView(R.layout.activity_main);
    // ...
  }

  void doSomething() {
    Log.d(TAG, "Log message, doSomething");
  }
}
```

You can define the TAG variable anywhere in the class, but in Listing 8-3, I defined it as a class member; Log.d() prints a debug message. You can use the other methods of the Log class to print warnings, info, or errors. The other methods are shown here:

```java
Log.v(TAG, message) // verbose
Log.d(TAG, message) // debug
Log.i(TAG, message) // info
Log.w(TAG, message) // warning
Log.e(TAG, message) // error
```

In each case, **tag** is a String literal or variable. You can use the tag for filtering the messages in the Logcat window. The **message** is also a String literal or variable which contains what you actually want to see in the log.

When you run your app, you can see the Log messages in the Logcat tool window. You can launch it either by clicking its tab in the menu strip at the bottom of the window (as shown in Figure 8-14) or from the main menu bar, **View ➤ Tool Windows ➤ Logcat**.

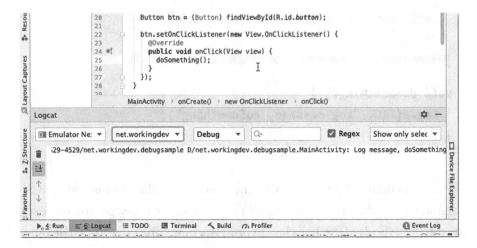

Figure 8-14. *Logcat tool window*

Walking through the Code

Android Studio includes an interactive debugger which allows you to walk and step through your code as it runs. With the interactive debugger, we can inspect snapshots of the application—values of variables, running threads, and so on—at specific locations in the code and at specific points in time. These specific locations in the code are called *breakpoints*; you get to choose these breakpoints.

To set a breakpoint, choose a line that has an executable statement, then click its line number in the gutter. When you set a breakpoint, there will be a pink circle icon in the gutter, and the whole line is lit in pink—as shown in Figure 8-15.

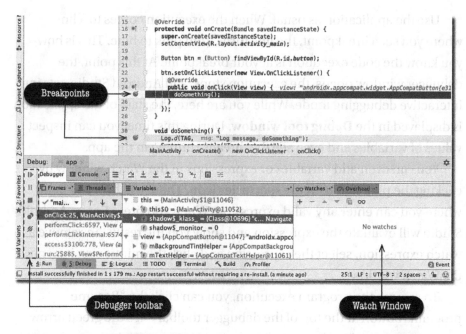

Figure 8-15. Debugger window

After the breakpoints are set, you have to run the app in debug mode. Stop the app if it is currently running, then from the main menu bar, click **Run ➤ Debug 'app'.**

Note   Running the app in debug mode isn't the only way to debug the app. You can also attach the debugger process in a currently running application. There are situations where this second technique is useful; for example, when the bug you are trying to solve occurs on very specific conditions, you may want to run the app for a while, and when you think you are close to the point of error, you can then attach the debugger.

Use the application as usual. When the execution comes to a line where you set a breakpoint, the line turns from pink to blue. This is how you know the code execution is at your breakpoint. At this point, the debugger window opens, the execution stops, and Android Studio gets into interactive debugging mode. While you are here, the state of the application is displayed in the **Debug tool window**. During this time, you can inspect values of variables and even see the threads running in the app.

You can even add variables or expressions in the Watch window by clicking the plus sign with the spectacles icon. There will be a text field where you can enter any valid expression. When you press **Enter**, Android Studio will evaluate the expression and show you the result. To remove a watch expression, select the expression and click the minus sign icon on the Watch window.

To resume the program execution, you can click the "Resume program" button at the top of the debugger toolbar—it's the green arrow pointing to the right. Alternatively, you can also resume the program from the main menu bar, **Run ➤ Resume Program**. If you want to halt the program before it finishes naturally, you can click the "Stop app" button on the debugger toolbar; it's the red square icon. Alternatively, you can do this also from the main menu bar, **Run ➤ Stop app**.

Profiler

The profiler gives us insights on how our app/game is using computing resources, like the CPU, memory, network bandwidth, and battery.

The Profiler is new in Android Studio 3. It replaces the Android monitor with its new unified and shared timeline view for the CPU, memory, network, and energy graphs. Figure 8-16 shows the Profiler.

You can get to the Profiler by going to the main menu bar, then selecting **View ➤ Tool Windows ➤ Profiler**.

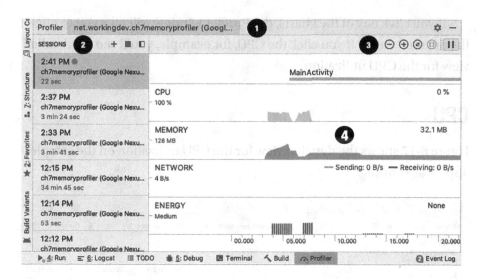

Figure 8-16. *Profiler*

❶   It shows the process and device being profiled.

❷   It shows you which sessions to view. You can also add new sessions from here by clicking the + button.

❸   Use the zoom buttons to control how much of the timeline to view.

❹   The new shared timeline view lets you see all the graphs for the CPU, memory, network, and energy usage. At the top, you will also see important app events, like user inputs or Activity state transitions.

As soon as you launch an application, either on an attached device or an emulator, you'll see its graph on the Profiler.

Note   If you try to profile an APK with a version lower than API level 26, you will see some warnings because Android Studio needs to fully instrument your code. You will need to enable "Advance profiling"; but, if your APK is Oreo or higher, you won't see any warnings.

If you click any of the charts, the Profiler window will take you to one of the detailed views. If you click the CPU, for example, you'll see the detailed view for the CPU utilization.

CPU

Figure 8-17 shows the detailed view for the CPU utilization on the sample app I was running.

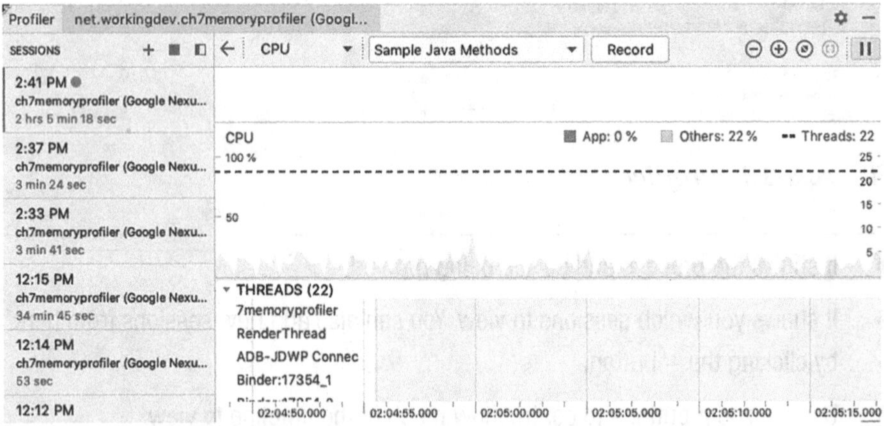

Figure 8-17. *CPU view*

Aside from the live utilization graph, the CPU detailed view also shows a list of all the threads in the app and their states—you can see if the threads are waiting for I/O or when they are active.

You might have noticed the "Record" button in Figure 8-17; if you click that button, you can get a report on all the methods that were executed in a given period. Notice also the selected trace type in the drop-down (Sample Java Methods); this *trace type* has a smaller overhead but not as detailed nor as accurate as the *instrumented type* (Trace Java Methods), meaning the sampled type may miss the execution of a very short-lived method. You might think, "just always use the instrumented type then"—you have to remember, though, that while instrumented type can record every method call, on Android devices before version 8, there is a limit on how much data can be captured; so, if you use the instrumented trace, that limit will be reached quickly. You can change that limit by editing the configuration for the instrumented capture. On the trace type drop-down, choose "Edit Configurations" as shown in Figure 8-18.

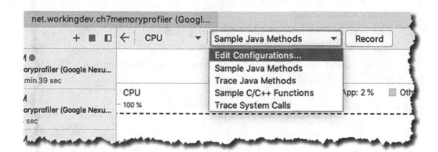

Figure 8-18. *Edit Configurations*

Figure 8-19 shows the "Sampling interval" and "File size limit" settings, which you can use to adjust how frequent the sampling will be and how big of a file size you'd like to allocate for the recording. Just to reiterate, the file size limitation is only present on Android devices that are running Android 8.0 or lower (< API level 26). If your device has a higher Android version, you're not constrained by these limitations.

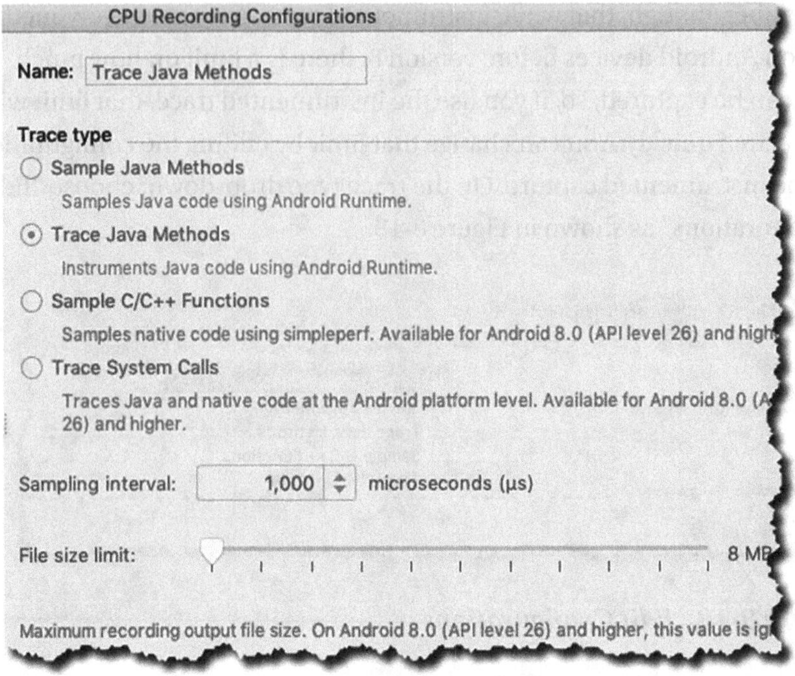

CPU Recording Configurations

Name: Trace Java Methods

Trace type

○ Sample Java Methods

Samples Java code using Android Runtime.

◉ Trace Java Methods

Instruments Java code using Android Runtime.

○ Sample C/C++ Functions

Samples native code using simpleperf. Available for Android 8.0 (API level 26) and high

○ Trace System Calls

Traces Java and native code at the Android platform level. Available for Android 8.0 (A 26) and higher.

Sampling interval: 1,000 ⬍ microseconds (µs)

File size limit: ⬦ ı ı ı ı ı ı ı ı ı ı 8 MB

Maximum recording output file size. On Android 8.0 (API level 26) and higher, this value is ig

Figure 8-19. *CPU Recording Configurations*

If you click record, Android Studio will begin capturing data. Click the "Stop" button when you'd like to stop recording, as shown in Figure 8-20.

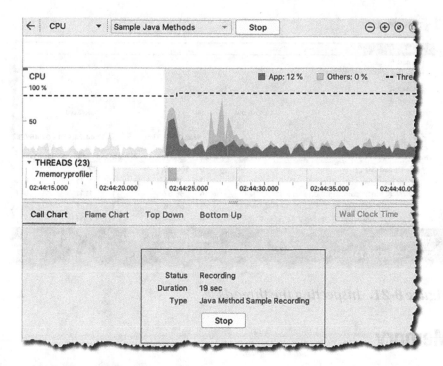

Figure 8-20. *Recording session*

When you hit stop, you can take a look at the individual threads, as shown in Figure 8-21.

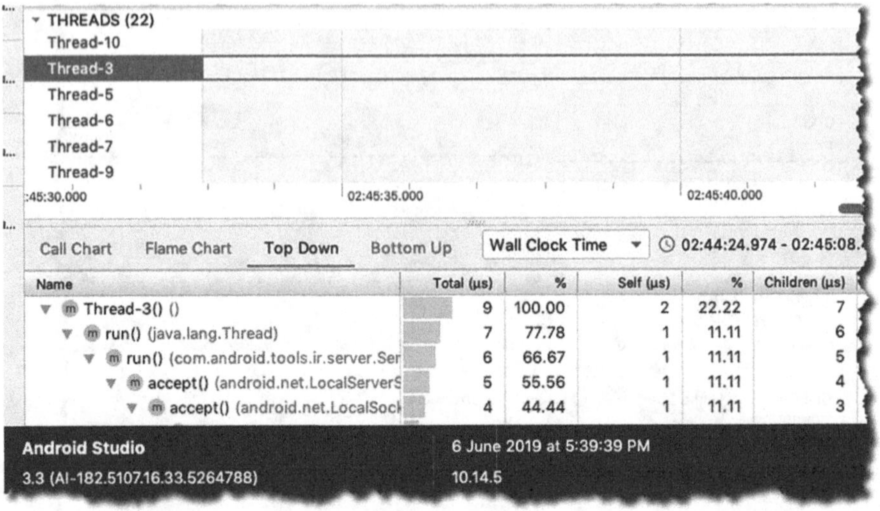

Name		Total (µs)	%	Self (µs)	%	Children (µs)
▼ ⓜ Thread-3() ()		9	100.00	2	22.22	7
▼ ⓜ run() (java.lang.Thread)		7	77.78	1	11.11	6
▼ ⓜ run() (com.android.tools.ir.server.Ser		6	66.67	1	11.11	5
▼ ⓜ accept() (android.net.LocalServerS		5	55.56	1	11.11	4
▼ ⓜ accept() (android.net.LocalSock		4	44.44	1	11.11	3

Figure 8-21. *Inspecting the threads*

Memory

The memory profiler shows, in real time, how much memory your app is consuming. Figure 8-22 shows a snapshot of the memory view as I captured the memory footprint of a test app. As you can see, not only does the graph show how much memory your app is gulping, it also shows the breakdown, for example, how much memory is used by the *code*, *stack*, *graphics*, *Java*, and so on.

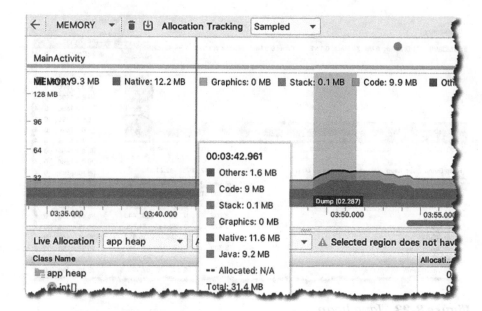

Figure 8-22. *Memory view*

You can force garbage collection (GC) in the memory view. See that garbage can icon at the top? Yup, if you click that, it'll force a GC. The button to its right is also useful—the icon with a down-pointing arrow inside a box is a *memory dump*. If you click that, the Java heap will be dumped, and then you can inspect it, as shown in Figure 8-23.

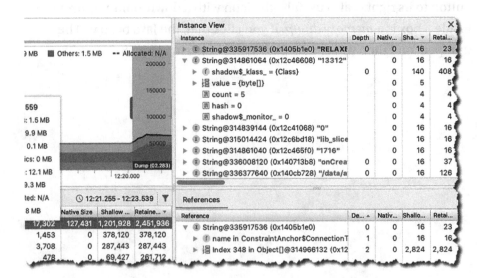

Figure 8-23. *Java heap*

The heap is a preserved amount of storage memory that the Android runtime allocates for our app. When we dumped the heap, it gave us a chance to examine instance properties of objects, as shown in Figure 8-24.

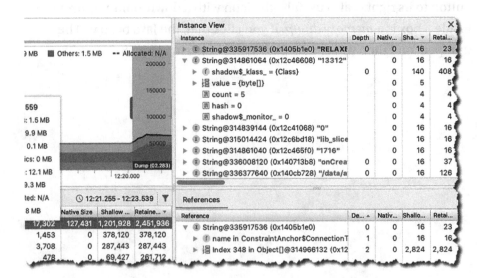

Figure 8-24. *Instance view, Reference tab*

The Reference tab can be very useful in finding memory leaks because it shows all the references pointing to the object you're examining.

Another useful tool in the memory view is the Allocation tracker, shown in Figure 8-25.

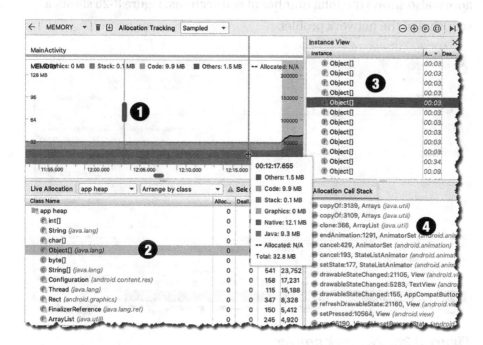

Figure 8-25. *Allocation tracker*

---

❶   Click anywhere in the timeline of the memory graph to view the allocation tracker. This will show you a list of all objects that were allocated and deallocated at that point in time.

❷   This shows a list of all classes being used by the app at a point in time.

❸   This shows the list of all those objects allocated and deallocated at a specific point in time.

❹   The tracker even includes the call stack of the allocation.

Network

Like the other views in the Profiler, the network view also shows real-time data. It lets you see and inspect data that is sent and received by your app; it also shows the total number of connections. Figure 8-26 shows a snapshot of the network profiler.

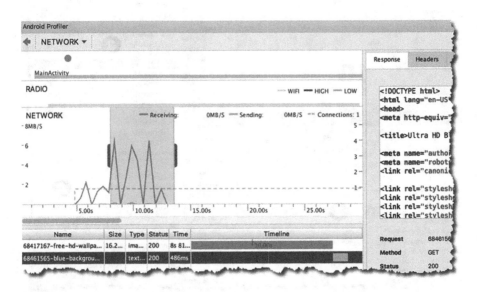

Figure 8-26. *Network profiler*

Every time your app makes a request to the network, it uses the WiFi radio to send and receive data—the radio isn't the most energy efficient; it's power-hungry, and if you don't pay attention to how your app makes network requests, that's a sure way of draining the device battery faster than usual.

When you use the network profiler, a good way to start is to look for short spikes of network activity. When you see sharp spikes that rise and fall abruptly and they're scattered all over the timeline, that smells like you could use some optimization by batching your network requests so as to reduce the number of times that the WiFi radio needs to wake up and send or receive data.

Energy

By now you're probably seeing a pattern on how the Profiler works. It shows you real-time data. In the case of the Energy profiler, it shows data on how much energy your app is guzzling—though it doesn't really show the direct measure of energy consumption, the Energy profiler shows an estimation of the energy consumption of the CPU, the radio, and the GPS sensor. Figure 8-27 shows a snapshot of the Energy profiler.

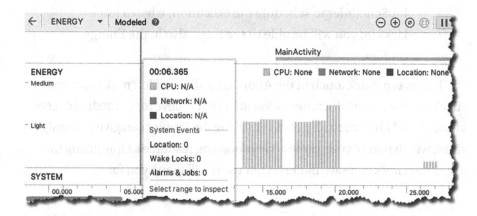

Figure 8-27. *Energy profiler*

You can also use the Energy profiler to find system events that affect energy consumption, for example, wake locks, jobs, and alarms.

- A *wake lock* is a mechanism for keeping the CPU of the screen on when the device would otherwise go to sleep, for example, when an app plays a video, it may use a wake lock to keep the screen on even when there's no user interaction—using a wake lock isn't a problem, but forgetting to release one is; it keeps the CPU on longer than necessary which will surely drain the battery faster.

- *Alarms* can be used to run background tasks that are outside your application's context at specific intervals. When an alarm goes off, it can run some tasks; in case it runs an energy-intensive piece of code, you'll definitely see it in the Energy profiler.

- A *job* can perform actions when certain conditions are met, for example, when the network becomes available. You would usually create a job with JobBuilder and use JobScheduler to schedule the execution; when a job kicks in, you will be able to see them also in the Energy profiler.

That was a quick touch of the Android Studio Profiler; make sure you check out the official documentation at `https://developer.android.com/studio/profile/android-profiler`. Using the Profiler can give you insights about which part of your game code is hogging resources. Optimizing the use of resources can save battery; your users will thank you for it.

Key Takeaways

- We've talked about various kinds of testing you can do for your games; you don't have to do them all, but make sure you do the test that applies to your game.

- Dev testing (unit testing) should be a core development task; try to get into the habit of writing your test cases together with your actual code.

- Android Studio Profile can inspect your app's behavior from under the hood. It can give you insights on how the app is consuming resources; use this tool when you're doing performance testing.

CHAPTER 9

Introduction to OpenGL ES

What we'll cover:

- About OpenGL ES

- OpenGL ES theories

- GLSurfaceView and GLSurfaceView.Renderer

- Using Blender data in OpenGL ES

Starting from API level 11 (Android 3), the 2D rendering pipeline already supports hardware acceleration. When you draw on the Canvas (which is what we used in the last two games we built), the drawing operation is already done on the GPU; but this also meant the app consumes more RAM because of the increased resources required to enable hardware acceleration.

Building games using the Canvas isn't a bad choice of tech if the game you're building isn't that complex; but when the level of visual complexities rises, the Canvas might run out of juice and won't be able to keep up with your game requirements. You'll need something more substantial. This is where OpenGL ES comes in.

© Ted Hagos, Mario Zechner, J.F. DiMarzio and Robert Green 2020
T. Hagos et al., *Beginning Android Games Development*,
https://doi.org/10.1007/978-1-4842-6121-7_9

What's OpenGL ES

Open Graphics Library (OpenGL) came from Silicon Graphics (SGI); they were makers of high-end graphics workstations and mainframes. Initially, SGI had a proprietary graphics framework called IRIS GL (which grew to be an industry standard), but as competition increased, SGI opted to turn IRIS GL to an open framework. IRIS GL was stripped down of nongraphics-related functions and hardware-dependent features and became OpenGL.

OpenGL is a cross-language, cross-platform application programming interface (API) for rendering 2D and 3D graphics. It's a lean mean machine for rendering polygons; it's written in C as an API for interacting with a graphics processing unit (GPU) to achieve hardware accelerated rendering. It's a very low-level hardware abstraction.

As small handheld devices became more and more common, OpenGL for Embedded Systems (OpenGL ES) was developed. OpenGL ES is a stripped-down version of the desktop version; it removed a lot of the more redundant API calls and simplified other elements to make it run efficiently on the less powerful CPUs in the market; as a result, OpenGL ES was widely adopted in many platforms such as HP webOS, Nintendo 3DS, iOS, and Android.

OpenGL ES is now an industry standard for (3D) graphics programming. It is maintained by the Khronos Group, which is an industry consortium whose members include, among others, ATI, NVIDIA, and Intel; together, these companies define and extend the standard.

Currently, there are six incremental versions of OpenGL ES: versions 1.0, 1.1, 2.0, 3.0, 3.1, and 3.2.

- **OpenGL ES 1.0 and 1.1**—This API specification is supported by Android 1.0 and higher.

- **OpenGL ES 2.0**—This API specification is supported by Android 2.2 (API level 8) and higher.

- **OpenGL ES 3.0**—This API specification is supported by Android 4.3 (API level 18) and higher.

- **OpenGL ES 3.1**—This API specification is supported by Android 5.0 (API level 21) and higher.

There are still developers, especially those who focus on games that run on multiple platforms, who write for OpenGL ES 1.0; this is because of its simplicity, flexibility, and standard implementation. All Android devices support OpenGL ES 1.0, some devices support 2.0, and any device after Jelly Bean supports OpenGL ES 3.0. At the time of writing, more than half of activated Android devices already support OpenGL ES 3.0. Table 9-1 shows the distribution and Figure 9-1 shows a nice pie chart to go with it; this data was taken from `https://developer.android.com/about/dashboards#OpenGL`.

Table 9-1. *OpenGL ES version distribution*

OpenGL ES Version	Distribution
GL 1.1 only	0.0%
GL 2.0	14.5%
GL 3.0	18.6%
GL 3.1	9.8%
GL 3.2	57.2%

Note   Support for one particular version of OpenGL ES also implies support for any lower version (e.g., support for version 2.0 also implies support for 1.1).

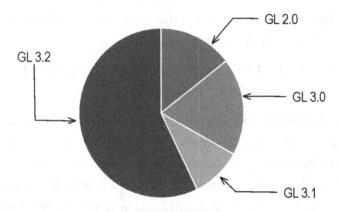

Figure 9-1. *OpenGL ES version distribution*

It's important to note that OpenGL ES 2.0 breaks compatibility with the 1.x versions. You can use either 1.x or 2.0, but not both at the same time. The reason for this is that the 1.x versions use a programming model called *fixed-function pipeline*, while versions 2.0 and up let you programmatically define parts of the rendering pipeline via *shaders*.

What does OpenGL ES do

The short answer is OpenGL ES just renders triangles on the screen, and it gives you some control on how those triangles are rendered. It's probably best also to describe (as early as now) what OpenGL ES is not. It is not

- A scene management API

- A ray tracer

- A physics engine

- A game engine

- A photorealistic rendering engine

OpenGL ES just renders triangles. Not much else.

Think of OpenGL ES as working like a camera. To take a picture, you have to go to the scene you want to photograph. Your scene is composed of objects that all have a position and orientation relative to your camera as well as different materials and textures. Glass is translucent and reflective; a table is probably made out of wood; a magazine has some photo of a face on it; and so on. Some of the objects might even move around (e.g., cars or people). Your camera also has properties, such as focal length, field of view, image resolution, size of the photo that will be taken, and a unique position and orientation within the world (relative to some origin). Even if both the objects and the camera are moving, when you press the shutter release, you catch a still image of the scene. For that small moment, everything stands still and is well defined, and the picture reflects exactly all those configurations of position, orientation, texture, materials, and lighting. Figure 9-2 shows an abstract scene with a camera, light, and three objects with different materials.

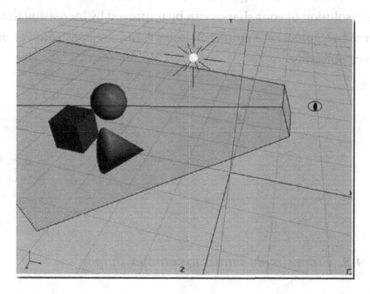

Figure 9-2. *Abstract scene*

Each object has a position and orientation relative to the scene's origin. The camera, indicated by the eye, also has a position in relation to the scene's origin. The pyramid in Figure 9-2 is called the *view volume* or *view frustum*, which shows how much of the scene the camera captures and how the camera is oriented. The little white ball with the rays is the light source in the scene, which also has a position relative to the origin.

We can map this scene to OpenGL ES, but to do so, we need to define (1) models or objects, (2) lights, (3) camera, and (4) viewport.

Models or Objects

OpenGL ES is a triangle rendering machine. OpenGL ES objects are a collection of points in 3D space; their location is defined by three values. These values are joined together to form faces, which are flat surfaces that look a lot like triangles. The triangles are then joined together to form objects or pieces of objects (polygons).

The resolution of your shapes can be improved by increasing the number of polygons in it. Figure 9-3 shows various shapes with varying number of polygons.

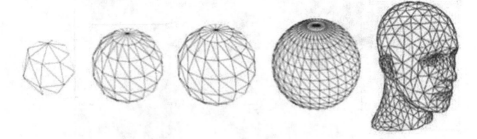

Figure 9-3. *From simple shapes to complex shapes*

On the far left of Figure 9-3 is a simple sphere; it doesn't really go over well as a sphere if you look closely at it. The shape next to it (right) is also a sphere but with more polygons. The shapes, as they progress to the right, form complex contours; this can be achieved by increasing the number of polygons in the shape.

Lights

OpenGL ES offers a couple different light types with various attributes. They are just mathematical objects with positions and/or directions in 3D space, plus attributes such as color.

Camera

This is also a mathematical object that has a position and orientation in 3D space. Additionally, it has parameters that govern how much of the image we see, similar to a real camera. All these things together define a view volume or view frustum (indicated by the pyramid with the top cut off in Figure 9-2). Anything inside this pyramid can be seen by the camera; anything outside will not make it into the final picture.

Viewport

This defines the size and resolution of the final image. Think of it as the type of film you put into your analog camera or the image resolution you get for pictures taken with your digital camera.

Projections

OpenGL ES can construct a 2D bitmap of a scene from the camera's point of view. While everything is defined in 3D space, OpenGL maps the 3D space to 2D via something called *projections*. A single triangle has three points defined in 3D space. To render such a triangle, OpenGL ES needs to know the coordinates of these 3D points within the pixel-based coordinate system of the framebuffer that are inside the triangle.

Matrices

OpenGL ES expresses projections in the form of matrices. The internals are quite involved; for our introductory purposes, we don't need to bother with the internals of matrices; we simply need to know what they do with the points we define in our scene.

- A matrix encodes transformations to be applied to a point. A transformation can be a projection, a translation (in which the point is moved around), a rotation around another point and axis, or a scale, among other things.

- By multiplying such a matrix with a point, we apply the transformation to the point. For example, multiplying a point with a matrix that encodes a translation by 10 units on the x axis will move the point 10 units on the x axis and thereby modify its coordinates.

- We can concatenate transformations stored in separate matrices into a single matrix by multiplying the matrices. When we multiply this single concatenated matrix with a point, all the transformations stored in that matrix will be applied to that point. The order in which the transformations are applied is dependent on the order in which we multiplied the matrices.

There are three different matrices in OpenGL ES that apply to the points in our models:

- **Model-view matrix**—This matrix is used to place a model somewhere in the "world." For example, if you have a model of a sphere and you want it located 100 meters to the east, you will use the model matrix to do this. We can use this matrix to move, rotate, or scale the points of our triangles (this is the *model* part of the model-view matrix). This matrix is also used to specify the position and orientation of our camera (this is the *view* part). If you want to view our sphere which is 100 meters to the east, we will have to move ourselves 100 meters to the east as well. Another way to think about this is that we remain stationary and the rest of the world moves 100 meters to the west.

- **Projection matrix**—This is the view frustum of our camera. Since our screens are flat, we need to do a final transformation to "project" our view onto our screen and get that nice 3D perspective. This is what the projection matrix is used for.

- **Texture matrix**—This matrix allows us to manipulate texture coordinates.

There's a lot more theories we need to absorb in OpenGL ES programming, but let's explore some of those theories alongside a simple coding exercise.

Rendering a Simple Sphere

OpenGL ES APIs are built into the Android framework, so we don't need to import any other libraries or include any other dependencies into the project.

OpenGL ES is widely supported among Android devices, but just to be prudent, if you want to exclude Google Play users whose device do not support OpenGL ES, you need to add a **uses-feature** in the Android Manifest file, like this:

```
<uses-feature android:glEsVersion="0x00020000"
              android:required="true" />
```

The manifest entry is basically saying that the app expects the device to support OpenGL ES 2, which is practically all devices at the time of writing.

Additionally (and optionally), if your application uses texture compression, you must also declare it in the manifest so that the app only installs on compatible devices; Listing 9-1 shows how to do this in the Android Manifest.

Listing 9-1. AndroidManifest.xml, texture compression

```
<supports-gl-texture android:name="GL_OES_compressed_ETC1_RGB8_
texture" />
<supports-gl-texture android:name="GL_OES_compressed_paletted_
texture" />
```

Assuming you've already created a project with an empty Activity and a default activity_main layout file, the first thing to do is to add **GLSurfaceView** to the layout file. Modify activity_main.xml to match the contents of Listing 9-2.

Listing 9-2. activity_main.xml

```xml
<?xml version="1.0" encoding="utf-8"?>
<androidx.constraintlayout.widget.ConstraintLayout
xmlns:android="http://schemas.android.com/apk/res/android"
  xmlns:app="http://schemas.android.com/apk/res-auto"
  xmlns:tools="http://schemas.android.com/tools"
  android:layout_width="match_parent"
  android:layout_height="match_parent"
  tools:context=".MainActivity">

  <android.opengl.GLSurfaceView
    android:layout_width="400dp"
    android:layout_height="400dp"
    android:id="@+id/gl_view"
  />

</androidx.constraintlayout.widget.ConstraintLayout>
```

I removed the default TextView object and inserted a GLSurfaceView element with 400dp by 400dp size. Let's keep it evenly square for now, so that our shape won't skew. OpenGL assumes that drawing areas are always square.

Figure 9-4 shows the activity_main layout in design mode.

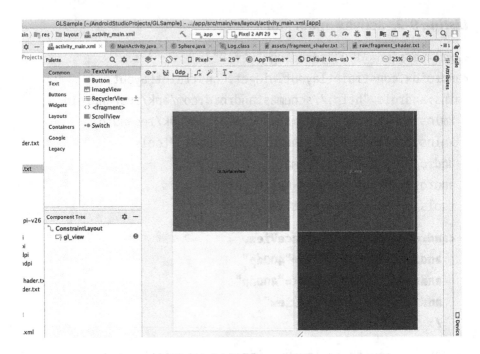

Figure 9-4. *activity_main.xml in design mode*

The GLSurfaceView is an implementation of the SurfaceView class that uses a dedicated surface for displaying OpenGL rendering; this object manages a surface, which is a special piece of memory that can be composited into the Android view system. The GLSurfaceView runs on a dedicated thread to separate the rendering performance from the main UI thread.

Next, in MainActivity, let's get a reference to the GLSurfaceView we just created. We can create a member variable on MainActivity that's of type GLSurfaceView, then in the **onCreate()** method, we'll get a reference to it using findViewByID. The code is shown in Listing 9-3.

Listing 9-3. Get a reference to the GLSurfaceView

```
public class MainActivity extends AppCompatActivity {

  private GLSurfaceView glView;

  @Override
  protected void onCreate(Bundle savedInstanceState) {
    super.onCreate(savedInstanceState);
    setContentView(R.layout.activity_main);

    glView = findViewById(R.id.gl_view);

  }
}
```

Next, still on MainActivity, let's determine if there's support for OpenGL ES 2.0. This can be done by using an ActivityManager object which lets us interact with the global system state; we can use this to get the device configuration info, which in turn can tell us if the device supports OpenGL ES 2. The code to do this is shown in Listing 9-4.

Listing 9-4. Determine support for OpenGL ES 2.0

```
ActivityManager am = (ActivityManager)
                  getSystemService(Context.ACTIVITY_
                  SERVICE);
ConfigurationInfo ci = am.getDeviceConfigurationInfo();

boolean isES2Supported = ci.reqGlEsVersion > 0x20000;
```

Once we know if the device supports OpenGL ES 2 (or not), we tell the surface that we'd like an OpenGL ES 2 compatible surface, and then we pass it in a custom renderer. The runtime will call this renderer whenever it's time to adjust the surface or draw a new frame. Listing 9-5 shows the annotated code for MainActivity.

Listing 9-5. MainActivity, creation of OpenGL ES 2 environment

```
import android.app.ActivityManager;
import android.content.Context;
import android.content.pm.ConfigurationInfo;
import android.opengl.GLES20;
import android.opengl.GLSurfaceView;
import android.os.Bundle;

import javax.microedition.khronos.egl.EGLConfig;
import javax.microedition.khronos.opengles.GL10;

import androidx.appcompat.app.AppCompatActivity;

public class MainActivity extends AppCompatActivity {

  private GLSurfaceView glView;

  @Override
  protected void onCreate(Bundle savedInstanceState) {
    super.onCreate(savedInstanceState);
    setContentView(R.layout.activity_main);

    glView = findViewById(R.id.gl_view);

    ActivityManager am = (ActivityManager)
        getSystemService(Context.ACTIVITY_SERVICE);
    ConfigurationInfo ci = am.getDeviceConfigurationInfo();

    boolean isES2Supported = ci.reqGlEsVersion > 0x20000;
    if(isES2Supported) {  ❶

      glView.setEGLContextClientVersion(2);  ❷
      glView.setRenderer(new GLSurfaceView.Renderer() {  ❸
        @Override
```

```
public void onSurfaceCreated(GL10 gl10, EGLConfig
eglConfig) {
  glView.setRenderMode(GLSurfaceView.RENDERMODE_WHEN_
  DIRTY); ❹
  // statements ❺
}

@Override
public void onSurfaceChanged(GL10 gl10, int width, int
height) {
  GLES20.glViewport(0,0, width, height); ❻
}

@Override
public void onDrawFrame(GL10 gl10) {
  // statements ❼
}
});
}
else {

}
}
}
```

---

❶ Once we know OpenGL ES 2 is supported, we proceed to creating an
   OpenGL ES 2 environment.

❷ We tell the surface view that we want an OpenGL ES 2 compatible surface.

❸ We create a custom renderer using an anonymous class, then passing an
   instance of that class to the **setRenderer()** method of the surface view.

283

❹   We're setting the render mode to draw only when there is a change to the drawing data.

❺   This is a good place to create objects you will use for drawing; think of this as the equivalent of the Activity's **onCreate()** method. This method may also be called if we lose the surface context and is later recreated.

❻   The runtime calls this method once when the surface has been created and subsequently when, for some reason, the size of the surface changes. This is where you set the view port, because by the time this is called, we've got the dimensions of the surface. Think of this as the equivalent of the **onSizeChanged()** of the View class. This may also be called when the device switches orientation, for example, from portrait to landscape.

❼   This is where we do our drawing. This is called when it's time to draw a new frame.

The **onDrawFrame()** method of the Renderer is where we tell OpenGL ES to draw something on the surface. We'll do this by passing an array of numbers which represents positions, colors, and so on. In our case, we're going to draw a sphere. We can hand-code the arrays of numbers—which represent X,Y,Z coordinates of the vertices—that we need to pass OpenGL ES, but that may not help us to envision what we're trying to draw. So, instead, let's use a 3D creation suite like Blender (www.blender.org) to draw a shape.

Blender is open source; you can use it freely. Once you're done with the download and installation, you can launch Blender, then delete the default cube by pressing **X**; next, press **Shift+A** and select **Mesh ➤ Ico Sphere**, as shown in Figure 9-5.

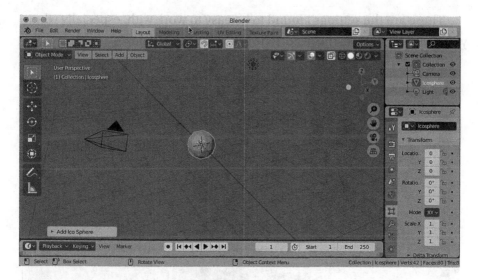

Figure 9-5. *Create an Icosphere*

Now we've got a moderately interesting object with a couple of vertices—it will be cumbersome to hand-code these vertices; that's why we took the Blender route.

To use the sphere in our app, we must export it as a Wavefront object. A Wavefront object is a geometry definition file format. It's an open format and is adopted by 3D graphics application vendors. This is a simple data format that represents 3D geometry, namely, the position of each vertex; the faces that make each polygon are defined as a list of vertices. For our purposes, we're only interested in the position of the vertices and the faces.

In Blender, go to **File ➤ Export Wavefront (.obj)** as shown in Figure 9-6. In the following screen, give it a name (sphere.obj) and save it in a location of your choice. Don't forget to note the export settings of Blender; check only the following:

- Export as OBJ object

- Triangulate faces

- Keep vertex order

These are the settings I found to be easy to work with, especially when you're about to parse the exported vertex and faces data.

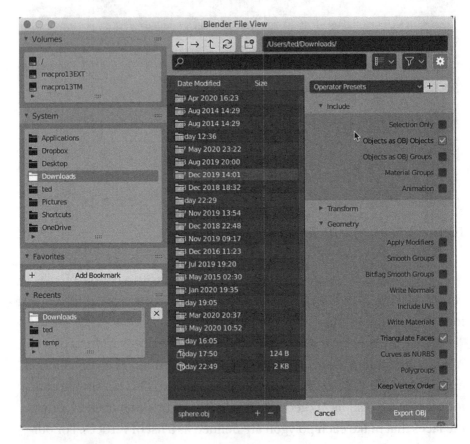

Figure 9-6. *Export the sphere to Wavefront object format*

The resulting object file is actually a text file; Listing 9-6 shows a partial listing of that **sphere.obj**.

Listing 9-6. Partial sphere.obj

```
# Blender v2.82 (sub 7) OBJ File: 'sphere.blend'
# www.blender.org
o Icosphere
v 0.000000 -1.000000 0.000000
v 0.723607 -0.447220 0.525725
v -0.276388 -0.447220 0.850649
v -0.894426 -0.447216 0.000000
v -0.276388 -0.447220 -0.850649
v 0.723607 -0.447220 -0.525725
v 0.276388 0.447220 0.850649
s off
f 1 14 13
f 2 14 16
f 1 13 18
f 1 18 20
f 1 20 17
f 2 16 23
f 3 15 25
f 4 19 27
f 5 21 29
```

Notice how each line starts with either a "v" or an "f". A line that starts with a "v" represents a single vertex, and a line that starts with an "f" represents a face. The vertex lines have the X, Y, and Z coordinates of a vertex, while the face lines have the indices of the three vertices (which together form a face).

To keep things organized, let's create a class that will represent our sphere object—we don't really want to write all the drawing code inside the **onDrawFrame()** method now, do we?

Let's create a new class and add it to the project. You can do this by using Android Studio's context menu; right-click the package name (as shown in Figure 9-7), then choose **New ➤ Java Class**.

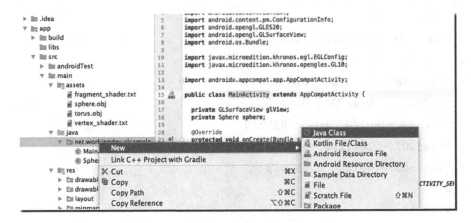

Figure 9-7. *Create a new class*

In the screen that follows, provide the name of the class (Sphere), as shown in Figure 9-8.

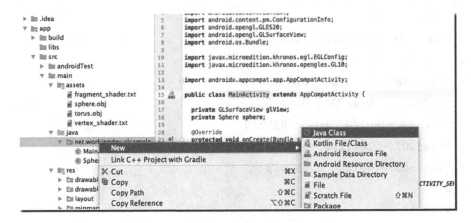

Figure 9-8. *Provide a name for the class*

We'll build the Sphere class a basic POJO that contains all the data that OpenGL ES requires to draw a shape. Listing 9-7 shows the starting code for **Sphere.java**.

Listing 9-7. Sphere.java

```java
public class Sphere {

  private List<String> vertList;
  private List<String> facesList;
  private Context ctx;
  private final String TAG = getClass().getName();

  public Sphere(Context context) {

    ctx = context;
    vertList = new ArrayList<>();
    facesList = new ArrayList<>();

  }
}
```

The Sphere class has two List objects which will hold the vertices and faces data (which we will load from the OBJ file). Apart from that, there's a Context object and a String object:

- **Context ctx**—The context object will be needed by some of our methods, so I made it a member variable.

- **String TAG**—I just need an identifying String for when we do some logging.

The idea is to read the exported Wavefront OBJ file and load the vertices and faces data into their corresponding List objects. Before we can read the file, we need to add it to the project. We can do that by creating an **assets** folder. An assets folder gives us the ability to add external files to the project and make them accessible to our code. If your project doesn't have an assets folder, you can create them. To do that, use the context menu; right-click the "app" in the Project tool window (as shown in Figure 9-9), then select **New ➤ Folder ➤ Assets Folder**.

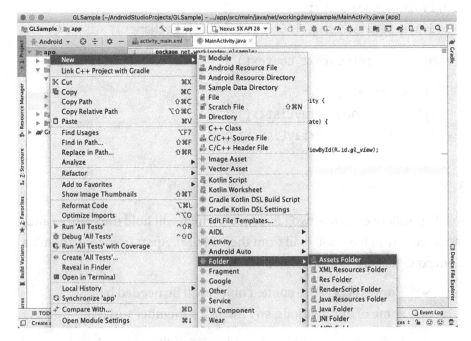

Figure 9-9. Create an assets folder

In the window that follows, click **Finish**, as shown in Figure 9-10.

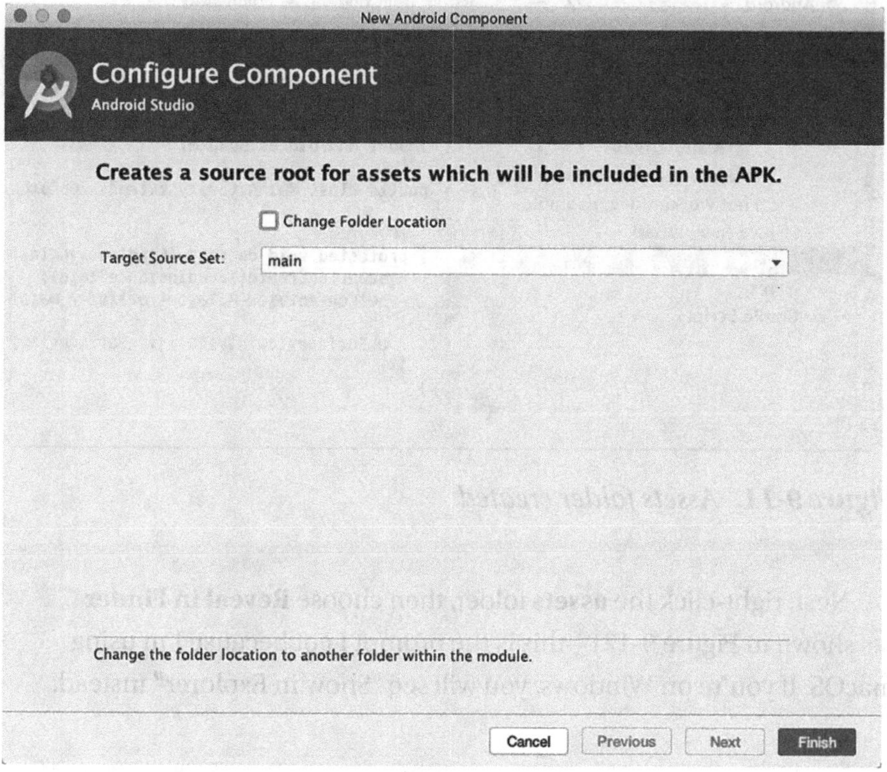

Figure 9-10. *New Android component*

Gradle will perform a "sync" after you've added a folder to the project. Figure 9-11 shows the Project tool window with the newly created **assets** folder.

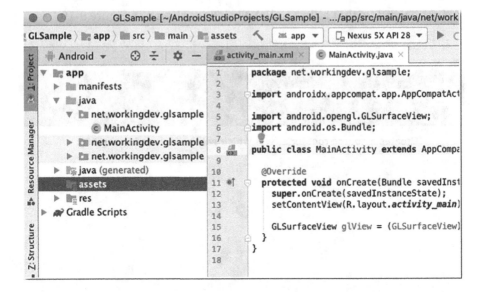

Figure 9-11. *Assets folder created*

Next, right-click the **assets** folder, then choose **Reveal in Finder**
(as shown in Figure 9-12)—this is the prompt I got because I'm using
macOS. If you're on Windows, you will see "Show in Explorer" instead.

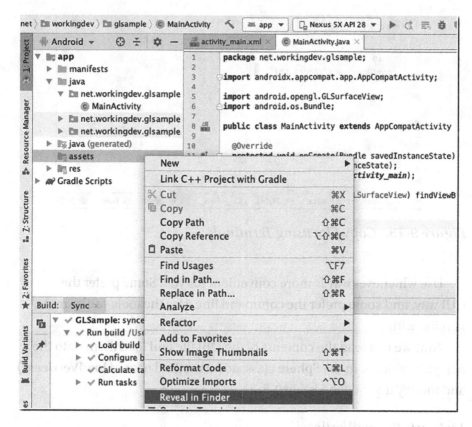

Figure 9-12. *Reveal in Finder or Show in Explorer (for Windows users)*

You can now transfer the **sphere.obj** file to the assets folder of the project.

Alternatively, you can copy the **sphere.obj** file to the assets folder using the Terminal of Android Studio (as shown in Figure 9-13).

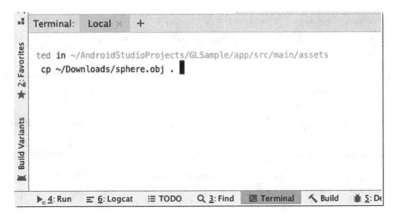

Figure 9-13. Copy files using Terminal

Use whichever way is more convenient for you. Some prefer the
GUI way, and some prefer the command line. Use the tools you're more
familiar with.

Now we can read the contents of the OBJ file and load them onto the
ArrayList objects. In the Sphere class, add a method named **loadVertices()**
and modify it to match Listing 9-8.

Listing 9-8. loadVertices()

```
import java.util.Scanner;

// class definition and other statements

private void loadVertices() {
  try {
    Scanner scanner = new Scanner(ctx.getAssets().open("sphere.
    obj")); ❶
    while(scanner.hasNextLine()) {  ❷
      String line = scanner.nextLine(); ❸
```

```
    if(line.startsWith("v ")) {
        vertList.add(line);  ❹
    } else if(line.startsWith("f ")) {
        facesList.add(line); ❺
    }
  }
  scanner.close();
}
catch(IOException ioe) {
    Log.e(TAG, ioe.getMessage()); ❻
  }
}
```

---

❶	Create a new Scanner object and open the **sphere.obj** text file.
❷	While we're not yet at the end of the file, **hasNextLine()** will always return true.
❸	Read the contents of the current line and save it to the *line* variable.
❹	If the line starts with a "v", add it to the **vertList** ArrayList.
❺	If the line starts with an "f", add it to the **facesList** ArrayList.

We're coding our app using the Java language, but you need to remember that OpenGL ES is actually a bunch of C APIs. We can't simply pass our list of vertices and faces to OpenGL ES directly. We need to convert our vertices and faces data into something OpenGL ES will understand.

Java and the native system might not store their bytes in the same order, so we use a special set of buffer classes and create a ByteBuffer large enough to hold our data and tell it to store its data using the native byte order. This is an extra step we need to do before passing our data to OpenGL. To do that, let's add another method to the Sphere class; Listing 9-9 shows the contents of the **createBuffers()** method.

Listing 9-9. createBuffers()

```
private FloatBuffer vertBuffer;  ❶
private ShortBuffer facesBuffer;

// some other statements

private void createBuffers() {

  // BUFFER FOR VERTICES
  ByteBuffer buffer1 = ByteBuffer.allocateDirect(vertList.
  size() * 3 * 4);  ❷
  buffer1.order(ByteOrder.nativeOrder());
  vertBuffer = buffer1.asFloatBuffer();

  // BUFFER FOR FACES
  ByteBuffer buffer2 = ByteBuffer.allocateDirect(facesList.
  size() * 3 * 2);  ❸
  buffer2.order(ByteOrder.nativeOrder());
  facesBuffer = buffer2.asShortBuffer();

  for(String vertex: vertList) {  ❹

    String coords[] = vertex.split(" ");  ❺
    float x = Float.parseFloat(coords[1]);
    float y = Float.parseFloat(coords[2]);
    float z = Float.parseFloat(coords[3]);
    vertBuffer.put(x);
    vertBuffer.put(y);
    vertBuffer.put(z);

  }

  vertBuffer.position(0);  ❻
```

```
for(String face: facesList) {
  String vertexIndices[] = face.split(" ");  ❼
  short vertex1 = Short.parseShort(vertexIndices[1]);
  short vertex2 = Short.parseShort(vertexIndices[2]);
  short vertex3 = Short.parseShort(vertexIndices[3]);
  facesBuffer.put((short)(vertex1 - 1));  ❽
  facesBuffer.put((short)(vertex2 - 1));
  facesBuffer.put((short)(vertex3 - 1));
 }
}
```

❶   You have to add FloatBuffer and ShortBuffer member variables to the
        Sphere class. We will use this to hold the vertices and faces data.

❷   Initialize the buffer using the **allocateDirect()** method. We're allocating
        4 bytes for each coordinate (because they are float numbers). Once
        the buffer is created, we convert it to a FloatBuffer by calling the
        asFloatBuffer() method.

❸   Similarly, we initialize a ByteBuffer for the faces, but this time, we allocate
        only 2 bytes for each vertex index, because the indices are unsigned
        short. Next, we call the **asShortBuffer()** method to convert the ByteBuffer
        to a ShortBuffer.

❹   To parse the vertices List object, we go through it using Java's enhanced
        for-loop.

❺   Each entry in the vertices List object is a line that holds the X,Y,Z position
        of the vertex, like **0.723607 -0.447220 0.525725**; it's separated by a
        space. So, we use the **split()** method of the String object using a white
        space as delimiter. This call will return an array of String with three
        elements. We convert these elements to float numbers and populate the
        FloatBuffer.

❻   Reset the position of the buffer.

❼   Same drill we did like in the vertices List, we split them into array
         elements, but this time convert them to short.

❽   The indices start from 1 (not zero); so, we subtract 1 to the converted
         value before we add it to the ShortBuffer.

The next step is to create the shaders. We can't render our 3D sphere
if we don't create the shaders; we need a vertex shader and a fragment
shader. A shader is written in a C-like language called OpenGL Shading
Language (GLSL for short).

A vertex shader is responsible for a 3D object's vertices, while a
fragment shader (also called a pixel shader) handles the coloring of the 3D
object's pixels.

To create the vertex shader, add a file to the project's assets folder and
name it **vertex_shader.txt**, as shown in Figure 9-14.

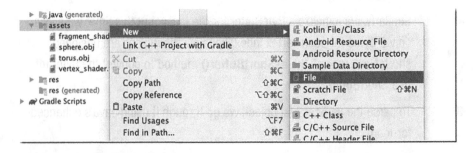

Figure 9-14. New file

In the window that follows (Figure 9-15), enter the name of the file.

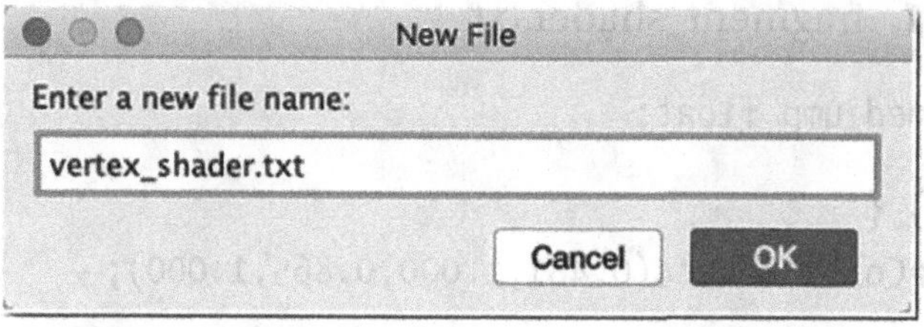

Figure 9-15. *Enter a new file name*

Modify the newly created **vertex_shader.txt** to match the contents of Listing 9-10.

Listing 9-10. vertex_shader.txt

```
attribute vec4 position; ❶
uniform mat4 matrix; ❷

void main() {
    gl_Position = matrix * position; ❸
}
```

---

❶   The **attribute** global variable receives the vertex position data from our Java program.

❷   This is the **uniform** global variable view-project matrix from our Java code.

❸   Inside the **main()** function, we set the value of **gl_position** (a GLSL built-in variable) to the product of the uniform and attribute global variables.

Next, we create the fragment shader. Like what we did in vertex_shader, add a file to the project and name it **fragment_shader.txt**. Modify the contents of the fragment shader program to match Listing 9-11.

Listing 9-11. fragment_shader.txt

```
precision mediump float;

void main() {
    gl_FragColor = vec4(0.481,1.000,0.865,1.000);
}
```

It's a minimalistic fragment shader code; it basically assigns a light green color to all the pixels.

The next step is to load these shaders into our Java program and compile them. We will add another method to the Sphere class named **createShaders()**; its contents are shown in Listing 9-12.

Listing 9-12. createShaders()

```
// class definition and other statements

private int vertexShader;   ❶
private int fragmentShader;

private void createShaders() {
  try {
    Scanner scannerFrag = new Scanner(ctx.getAssets()
                              .open("fragment_shader.txt"));  ❷
    Scanner scannerVert = new Scanner(ctx.getAssets()
                              .open("vertex_shader.txt"));  ❸

    StringBuilder sbFrag = new StringBuilder();  ❹
    StringBuilder sbVert = new StringBuilder();

    while (scannerFrag.hasNext()) {
      sbFrag.append(scannerFrag.nextLine());  ❺
    }
```

```
  while(scannerVert.hasNext()) {
    sbVert.append(scannerVert.nextLine());
  }
  String vertexShaderCode = new String(sbVert.toString()); ❻
  String fragmentShaderCode = new String(sbFrag.toString());

  Log.d(TAG, vertexShaderCode);

  vertexShader = GLES20.glCreateShader(GLES20.GL_VERTEX_
  SHADER); ❼
  GLES20.glShaderSource(vertexShader, vertexShaderCode);

  fragmentShader = GLES20.glCreateShader(GLES20.GL_FRAGMENT_
  SHADER);
  GLES20.glShaderSource(fragmentShader, fragmentShaderCode);
  GLES20.glCompileShader(vertexShader);   ❽
  GLES20.glCompileShader(fragmentShader);
}
catch(IOException ioe) {
  Log.e(TAG, ioe.getMessage());
}
}
```

---

❶   Add member variable declarations for **vertexShader** and **fragmentShader**.

❷   Open **fragment_shader.txt** for reading.

❸   Open **vertex_shader.txt** for reading.

❹   Create a StringBuffer to hold the partial Strings we will read from the Scanner object; do this for both fragment_shader.txt and vertex_shader.txt.

❺   Append the current line to the StringBuffer (do this for both StringBuffer objects).

301

❻   When all the lines in the Scanner object have been read and appended to the StringBuffer, we create a new String object. Do this for both StringBuffers.

❼   The shader's code must be added to the shader objects of OpenGL ES. We create a new shader using the **glCreateShader()** method, then we set the shader source using the newly created shader and the shader program code; do this for both vertex_shader and fragment_shader.

❽   Finally, compile the shaders.

Before we can use the shaders, we need to link them to a program. We can't use the shaders directly. This is what connects the output of the vertex shader with the input of the fragment shader. It's also what lets us pass an input from our program and use the shader to draw our shapes.

We'll create a new program object, and if that turns out well, we'll attach the shaders. Let's add a new method to the Sphere class and name it **runProgram()**; the code for this method is shown in Listing 9-13.

Listing 9-13. runProgram()

```
private int program; ❶

// other statements

private void runProgram() {

  program = GLES20.glCreateProgram(); ❷
  GLES20.glAttachShader(program, vertexShader); ❸
  GLES20.glAttachShader(program, fragmentShader); ❹

  GLES20.glLinkProgram(program); ❺
  GLES20.glUseProgram(program);
}
```

---

❶   You need to create the **program** as a member variable in the Sphere class.

❷   Use the **glCreateProgram()** method to create a program.

❸   Attach the vertex shader to the program.

❹   Attach the fragment shader to the program.

❺   To start using the program, we need to link it using the **glLinkProgram()** method and put it to use via the **glUseProgram()** method.

Now that all the buffers and the shaders are ready, we can finally draw something to the screen. Let's add another method to the Sphere class and name it **draw()**; the code for this method is shown in Listing 9-14.

Listing 9-14. draw()

```
import android.opengl.Matrix; ❶

// class definition and other statements

public void draw() {

    int position = GLES20.glGetAttribLocation(program,
    "position"); ❷
    GLES20.glEnableVertexAttribArray(position);
    GLES20.glVertexAttribPointer(position, 3, GLES20.GL_FLOAT,
    false, 3 * 4, vertBuffer); ❸

    float[] projectionMatrix = new float[16]; ❹
    float[] viewMatrix = new float[16];
    float[] productMatrix = new float[16];

    Matrix.frustumM(projectionMatrix, 0, -1, 1, -1, 1, 2, 9); ❺
    Matrix.setLookAtM(viewMatrix, 0, 0, 3, -4, 0, 0, 0, 0, 1,
    0f); ❻
```

```
Matrix.multiplyMM(productMatrix, 0, projectionMatrix, 0,
viewMatrix, 0);

int matrix = GLES20.glGetUniformLocation(program, "matrix"); ❼
GLES20.glUniformMatrix4fv(matrix, 1, false, productMatrix, 0);

GLES20.glDrawElements(GLES20.GL_TRIANGLES, facesList.size() * 3,
                      GLES20.GL_UNSIGNED_SHORT,
                      facesBuffer); ❽
GLES20.glDisableVertexAttribArray(position);

}
```

❶   You need to import the Matrix class.

❷   If you remember in the **vertex_shader.txt**, we defined a **position** variable
      that's supposed to receive vertex position data from our Java code; we're
      about to send that data to this **position** variable. To do that, we must first
      get a reference of the **position** variable in the vertex_shader. We do that
      using the **glGetAttribLocation()** method, and then we enable it using the
      glEnableVertexAttribArray() method.

❸   Point the **position** handle to the vertices buffer. The **glVertexAttribPointer()**
      method also expects the number of coordinates per vertex and the byte offset
      per vertex. Each coordinate is a float, so the byte offset is **3 * 4**.

❹   Our vertex shader expects a view-projection matrix, which is the product
      of the view and projection matrices. A **view matrix** allows us to specify the
      locations of the camera and the point it's looking at. A **projection matrix** lets
      us map the square coordinates of the Android device and also specify the
      near and far planes of the viewing frustum. We simply create float arrays for
      these matrices.

❺   Initialize the projection matrix using the **frustumM()** method of the Matrix class. You need to pass some arguments to this method; it expects the locations of the left, right, bottom, top, near, and far clip planes. When we defined the GLSurfaceView in our activity_main layout file, it's already a square, so we can use the values **-1 and 1** for the near and far clip planes.

❻   The **setLookAtM()** method is used to initialize the view matrix. It expects the positions of the camera and the point it is looking at. Then calculate the product matrix using the **multiplyMM()** method.

❼   Let's pass the product matrix to the shader using the **glGetUniformLocation()** method. When we get the handle (the **matrix** variable), point it to the product matrix using the **glUniformMatrix4fv()** method.

❽   The **glDrawElements()** method lets us use the faces buffer to create triangles; its arguments expect the total number of vertex indices, the type of each index, and the faces buffer.

Now that we've got the methods to load the vertices from a blender file, create all the buffers, compile the shaders, and create an OpenGL program, we can now tie all these methods together in the constructor of the Sphere class, as shown in Listing 9-15.

Listing 9-15. Constructor of the Sphere class

```
public Sphere(Context context) {

  ctx = context;
  vertList = new ArrayList<>();
  facesList = new ArrayList<>();
```

```
loadVertices();
createBuffers();
createShaders();
runProgram();
```

}

After adding all these methods, it may be difficult to keep the code straight. So, I'm showing all the contents of the Sphere class in Listing 9-16, for your reference.

Listing 9-16. Complete code for the Sphere class

```java
import android.content.Context;

import java.io.IOException;
import java.nio.ByteBuffer;
import java.nio.ByteOrder;
import java.nio.FloatBuffer;
import java.nio.ShortBuffer;
import java.util.ArrayList;
import java.util.List;
import java.util.Scanner;
import android.opengl.GLES20;
import android.opengl.Matrix;
import android.util.Log;

public class Sphere {
    private FloatBuffer vertBuffer;
    private ShortBuffer facesBuffer;
    private List<String> vertList;
    private List<String> facesList;
    private Context ctx;
    private final String TAG = getClass().getName();
```

```java
private int vertexShader;
private int fragmentShader;

private int program;

public Sphere(Context context) {

  ctx = context;
  vertList = new ArrayList<>();
  facesList = new ArrayList<>();

  loadVertices();
  createBuffers();
  createShaders();
  runProgram();

}

private void loadVertices() {

  try {
    Scanner scanner = new Scanner(ctx.getAssets().
    open("sphere.obj"));
    while(scanner.hasNextLine()) {
      String line = scanner.nextLine();
      if(line.startsWith("v ")) {
        vertList.add(line);
      } else if(line.startsWith("f ")) {
        facesList.add(line);
      }
    }
    scanner.close();
  }
```

```java
catch(IOException ioe) {
  Log.e(TAG, ioe.getMessage());
}
}

private void createBuffers() {

  // BUFFER FOR VERTICES
  ByteBuffer buffer1 = ByteBuffer.allocateDirect(vertList.
  size() * 3 * 4);
  buffer1.order(ByteOrder.nativeOrder());
  vertBuffer = buffer1.asFloatBuffer();

  // BUFFER FOR FACES
  ByteBuffer buffer2 = ByteBuffer.allocateDirect(facesList.
  size() * 3 * 2);
  buffer2.order(ByteOrder.nativeOrder());
  facesBuffer = buffer2.asShortBuffer();

  for(String vertex: vertList) {
    String coords[] = vertex.split(" ");
    float x = Float.parseFloat(coords[1]);
    float y = Float.parseFloat(coords[2]);
    float z = Float.parseFloat(coords[3]);
    vertBuffer.put(x);
    vertBuffer.put(y);
    vertBuffer.put(z);

  }

  vertBuffer.position(0);

  for(String face: facesList) {
    String vertexIndices[] = face.split(" ");
    short vertex1 = Short.parseShort(vertexIndices[1]);
```

```
    short vertex2 = Short.parseShort(vertexIndices[2]);
    short vertex3 = Short.parseShort(vertexIndices[3]);
    facesBuffer.put((short)(vertex1 - 1));
    facesBuffer.put((short)(vertex2 - 1));
    facesBuffer.put((short)(vertex3 - 1));
  }

  facesBuffer.position(0);
}

private void createShaders() {

  try {
    Scanner scannerFrag = new Scanner(ctx.getAssets()
                                  .open("fragment_shader.txt"));
    Scanner scannerVert = new Scanner(ctx.getAssets()
                                  .open("vertex_shader.txt"));

    StringBuilder sbFrag = new StringBuilder();
    StringBuilder sbVert = new StringBuilder();

    while (scannerFrag.hasNext()) {
      sbFrag.append(scannerFrag.nextLine());
    }

    while(scannerVert.hasNext()) {
      sbVert.append(scannerVert.nextLine());
    }

    String vertexShaderCode = new String(sbVert.toString());
    String fragmentShaderCode = new String(sbFrag.toString());

    Log.d(TAG, vertexShaderCode);
```

```java
    vertexShader = GLES20.glCreateShader(GLES20.GL_VERTEX_
    SHADER);
    GLES20.glShaderSource(vertexShader, vertexShaderCode);

    fragmentShader = GLES20.glCreateShader(GLES20.GL_
    FRAGMENT_SHADER);
    GLES20.glShaderSource(fragmentShader, fragmentShaderCode);

    GLES20.glCompileShader(vertexShader);
    GLES20.glCompileShader(fragmentShader);
  }
  catch(IOException ioe) {
    Log.e(TAG, ioe.getMessage());
  }
}

private void runProgram() {
  program = GLES20.glCreateProgram();
  GLES20.glAttachShader(program, vertexShader);
  GLES20.glAttachShader(program, fragmentShader);
  GLES20.glLinkProgram(program);

  GLES20.glUseProgram(program);
}

public void draw() {
  int position = GLES20.glGetAttribLocation(program,
  "position");
  GLES20.glEnableVertexAttribArray(position);
  GLES20.glVertexAttribPointer(position, 3, GLES20.GL_FLOAT,
  false, 3 * 4, vertBuffer);
```

```java
float[] projectionMatrix = new float[16];
float[] viewMatrix = new float[16];
float[] productMatrix = new float[16];

Matrix.frustumM(projectionMatrix, 0, -1, 1, -1, 1, 2, 9);

Matrix.setLookAtM(viewMatrix, 0, 0, 3, -4, 0, 0, 0, 0, 1, 0f);

Matrix.multiplyMM(productMatrix, 0, projectionMatrix, 0,
viewMatrix, 0);

int matrix = GLES20.glGetUniformLocation(program, "matrix");
GLES20.glUniformMatrix4fv(matrix, 1, false, productMatrix, 0);

GLES20.glDrawElements(GLES20.GL_TRIANGLES, facesList.
size() * 3, GLES20.GL_UNSIGNED_SHORT, facesBuffer);
GLES20.glDisableVertexAttribArray(position);

    }
}
```

Now that all of the code for the Sphere class is complete, we can go back to MainActivity. Remember in MainActivity that we created a Renderer object using an anonymous inner class. We created that renderer because a GLSurfaceView needs a renderer object so that it can, well, render 3D graphics. Listing 9-17 shows the complete code for MainActivity.

Listing 9-17. MainActivity, complete

```java
public class MainActivity extends AppCompatActivity {

    private GLSurfaceView glView;
    private Sphere sphere;   ❶
```

```
@Override
protected void onCreate(Bundle savedInstanceState) {
  super.onCreate(savedInstanceState);
  setContentView(R.layout.activity_main);

  glView = findViewById(R.id.gl_view);

  ActivityManager am = (ActivityManager)
getSystemService(Context.ACTIVITY_SERVICE);
  ConfigurationInfo ci = am.getDeviceConfigurationInfo();

  boolean isES2Supported = ci.reqGlEsVersion > 0x20000;

  if(isES2Supported) {

    glView.setEGLContextClientVersion(2);
    glView.setRenderer(new GLSurfaceView.Renderer() {
      @Override
      public void onSurfaceCreated(GL10 gl10, EGLConfig
      eglConfig) {
        glView.setRenderMode(GLSurfaceView.RENDERMODE_WHEN_
        DIRTY);
        sphere = new Sphere(getApplicationContext()); ❷
      }

      @Override
      public void onSurfaceChanged(GL10 gl10, int width,
      int height) {
        GLES20.glViewport(0,0, width, height);
      }
```

```
  @Override
  public void onDrawFrame(GL10 gl10) {
    sphere.draw(); ❸
  }
});
}
else {

}
}
}
```

---

❶   Create a member variable as a reference to the sphere object we're about to create.

❷   Create the sphere object; pass the current context as an argument.

❸   Call the **draw()** method of the sphere.

At this point, you're ready to run the app. Figure 9-16 shows the app at runtime.

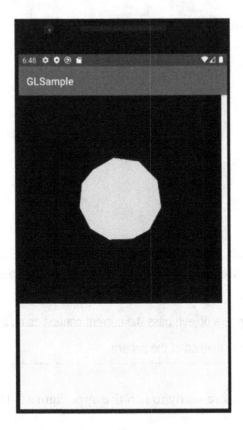

Figure 9-16. *Icosphere rendered in OpenGL ES*

After nearly 300 lines of code, all we got was a little green Icosphere without much definition. Welcome to OpenGL ES programming. This should give you an idea how involved and how much work goes into an OpenGL ES game.

Key Takeaways

- Starting with Android 3 (API level 11), drawings done on the Canvas already enjoy hardware acceleration, so it's not a bad choice of tech for game programming. However, if the visual complexities of your game exceed the capabilities of the Canvas, you should consider drawing the graphics using OpenGL ES.

- OpenGL ES is really good at just drawing triangles, not much else. It gives you a lot of control though on how you draw those triangles. With it, you can control the camera, the light source, and the texture, among other things.

- Android SDK already has built-in support for OpenGL ES. The GLSurfaceView, which is what you will typically use for drawing OpenGL ES objects, is already included in the SDK.

CHAPTER 10

Monetization

If you want to release your game for free, after pouring blood, sweat, and tears into it, that's cool! Everybody wants a free game. You can skip this chapter altogether. On the other hand, if you want some ideas on how you can get paid, then read on. This chapter is about that. Here's what we'll cover:

- Pricing models
- Freemium
- Advertising
- Discoverability

Paid or Free

You must decide whether the game is paid or released for free. Once the app has been released for free, it cannot be changed to paid. A paid app, however, may be switched to free at a later time. Releasing the app as paid is a straightforward way of getting paid for your efforts; build the app, release the app, and ask money for it.

© Ted Hagos, Mario Zechner, J.F. DiMarzio and Robert Green 2020
T. Hagos et al., *Beginning Android Games Development*,
https://doi.org/10.1007/978-1-4842-6121-7_10

You can also release your game for free, but how can you build an income stream if you're giving it away? Some developers have taken the "free with ads" route, and while many are still doing this, you might want to consider other forms of income stream because of sheer competition. The prevailing thought is there are a lot of mobile apps advertising and not a lot of money behind the ads, so money is spread thinly. The basic idea is you offer the game for free and you display adverts to generate income. The key measurement to watch for here is CTR, which is short for click-through rate. CTR is the number of ads that were tapped divided by the number of ads displayed (impressions) expressed as a percentage. If you displayed 100 adverts and the user tapped twice, the CTR is 2%; the more people playing your game, the more adverts you display and the more chances for a higher CTR; that's the basic idea.

Ads aren't all created equal; some have higher potential than others. A banner ad, let's say, for example, has a CTR of 0.02%; if your game displays 100,000 impressions, you get 200 clicks; at $0.05 per click, that's $10. If your app is getting 100,000 impressions per month, you might want to think first before giving up that day job. Just doing this math, you can figure out how much impressions a game needs to get to a $1000 revenue.

Fortunately, adverts aren't the only way to make money with free games. A decade or so ago, the freemium pricing model got into mainstream consciousness. Freemium is a portmanteau of the words "free" and "premium." It's a pricing strategy where you can release a game for free and derive income somewhere else, like in-app purchases, virtual currencies, and so on.

Freemium

If you look at Google's top grossing apps (`https://bit.ly/topgrossingapps`), you'll find that quite a few of them are free; to be more precise, they're freemium. They're free to use and download, but they also have in-app purchases that cost real money. These purchases allow the users to buy extra content, for example, levels, new characters, costumes, virtual currencies, or coins, which can be used for upgrades. There are many more that you can buy in an in-app purchase, but these are the popular ones. The freemium model is very successful, but it requires more development work. On the side of the users, it works to their advantage because there is no cost in trying out the game. If they like it and they've invested some playing hours already, they're more likely to spend real money to buy more content. Going freemium is more work because of two things:

1. The extra content isn't defined in the game itself, it's defined somewhere in Google Play, which means you need to spend time in administering Google Play. When the items are defined, your game can then query Google Play to get a list of items available for purchase.

2. When new game content has been bought (and downloaded), the game needs to change its behavior. The changes in game behavior depending on the content available need to factor into the overall structure of the game; this adds to the programming complexity.

By the way, going for the freemium model isn't mutually exclusive with adverts, neither is it mutually exclusive with paid apps. There are shady developers who might release a paid app with adverts and then offer an in-app purchase to remove the ads. It's not difficult to see how this can backfire. When the users start leaving comments and tell other users of the unsavory maneuver, it's game over.

In-app Purchase

In-app purchases (IAP) or in-app products refer to the buying of goods and services from inside an application on a mobile device. The idea is that the player wants something that's offered in your game, and he's willing to pay a small amount of money to get it. There are two types of in-app product options given on the Google Play Store:

- **Managed items**—These are items that can only be purchased once. They are attached to the buyer and not the device. Google Play keeps track of these purchases, which allows the user to query these items at a later time for restoration; also, if the buyer tries to purchase an item that they have already purchased, Google Play will respond that "the item has already been purchased." Examples of managed items are levels, characters, or abilities.

- **Unmanaged items**—These are items that get used up by the user, like coins, virtual currencies (VC), or anything that needs to be "refilled." Unmanaged items aren't tracked by Google Play; the user cannot "restore" these purchases at a later time. If you wish to track unmanaged items, you need to write code for that in your game. Like managed items, these items are also attached to the Google account and not the device.

Another monetization option related to IAPs is "subscriptions." Google Play allows you to set up subscriptions that bill at regular intervals. A subscription is seen by your app as simply "on" or "off." When it's "on," the user is allowed continuous access to content or services for a fee. The player can enjoy whatever your game has to offer while they are subscribed.

Virtual Currency

Virtual currency is in-game money. They're called by many names; in some games, they're called gold, coins, rubies, credits, and so on. VCs are points or numbers that your game stores for the player; and it allows the player to do or buy things while in the game. With VCs, the player can buy hints, upgraded weaponry, more health, and so on.

VCs can (usually) be acquired either by earning them while playing the game or by simply buying them (from Google Play, as unmanaged items) in exchange for real money.

Advertising

If you're considering putting ads on the game, you need to get familiar with the ad providers; they deliver the ads from advertisers and pay you for the clicks. The money is split between you and the ad provider (it's not split in the middle). A portion of the money goes to you (the game publisher) and the rest of the money goes to the ad provider, which is how the provider makes money. You'll need to configure some keywords for the app, so the ads are more relevant; this is where you need a bit of SEO background and keyword wizardry. The ads can be in a variety of formats, but the common ones are banner and full-page ads. Here are some of the major ad providers and aggregators:

- AdMob (https://admob.google.com)
- Verizon Media (https://bit.ly/verizonmedia)
- MoPub (www.mopub.com/)

These services have their own APIs which are generally easy to use. Visit their websites for the technical documentation.

It's easy to get excited when implementing ads, and you might overdo it. Just remember that the goal for displaying ads is to make money. There's a sweet spot between displaying ads and irritating your users; the law of diminishing returns clearly applies here. Users can get annoyed if there's too much interruption brought about by ads; when that happens, the user base could shrink—your revenues will follow.

Getting your Game Discovered

There are thousands of games available already (approx. 300,000 in Google Play, at the time of writing) with many more on the way. This is red ocean territory; it's a very crowded place; but there is no shortage of success stories. So, how do you get your games noticed? How do you make people aware that your game is out in Google Play and that it's awesome? Well, you can always spend a lot of money on advertisements, or you can try the things outlined in this section.

Social Network

Facebook and Twitter are heavy hitters in social media. I'm assuming you've already used these platforms by now. There are many tactics in using social media to get your game some mindshare. You could always do what a lot of people are already doing, like building a Facebook page and "boosting" the page (you have to pay for that). Together with that, you can tell your friends to like that page. That may get you a couple of downloads, but that's it—unless you have millions of friends or followers. I'm assuming you don't have that many, so let's keep looking.

A few of the great things about these two social networking sites from a marketing perspective are that nearly everyone uses them, they are free to use, and they are friendly to more creative solutions. Here are some examples of how you can exploit these websites to market your game: Give 50 free VC credits to users who "like" your game on Facebook. Give 50 free VC credits to users who mention your game in a tweet.

Hold a high-score contest once a month where the prize is a new Android device, and only allow people to register if they've liked you on Facebook. In the last example, you'd have to actually purchase a device to give away as a prize, of course, but as far as incentivizing "likes" goes, such a strategy can work really well. It's easy to create incentives to get people to share your game with each other, and these networks are the perfect platform for that kind of information sharing.

Both Facebook and Twitter provide Android SDKs that you can download and use to integrate the networks with your game. The API integration docs are generally easy to follow, so make sure to try them out.

Discovery Services

There are companies such as AppBrain (`https://appbrain.com`) whose sole purpose is to help you get your game discovered. Other companies, such as Tapjoy (`www.tapjoy.com`) and Flurry (`www.flurry.com`), also have discovery services. Most of these services provide ways to put your game "in network" so that it will be promoted by other games. You can pay for installs and control a campaign to get your game into the hands of numerous people.

Different companies offer different methods of discovery, but, in short, if you're looking to get your game discovered and you have a budget to work with, you may want to look into one or more of these services. When you combine such a service with a good social networking strategy, you might just get the snowball rolling and create a buzz about your game.

Blogs and Web Media

Another strategy for getting your game discovered is to put together pilots for stories, create videos for demos, and send all of this to blogs that review new Android apps and games. The editors of these sites are bombarded with requests to review apps and games, so do as much work for them as possible by giving them all the information they need up front.

Game Design

I mentioned earlier that a game with in-app purchase capabilities is more complex to develop and administer. It's better to anticipate the structural complexities warranted on the outset if you want to monetize the game rather than retrofitting an already finished game for monetization. A game that's designed for monetization may have one or more of the following elements:

- Optional modifiers that affect gameplay
  - Boost
  - Upgrades
  - Cheats
- Optional content that does not affect gameplay
  - Skins
  - Characters
- Additional content
  - New levels
  - New cinematics
  - New parts
  - Unlockable parts of levels

- Virtual currency that

  - Can be acquired by simply playing the game

  - Can be purchased using real money

  - Can be used to purchase upgrades in the game

  - Can be used to purchase additional content

Also, during the early planning stage, make the game discoverable by design; these kinds of games provide incentives for players to tell other people about the game. Much like a game that's designed to be monetized, a game that's designed to be discoverable incorporates most or all of the same elements (virtual currency, virtual goods, unlockables, additional content, etc.) as incentives for telling other people about the game. Here are some ideas on how to do this:

- Make a piece of content that can only be unlocked by entering a referral code received from another player.

- Give additional content or VC for tweeting about the game or sharing or liking it on Facebook.

- Award players with VC for all referrals they make to other players.

- Integrate with Facebook or other social media to post achievements and new high scores.

- Create another part of the game that is played as a Facebook app but ties into the mobile game in some way.

Key Takeaways

- There are plenty of ways to monetize your game; you can straight up just sell it for a few dollars a pop; that's it and that's all. You can release it for free and offer in-app purchases within the game. You can also release the game for free and get revenue by displaying adverts; or you can use a combination of all three.

- Use social networking creatively when promoting your game; there are far more cost-effective ways than simply throwing money on adverts.

- A monetizable game is more complex and hence more difficult to develop; but make sure that monetizing the game isn't an afterthought. You need to include monetization strategies during the planning stage of game development and design.

CHAPTER 11

Publishing the Game

You can distribute your games quite freely and without much restrictions; you can let your users download it from your website, Google Drive, Dropbox, and so on; you may even email the game APK directly to the users, if you wish; but many developers choose to distribute their apps or games on a marketplace like Google or Amazon to maximize reach.

In this chapter, we'll discuss the things you need to do to get your game out in Google Play. Here's what we'll cover:

- Preparing for release

- Signing the app

- Google Play

- App bundle

Prepare the Project for Release

There are three things you need to keep in mind when preparing for release; these are

- Prepare the material and assets for release

- Configure the project for release

- Build a release-ready app

© Ted Hagos, Mario Zechner, J.F. DiMarzio and Robert Green 2020
T. Hagos et al., *Beginning Android Games Development*,
https://doi.org/10.1007/978-1-4842-6121-7_11

Prepare Material and Assets for Release

Your code is great and you might even think it's clever, but the user will never see it. What they will see are your View objects, the icons, and the other graphical assets. You should polish them.

If you think the app's icon isn't a big deal, that could be a mistake. The icons help the users identify your app as it sits on the home screen. This icon also appears on other areas like the launcher window and the downloads section, and more importantly, it appears on Google Play. The icon weighs in a lot in creating the first impressions of the users about your game. It's a good idea to put some work into this and read Google's guidelines for icons which can be found here: `http://bit.ly/ androidreleaseiconguidelines`.

Other things to consider if you will publish in Google's marketplace are graphical assets like screen captures and the text for promotional copy. Make sure to read Google's guidelines for graphical assets which can be found here: `http://bit.ly/androidreleasegraphicassets`.

Configure the App for Release

1. **Check the package name**—You may want to check the package name of the app. Make sure it isn't still com.example.myapp. The package name makes the app unique across Google marketplace; and once you decide on a package name, you can't change it anymore. So, give it some thought.

2. **Deal with the debug information**—Make sure you remove the `android:debuggable` attribute in the `<application>` tag of the Manifest file.

3. **Remove the log statements**—Different developers do this differently. Some would painstakingly go through the code and remove the statements manually. Some would write sed or awk programs to strip away the log statements. Some would use ProGuard, and others would use third-party tools like Timber to take care of logging activities. It's up to you which you will use; but make sure that your users won't accidentally see the log information.

4. **Check the application's permissions**—Sometime during development, you may have experimented on some features of the application, and you may have set permissions on the manifest like permission to use the network, write to external storage, and so on. Review the **<uses-permission>** tag on the manifest and make sure that you don't grant permissions that the game does not need.

5. **Check remote servers and URLs**—If the game relies on web APIs or cloud services, make sure that the release build is using production URLs and not test paths. You may have been given sandboxes and test URLs during development; you need to switch them up to the production version.

Build a Release-Ready Application

During development, Android Studio did quite a few things for you; it

- Created a debug certificate
- Assembled all your project's assets, config files, and runtime binaries into an APK

- Signed the APK using a debug certificate

- Deployed the APK to an emulator or a connected device

All these things happened in the background; you didn't have to do anything else but write your code. Now, you need to take care of that certificate. Google Play and other similar marketplaces won't distribute an app that's signed with a debug certificate. It needs to be a proper certificate. You don't need to go to a certificate authority like Thawte or Verisign; a self-signed certificate will suffice. Also, make sure to keep that certificate; when you make updates to the app, you will need to sign it with the same certificate.

In the next steps, you'll see how to generate a signed bundle or APK; you already know what an APK is—it's the package that contains your application. It's what you upload to Google Play. A bundle, on the other hand, is a lot like an APK but it's a newer upload format. Like the APK, it also includes all your app's compiled code and resources, but it defers APK generation. It's Google Play's new app serving model called Dynamic Delivery. It uses your app bundle to generate and serve optimized APK for each user's device configuration—so they download only the code and resources that they need to run your app. You don't have to build, sign, and manage multiple APKs anymore.

In Android Studio, the steps to generate an APK and a bundle are almost identical. In the following steps, we'll see how to generate both the bundle and an APK.

Launch Android Studio, if you haven't done so yet. Open the project, then from the main menu bar, go to **Build ➤ Generate Signed Bundle/ APK**, as shown in Figure 11-1.

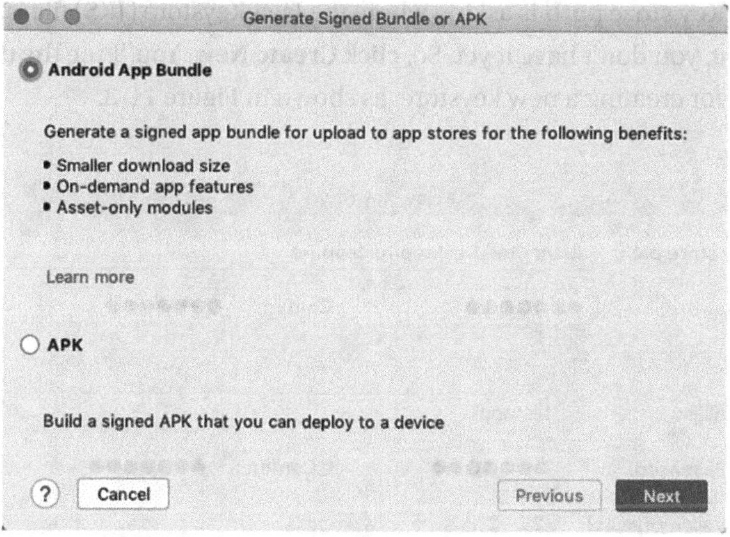

Figure 11-1. *Generate signed APK*

Choose either **Bundle** or **APK**, then click **Next**; in this example, I chose to create a bundle. When you click **Next**, you will see the "Keystore" dialog, as shown in Figure 11-2.

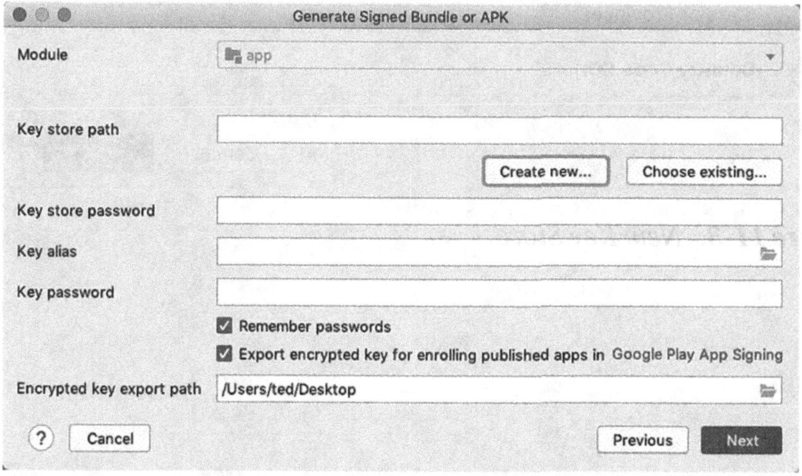

Figure 11-2. *Keystore dialog*

The **Key store path** is asking where the Java Keystore (JKS) file is. At this point, you don't have it yet. So, click **Create New**. You'll see the dialog window for creating a new keystore, as shown in Figure 11-3.

Figure 11-3. *New Key Store*

Table 11-1 shows the description for the input items of the keystore.

Table 11-1. *Keystore items and description*

Keystore items	Description
Keystore path	The location where you want to keep the keystore. This is entirely up to you. Just make sure you remember this location
Password	This is the password for the keystore
Alias	This alias identifies the key. It's just a friendly name for it
(Key) Password	This is the password for the key. This is **NOT** the same password as the keystore's (but you can use the same password if you like)
Validity, in years	The default is 25 years; you can just accept the default. If publish on Google Play, the certificate must be valid until October of 2033—so, 25 years should be fine
Other information	Only the first and last name fields are required

When you're done filling up the New Key Store dialog, click OK. This will bring you back to the Generate Signed Bundle or APK window, as shown in Figure 11-4; but now, the JKS file is created and the Keystore dialog is populated with it.

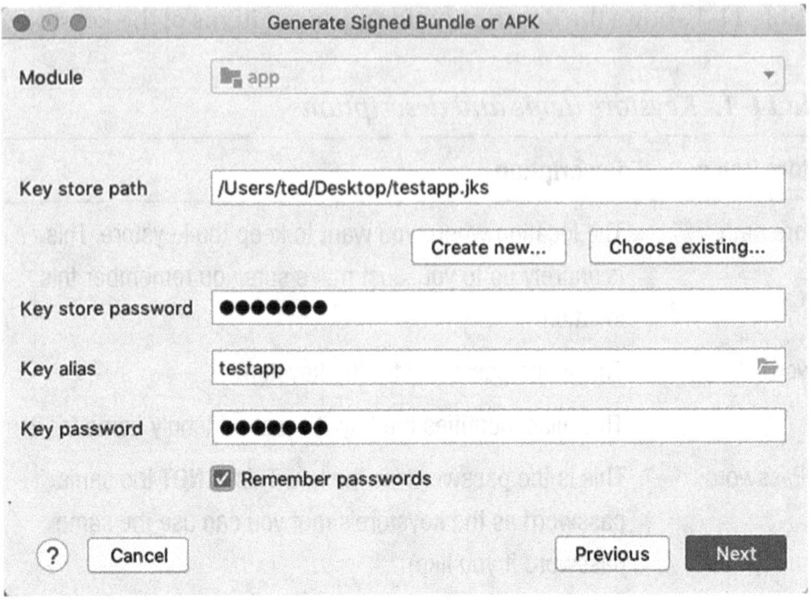

Figure 11-4. Generate Signed Bundle or APK, populated

Click Next. Now we choose the destination of the signed bundle as shown in Figure 11-5.

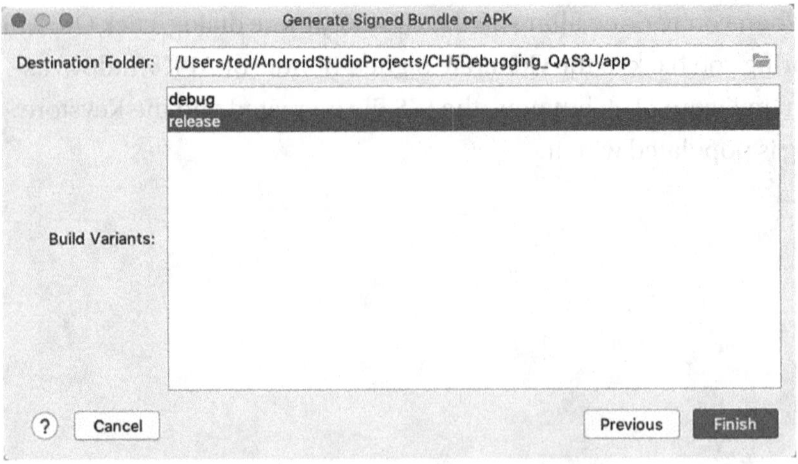

Figure 11-5. Signed APK, APK destination folder

You need to remember the location of the "Destination Folder," as shown in Figure 11-5. This is where Android Studio will store the signed bundle. Also, make sure that the **Build Variants** is set to "release."

When you click Finish, Android Studio will generate the signed bundle for your app. This is the file that you will submit to Google Play.

Releasing the App

Before you can submit an app to Google Play, you'll need a developer account. If you don't have one yet, you can sign up at https://developer. android.com. There's a lot of assumptions I'm making about the next activities. I'm assuming that

1. You already have a Google account (Gmail).

2. You're using Google Chrome to go to https:// developer.android.com.

3. Your Google account is logged in to Chrome.

If your Google account isn't logged in to Chrome, you might see something like Figure 11-6. Chrome will ask you to go select an account (or create one).

Figure 11-6. *Choose an account*

When you get your Google account sorted out, you'll be taken to the **developer.android.com** website, as shown in Figure 11-7.

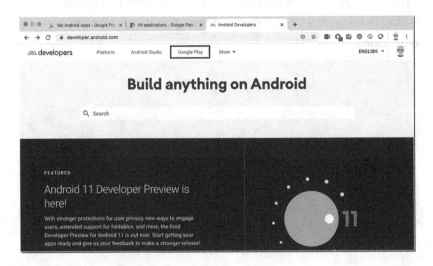

Figure 11-7. *developer.android.com*

Click **Google Play**, as shown in Figure 11-7.

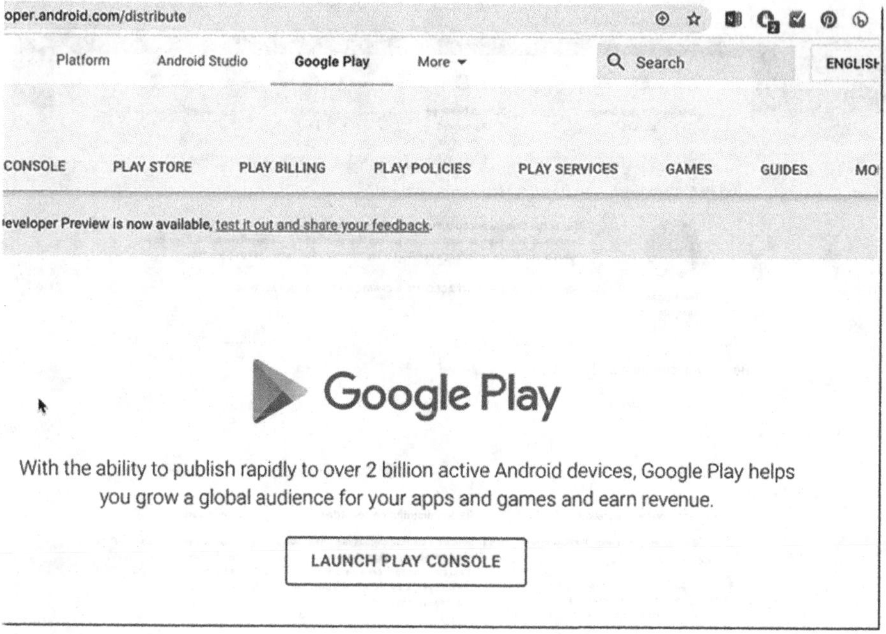

Figure 11-8. *Launch Play Console*

Click **Launch Play Console**, as shown in Figure 11-8.

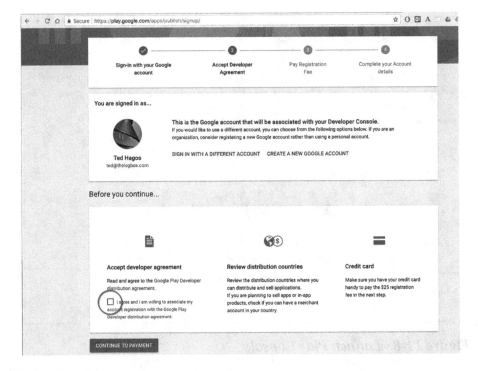

Figure 11-9. *Google Play Console, sign up*

You need to go through four steps to complete the registration, (shown in Figure 11-9):

- Sign in with your Google account.

- Accept the developer agreement.

- Pay the registration fee.

- Complete your account details.

Once you have completed the registration and payment, you will now have access to the Google Play Console, as shown in Figure 11-10.

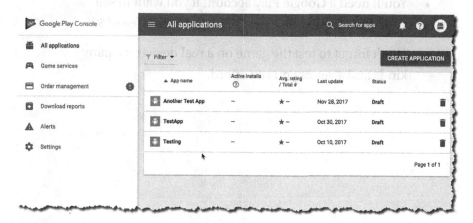

Figure 11-10. *Play Console*

This is where you can start the process of submitting your app to the store. Click the "Create Application" button to get started.

Key Takeaways

- Before the users can experience your game, they will see the icons and other graphical assets first—make sure the graphical assets are just as polished as your code.

- Strip your code of all debug info and log statements before you build a release.

- Code review your own work. If you have buddies or other people who can review the code with you, that's much better. If your app uses servers, RESTful URLs, and so on, make sure they are production ready and not sandboxes.

- Before you can upload your app to Google Play, you need to sign your app with a proper certificate.

- You'll need a Google Play account if you want to sell your apps on Google Play. I paid a one-time fee of $25.

- Don't forget to test the game on a real device, as many kinds and sizes as you can afford.

CHAPTER 12

What's Next

After 11 chapters of learning the basics of Android programming, learning Android Studio, a bit of theory about game development, and two games that were built from scratch, we're just about ready to conclude.

I'm sure you've got some newfound confidence after building those two games from scratch. It's a nice warm feeling when you get to see your work running and humming on that emulator or device; but the learning curve for game programming is steep. The bar is already very high on the quality of games being released nowadays.

In this chapter, we'll look at some areas of interest that you can add to your game programming arsenal. We'll cover the following:

- Android NDK

- Vulkan introduction and basic setup

- Game engines and game frameworks

Android NDK

Quite a few of the gaming resources, libraries, frameworks, or even engines that you'll encounter in game programming will either be written in C or C++. So, you'll need to know how to play nice with these libraries and the languages themselves. Android has a way to work side by side with C/C++. That's the NDK, which is short for Native Development Kit.

© Ted Hagos, Mario Zechner, J.F. DiMarzio and Robert Green 2020
T. Hagos et al., *Beginning Android Games Development*,
https://doi.org/10.1007/978-1-4842-6121-7_12

The NDK is an addition to the Android SDK that lets you write C/
C++ and assembly code that you can then integrate into your Android
application. The NDK consists of a set of Android-specific C libraries, a
cross-compiler toolchain based on the GNU Compiler Collection (GCC)
that compiles to all the different CPU architectures supported by Android
(ARM, x86, and MIPS), and a custom-built system (`https://developer.`
`android.com/ndk/guides/ndk-build`) that should make compiling C/C++
code easier when compared to writing your own make files.

The NDK doesn't expose most of the Android APIs, such as the UI
toolkit. It is mostly intended to speed up some code that can benefit by
writing them in C/C++ and calling them from within Java. Since Android
2.3, Java can be bypassed almost completely by using the NativeActivity
class instead of Java activities. The NativeActivity class is specifically
designed to be used for games with full window control, but it does not
give you access to Java at all, so it can't be used with other Java-based
Android libraries. Many game developers coming from iOS choose that
route because it lets them reuse most of the C/C++ on Android without
having to go too deep into the Android Java APIs. However, the integration
of services such as Facebook authentication or ads still needs to be done
in Java, so designing the game to start in Java and call into C++ via the JNI
(Java Native Interface) is often the most preferred way. With that said, how
does one use the JNI?

The JNI is a way to let the virtual machine (and hence Java code)
communicate with C/C++ code. This works in both directions; you can call
C/C++ code from Java, and you can call Java methods from C/C++. Many
of Android's libraries use this mechanism to expose native code, such as
OpenGL ES or audio decoders.

Once you use JNI, your application consists of two parts: Java code
and C/C++ code. On the Java side, you declare class methods to be
implemented in native code by adding a special qualifier called native. The
code could look like the one in Listing 12-1.

Listing 12-1. NativeSample.java

```
class NativeSample {
  public native void doSomething(String a);
}
```

As you can see, the method we declared doesn't have a method body. When the JVM running your Java code sees this qualifier on a method, it knows that the corresponding implementation is found in a shared library instead of in the JAR file or the APK file.

A shared library is very similar to a Java JAR file. It contains compiled C/C++ code that can be called by any program that loads this shared library. On Windows, these shared libraries usually have the suffix .dll; on Unix systems, they end in .so.

On the C/C++ side, we have a lot of header and source files that define the signature of the native methods in C and contain the actual implementation. The header file for our class in the preceding code would look something like Listing 12-2.

Listing 12-2. NativeSample.h

```
/* DO NOT EDIT THIS FILE - it is machine generated */
#include <jni.h>
/* Header for class NativeSample */

#ifndef _Included_NativeSample
#define _Included_NativeSample
#ifdef __cplusplus
extern "C" {
#endif
/*
```

```
* Class:      NativeSample
* Method:     doSomething
* Signature: (Ljava/lang/String;)V
*/
JNIEXPORT void JNICALL Java_NativeSample_doSomething
  (JNIEnv *, jobject, jstring);

#ifdef __cplusplus
}
#endif
#endif
```

Before Java 10, programmers used **javah** to generate header files like the preceding code, but **javah** became obsolete when Java 10 came about. To generate this header files for JNI, we now use

```
javac NativeSample.java -h .
```

The tool takes a Java class as input and generates a C function signature for any native methods it finds. There's a lot going on here, as the C code needs to follow a specific naming schema and needs to be able to marshal Java types to their corresponding C types (e.g., Java's int becomes a jint in C). We also get two additional parameters of type JNIEnv and jobject. The first can be thought of as a handle to the VM. It contains methods to communicate with the VM, such as to call methods of a class instance. The second parameter is a handle to the class instance on which this method was invoked. We could use this in combination with the JNIEnv parameter to call other methods of this class instance from the C code.

Of course you still need to write the C source file that actually implements the function and compile it before the Java code can use it.

To install the NDK, you need to go to the SDK manager. If you have an open project in Android Studio, go to Preferences or Settings (Windows and Linux); then choose Android SDK, then check the boxes **NDK (Side by side)** and **CMake**, as shown in Figure 12-1, then click OK.

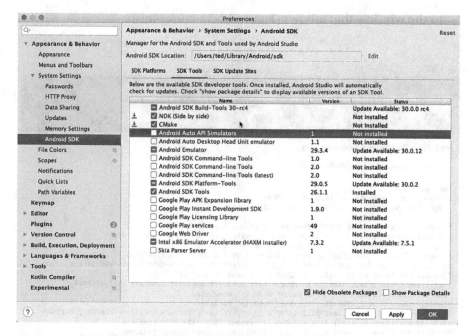

Figure 12-1. *Install CMake and NDK (Side by side)*

In the window that follows (Figure 12-2.), click OK to confirm the change and proceed.

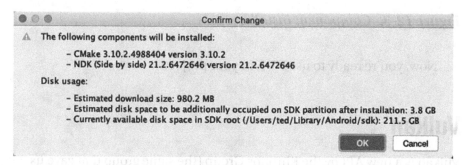

Figure 12-2. *Confirm change*

In the window that follows (Figure 12-3), click Finish.

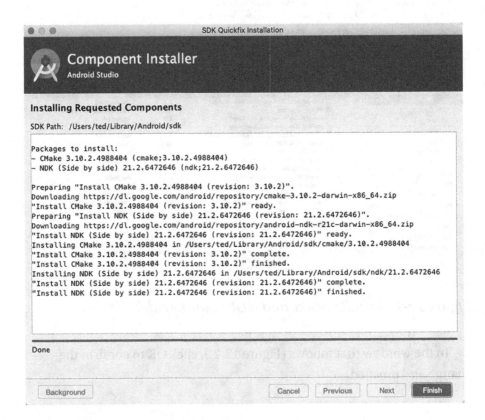

Figure 12-3. *Component installer*

Now, you're ready to use NDK in your projects.

Vulkan

Vulkan is a new API by the Khronos Group (the same group that gave us OpenGL) that provides a much better abstraction for modern graphics cards. This new interface allows us to better describe what the application intends to do, which can lead to better performance and less surprising driver behavior compared to existing APIs like OpenGL and Direct3D. The ideas behind Vulkan are similar to those of **Direct3D** 12 (which you can only use on Windows) and **Metal** (a graphics API that can only be used on the Apple ecosystem), but Vulkan has the advantage of being fully cross-platform and allows you to develop for Windows, Linux, and Android at the same time.

The price to pay for these benefits is that we have to work with a significantly more verbose API. Every detail related to the graphics API needs to be set up from scratch by your application, including initial frame buffer creation and memory management for objects like buffers and texture images. The graphics driver will do a lot less hand holding, which means that we need to do more work in our app to ensure correct behavior.

Vulkan may not be for everyone. If you're geeked up about high-performance graphics and are willing to put some work in, this may be right down your alley. On the other hand, if you're more interested in game development rather than computer graphics, you can always stay with OpenGL ES—it won't be deprecated in favor of Vulkan anytime soon.

The Android platform includes an Android-specific implementation of the Vulkan API.

To get started with Vulkan on Android, you can download the LunarG Vulkan repository. You'll need to download the project from GitHub. You can simply download the git file from https://github.com/LunarG/VulkanSamples. Click the "Clone or download" button as shown in Figure 12-4.

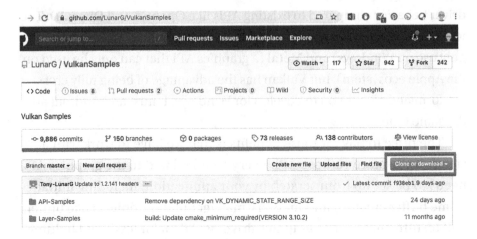

Figure 12-4. *VulkanSamples.git*

Or use git on a command line, like this (this was done on a Mac; same commands will work on Linux):

```
mkdir vulkan
cd vulkan
git clone --recursive https://github.com/LunarG/VulkanSamples.
git

cd VulkanSamples/API-Samples
cmake -DANDROID=ON -DABI_NAME=abi

cd android
python3 compile_shaders.py
```

Note   You will need to install Python 3 on your system, if you don't have it yet. You can get it from the Python website www.python.org/downloads/.

Next, open Android Studio, if you haven't launched it yet. Choose **File**
➤ **Open** and select VulkanSamples/API-Samples/android/build.gradle.
The project looks like the window shown in Figure 12-5.

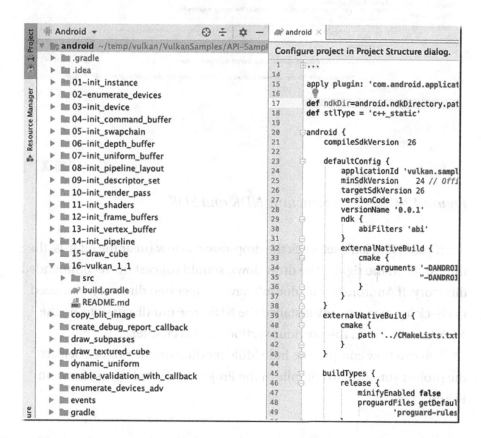

Figure 12-5. *Project pane displaying samples after the import*

We need to configure the SDK and NDK directories; to do that, go to
File ➤ Project Structure and then ensure that the SDK and NDK locations
are set (as shown in Figure 12-6).

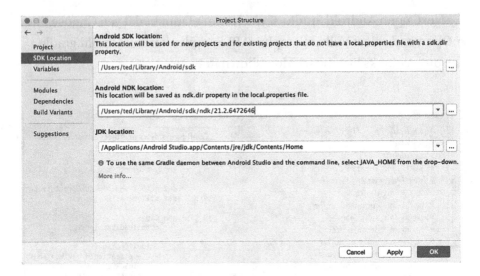

Figure 12-6. *Project Structure, NDK and SDK*

If your NDK isn't set, click the drop-down arrow (near the ellipsis, the three dots on the right). The drop-down should suggest the recommended directory. If Android Studio doesn't have a suggested directory, you need to check if you've already installed the NDK. See our discussions on the NDK installation in the previous sections of this chapter.

You can now compile the individual modules in the project. Select the project you want to compile in the Project tool window, as shown in Figure 12-7.

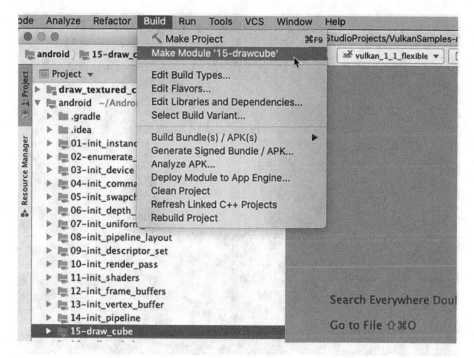

Figure 12-7. *Make module*

From the Build menu, choose Make Module **<module name>**. Resolve any dependency issues, then compile. Most of the samples have simple functionality. The drawcube example is one of the visually interesting examples (shown in Figure 12-8).

These instructions on how to set up a Vulkan environment in Android came from the Android Development website (https://developer. android.com/ndk/guides/graphics/getting-started); the instructions may change by the time this book goes to print; so, make sure to visit the page when you set up your Vulkan environment.

Figure 12-8. *drawcube module*

Game Engines and Frameworks

You had a tiny slice of a game developer's life in Chapters 6 and 7 because we built two small games, but we built them from scratch. Though the games were not very sizable, as lines of code and assets go, we had to do everything. We had to tell the program where to get the graphics file, load them on specific coordinates on the screen, play some audio during specific timings in the game, and so on. It's like painting a house using a toothbrush—yes, you have a lot of control over every aspect of the game, but it's just a lot of work too. You can bet that most of the AAA games you played weren't built that way.

Most modern games either use a game framework or a game engine. A game engine is a complete package. It's a comprehensive set of tools to help you build a game from scratch. Engines typically contain some scene or level editor, tools to import game assets (models, textures, sounds, sprites, etc.), an animation system, and a scripting language or API to program the game logic. You will still need to write code to use an engine, but most of it will be focused on the game logic. The system-level boilerplate code will be facilitated for you by the game engine.

The Android SDK provides a decent framework for games. Remember when we used the View objects and the ImageView objects? The Android SDK also provided some decent support so we can handle events, get the window to full size, and draw some rudimentary graphics on the screen. Those are the things a framework does; but there are other frameworks apart from what the Android SDK offers.

To be honest, you don't really need a game engine nor a framework; but they do make your life a lot easier during game programming. Building a nontrivial game without an engine or framework can be arduous and perilous. If your end goal is to build a game, you will be better served to consider using third-party tools.

There are many frameworks and engines out there; I've compiled only those that include Android as a target platform; not all of them will use Java or the Android SDK for development. You should remember that this list is not comprehensive at all, but it should get you started.

Frameworks

HaxeFlixel. http://haxeflixel.com/

It's a 2D game framework. You can deploy it on HTML5, Android, iOS, and Desktop. If you don't mind learning the Haxe language, you can try this out.

LÖVE. https://love2d.org/

It's also a 2D framework. You'll have to use the Lua language, but you can deploy it on Android, iOS, Linux, macOS, and Windows. This framework has already been used on some commercial games; check out Figure 12-9.

Figure 12-9. *Commercial games done with LÖVE*

MonoGame. www.monogame.net/

It's another 2D framework that targets iOS, Windows, Android, macOS, PS4, PSVita, Xbox One, and Switch. The language used is C# (which shares a lot of language element similarities with Java).

Engines

Cocos2D. http://cocos2d.org/

It's a 2D engine that targets Android (in development), PC, macOS, and iOS. Depending on your platform, you'll have to use either C++, C#, or Objective-C.

CopperCube. www.ambiera.com/coppercube

This is a 3D engine that you can use for games that will run on Windows, macOS, Android, and the Web. It supports the languages C++, JavaScript, and Visual Scripting.

Defold. www.defold.com/

You can target Windows, macOS, Linux, iOS, Android, and HTML with this 2D engine if you don't mind using the Lua language.

Esenthel. www.esenthel.com/

It's a 2D/3D engine that targets Windows, Xbox, Mac, Linux, Android, iOS, and the Web. You'll have to code on C++.

GameMaker Studio 2. www.yoyogames.com/

This is a commercial 2D engine that targets Windows, Mac, Android, iOS, Windows Phone 8, HTML5, Ubuntu, Tizen, and Windows UWP. It uses a custom language called GML. There is a free (but limited) trial.

Unity. http://unity3d.com/

This is a 2D/3D engine that targets Windows, macOS, Linux, HTML5, iOS, Android, PS4, XB1, N3DS, Wii U, and Switch. C# is the language of choice here. This is free to use up until the first $100,000 revenue. Check out their website for more details.

Unreal Engine 4. www.unrealengine.com/

You can target Windows, iOS, Mac, PS4, XB1, Switch, HTML5, HoloLens, Lumin, Android, and Linux. This is a 2D/3D engine. You'll have to use either C++ or Blueprints Visual Scripting (JavaScript language can be used with the use of some plugins). It's free to use until the project makes more than $1M. Check the website for more details.

Key Takeaways

In this final chapter, we learned a little bit about the NDK, Vulkan, and game engines and frameworks. Game programming is a big topic; we've only scratched the surface in this book. I hope you continue your journey to building interesting and engaging games. May the force be with you!

Index

C

U

V, W, X, Y, Z

Printed in the United States
By Bookmasters